DOCTOR WHO
THE HANDBOOK
The Sixth Doctor

DOCTOR WHO THE HANDBOOK

The Sixth Doctor

David J. Howe
Mark Stammers
Stephen James Walker

First published in Great Britain in 1993 by
Doctor Who Books
an Imprint of Virgin Publishing Ltd
332 Ladbroke Grove
London W10 5AH

A catalogue record for this book is available from the British Library

ISBN 0 426 20400 X

Typeset by D&S Design
1 Edith Grove, London SW10 0JY

Printed and bound in Great Britain by
Cox & Wyman Ltd, Reading, Berks

For Andrew Pixley – DJH

For Susan, Julie, Teresa and Kimberlie – MS

For everyone who ever contributed to *The Frame* – SJW

Acknowledgements

We are indebted this time around to: Colin Baker for his support and enthusiasm, Richard Bignell, John Brace, Austen Atkinson Broadbelt, Nicola Bryant for her long-distance assistance, David Gibbes-Auger, Pat Godfrey, Graeme Harper, John Nathan-Turner for all his help in the past, Barry Newbery, Alister Pearson, Andrew Pixley for again allowing us to draw on his encyclopaedic memory, Jon Preddle, Gary Russell of *Doctor Who Magazine,* Eric Saward, Paul Scoones, Alan Spalding, Patrick White, Martin Wiggins for supplying us with so much helpful reference material, and Graeme Wood. Thanks also to all those unsung *Doctor Who* fanzine editors and writers for providing many happy hours of entertainment and education.

Contents

Introduction

On 10 June 1983, I went to visit John Nathan-Turner at the BBC at his request, not in any way suspecting that that visit would result in my sitting at this word-processor ten years later reflecting on the fact that the work of this 'jobbing' actor could result in a book containing such meticulous and detailed research as that which follows this introduction.

And certainly when exactly six months later I stepped into BBC's Rehearsal Room 202 in Acton, I would have perhaps been a little more unnerved, rather than elated and nervous, had I known the exact course of events that would follow over the next three years, culminating in that 29 October 1986 phone call from John Nathan-Turner informing me of the order from above to 'regenerate'!

Now that the moving finger has written and moved inexorably onwards, it is, I am happy to say, predominantly the happy memories which endure, both in the making of the programme and in the warmth and generosity of many of the people I have met as a result of making it.

Having been a guest actor in other series in the past, I was very aware that the regular performer/performers in a series dictate to a certain extent the working atmosphere at rehearsals and in the studio. I was therefore delighted to have the opportunity of ensuring that the atmosphere during the time of the sixth Doctor should be conducive to everyone giving their best, whilst enjoying themselves at the same time. Arguably we sometimes enjoyed ourselves inordinately, particularly when Pat Troughton and Frazer Hines joined us or when we joined Brian Blessed (it would almost be *lèse majesté* to envisage it the other way round)! But I like to think that the work was enhanced rather than suffered as a result of all the good humour.

I was also extremely lucky in my companion. Nicola Bryant had received a lot of good-natured chaffing from Peter Davison along the lines of 'Colin Baker eh???' followed by a lot of head-shaking and sucking in of air through the teeth – much in the same way as any *soi-disant* expert does when I tell them what car, computer or lawn-mower I have just bought. (Long suck – 'Oh, I could have got that for you for next to nothing, they're phasing them out because the technology . . .' etc . . . etc).

So Nicola, whilst being aware that she was being wound up, nonetheless viewed the impending regeneration with a little uncertainty. And, of course, from my point of view she was the old hand and I was replacing her Doctor! But we very soon realised that we worked well together, after she had discovered that there was a slight difference between the Doctor and the actor. At least I hope there is, even if only in terms of dress sense.

It didn't take long before going to work became like going to another home. There are those, I suppose, who might not find that desirable, but I like to feel surrounded by kindred spirits when working. I found John Nathan-Turner a very supportive producer to work with and whilst he could quite properly crack the whip on occasion, nonetheless he would happily enter into the badinage at other times. He was also very much a part of the team, putting in regular appearances at rehearsals rather than simply turning up for the 'producer's run', with that 'Right, let's see you earn your money' attitude which can be somewhat intimidating when that is the only time a producer puts in an appearance. The crew were also a welcome constant. We developed a great rapport with Alec Wheal and his camera team, which saved a lot of time in the studio and added to the enjoyment.

We had some splendid guests on the show – I have very fond memories of working with Maurice Denham, a gentle and understated genius, and Kevin McNally, with whom we laughed a lot on *The Twin Dilemma;* with the inventive and talented Nabil Shaban, the deceptively effortless Martin Jarvis and the refreshingly charming and unaffected Jason Connery in *Vengeance on Varos;* with Sarah Green,

Faith Brown and David Banks in *Attack of the Cybermen*; the irreplaceable Pat Troughton, the irrepressible Frazer Hines and the irredeemable Jackie Pearce in *The Two Doctors*; with the under-used Anthony Ainley and my former sparring partner from the days of *The Brothers* the eternally glamorous and versatile Kate O'Mara in *The Mark of the Rani*; with that eschewer of understatement Paul Darrow in *Timelash*; and marvellous William Gaunt, Eleanor Bron and Clive Swift in *Revelation of the Daleks* – not to mention the odd Dalek!

In the Trial season the team was joined by Lynda Bellingham, Michael Jayston and Tony Selby, all of whom became very good friends. I think the memories of Michael's and my attempts to invent rhyming slang to baffle Tony were highlights of my entire time as the Doctor. (As in: 'Me carrots are really giving me gyp today.' 'Carrots?' 'Yeah, carrots and onions – bunions.' Well, you should have been there!!) Michael is one of the great 'twinklers' of this business, with a great talent and refreshing lack of ego combined with a finely tuned humour – *and* he likes cricket! The visiting artists included wonderful Joan Sims, BRIAN BLESSED, for whom there are no words that do not draw on the epic, the dashing and perplexed Patrick Rycart, Trevor Laird with his infectious laugh, splendid Adam Blackwood, the impossibly divine Honor Blackman, the dry and very funny Malcolm Tierney and the ditto Geoff Hughes, who had the added advantage of making me look like a bantamweight!

And, of course, that season brought Bonnie Langford into the long list of companions. I had worked with Bonnie before in *Goldilocks* at Lincoln, when I could only marvel at her sheer professionalism and all-round niceness. In a way she was an easier companion for the sixth Doctor because she was in a sense less of a 'woman' than Nicola, so it was easier for the Doctor to be protective, in an avuncular way, which might have been susceptible to misconstruction with the undeniably more nubile Peri. And she lacked her predecessor's advantage of being previously unknown. Everyone knows Bonnie and so she had a hard task to show us a Mel unencumbered by the baggage of her many outstanding previous roles in many areas of the acting profession. That she succeeded so well is a tribute to her.

I was very impressed by another rare quality of John Nathan-Turner's – he spent a lot of time going around drama schools and spotting and encouraging new young talent, resulting in many new faces that have since become well known making their first appearance on *Doctor Who*. This was a splendid counter-balance against the fact that very popular and 'name' artists were queuing up to appear on the programme. John also had the happy knack of persuading the best directors to take on the very specialised job of directing *Doctor Who*. In the past highly respected directors had balked at the challenge of bringing to the screen a programme that demanded so much from what, it must be admitted, was not always an adequate budget. Each director with whom I worked rose to the occasion admirably and I am sure the others will forgive me if I single out Peter Moffatt, who made my first story such a delight to do by trusting me and encouraging me to be my own Doctor. I think he knows how much that helped me through those first few difficult episodes – I imagine that as an actor of no mean reputation himself, he sensed how best to assist those first few faltering steps! Also I must mention Graeme Harper, whom I knew as a young assistant floor manager on *War and Peace* in 1971. He was an amazingly resilient campaigner in a very difficult, whipping-boy position. I was not surprised to find that his energy and enthusiasm had not dimmed over fifteen years and that his boundless appetite for the job and ability to create on the hoof, as it were, made him a delight to work with. And the end results were original and vital.

I cannot recall once during my tenure in the role wishing that I were doing anything else. In a sense, it was as well that Michael Grade and Jonathan Powell decided that three years was the optimum gap between regenerations otherwise I might have been sorely tempted to try to match my foolishly declared ambition of beating Tom Baker's impressive seven years as the Doctor.

Given the enduring popularity of *Doctor Who*, it is inevitable, I must concede, that I am frequently and sometimes uncomfortably reminded of the less pleasant elements of my brief time in 'the best role on television'. It is still a great sadness to me that there is a handful of people on the fringes of the programme whose misguided devotion to it has led them to engage in behaviour which can at best be described as selfish and arrogant and at worst pathological and vindictive. Whilst I myself have suffered only slightly from the effect of this blinkered obsession, it pains me to see that others have been hounded quite so mercilessly for that great crime – having a different belief. I would draw the attention of those concerned to the effects of intolerance and vendetta on the world around us today and in our daily news. Whilst the plights of Yugoslavia and Salman Rushdie may seem far removed from the subject of this book, and I have no wish to diminish them by this seemingly banal comparison, it is assuredly from the smallest of such seeds of envy and bigotry that grow the forests of hatred and destruction.

It would be inappropriate to end this introduction without paying a tribute to the many members of the *Doctor Who* Appreciation Society and other unaligned fans of *Doctor Who,* worldwide, who have been kind enough not only to write and tell me that they have found my work not unwatchable, but who have also been warm-hearted enough to take on board a charity which means a lot to me. The Foundation for the Study of Infant Deaths has repeatedly benefited from the generosity and industry of fans of the programme who have pushed Daleks, run conventions, held raffles, made films, sold memorabilia and generally harassed people into giving to this very worthy cause. I know that the recent drop in the incidence of cot-deaths is due in part to money raised in this way to fund the research that led to the recognition that sleeping position, temperature and cigarette smoking in pregnancy were significant and avoidable contributory factors. For that I will be eternally in their debt.

Finally I would like to commend this book to you. I know the authors. They are honourable men. I may not agree with every opinion expressed herein, but like many others before me I will defend to their last drop of blood their right to hold those opinions. I am grateful to them for the opportunity to write this introduction and hope that you will be as stimulated and intrigued as I have been to read the results of their endeavours. I am amazed how much I didn't know! I know you will find it fascinating and eminently readable.

Colin Baker 20/05/1993.

Foreword

Kneeling over the body of the Doctor, Peri realised that her friend had sacrificed himself for her. He had obtained the bat's milk from the bowels of Androzani Minor, but there had been only enough for one. He had saved her life, but forfeited his own.

Peri reached down and grasped his blood-smeared hand. 'No,' she protested. 'There must be something I can do – tell me!'

'Too late, Peri. Going soon.' He raised his eyes to gaze at her face. 'It's time to say goodbye.'

The shocking realisation that the Doctor was talking about dying cut deeply. 'Don't give up,' she pleaded, close to tears. 'You can't leave me now!'

The Doctor's brow furrowed momentarily as a strange sensation passed through his body. 'I might regenerate,' he muttered with breathless difficulty. 'I don't know.'

Peri watched as the Doctor's face creased again in confusion and pain. He seemed to convulse slightly, then the strength drained from his body. Shaking her head in denial of the situation facing her, she let his blond head slip to the TARDIS floor. What should she do now? In her confusion she pulled herself to the TARDIS wall and huddled there, stunned.

For the Doctor, this was like nothing he had experienced before – and he had experienced a lot. As his strength failed him, he gazed up at the ceiling of his beloved TARDIS. His ship had helped him before, but his body had been less ravaged with illness, and there had been others there to help him. In any case, it felt different this time. Had he spoken this fact out loud? He didn't know. He let his hand slip to the TARDIS floor, all his strength now gone.

Thoughts flooded the Time Lord's brain. Would he die? Should he die? Then, a voice:

'What was it you always told me Doctor? Brave heart?'

Brave heart. Yes. Tegan. He felt he could see again her cropped black hair and pretty features and hear the distinctive Australian twang in her voice. Then another spoke:

'You must survive. Too many of your enemies would delight in your death, Doctor.'

Turlough. The boy from Trion whom the Black Guardian had tried to use as an unwilling pawn in his game with the Doctor. And then, affirmation:

'Turlough speaks the truth Doctor.'

The robotic cadences of Kamelion, the shape-shifting robot that the Doctor had wrested from the Master. And another:

'You're needed. You mustn't die Doctor.'

Nyssa. Sweet, innocent Nyssa. Again, confirmation:

'You know that Doctor.'

Adric! The Alzarian boy who had willingly given his young life to save the Doctor's. Could the Doctor now let that sacrifice have been in vain?

The Doctor's mind reeled. The faces of his recent friends spun before his eyes, offering advice, encouragement, support. But then there was another. Mocking laughter. No, not a friend, but one who had good reason to see the Doctor give up the fight for life. The Master. His face appeared before the Doctor now: sly and devious as ever, the black beard and moustache giving him a satanic visage. And his advice:

'No, my dear Doctor, you must die! Die Doctor! Die Doctor!' The Master's face expanded, filling the Doctor's consciousness. Mocking laughter echoed through his brain, blotting out the support from his friends. Was he going to let the Master win? How could he prevent it?

Then: colour. Colour, shape and light. A vortex unravelled itself in the Doctor's mind. Brain synapses aligned themselves into a familiar reflexive pattern for the fifth time in his life. He was falling. Falling into oblivion. He felt the change overtake him. His skin tingled and itched as the very essence of his being shifted. His mind flexed and the vortex rapidly expanded, flooding every pore, every atom of his being.

Then his mind. Strange thoughts and desires flooded through and battled with each other, some submerging to resurface later. A momentary alien impulse to kill and to destroy; the familiar feelings of love and friendship; a sudden appreciation of poetry, of language; and an obscure desire to keep a cat. On top of all this, the most familiar feeling of all. A frustrating, niggling, tugging-at-the-corners-of-his-mind feeling.

Suddenly there is a question. A single, mind-engulfing question of shattering importance. The answer is there and it is not there. The realignment is complete but a question needs an answer. The question: *Who am I?*

The Doctor sat up.

Who am I?

He glanced at his bloodied hands and dismissed them. He drew a deep breath and scanned the strangely familiar wall facing him.

Who am I?

Behind him, Peri had been startled from her introspective reverie by his sudden movement. He had his back to her so she couldn't see his face, but the hair . . . the build . . . This was a different person – but how?

Who am I?

'Doctor?'

An answer! The Doctor accepted this instantly. 'You were expecting someone else?'

The voice was different. More mellow, distinguished even, but with a hint of sarcasm.

The Doctor sat where he was, listening as the owner of the other voice which had provided his name edged closer to him. Peri was lost for words. 'I . . . I . . . I' was all she could stammer before the Doctor interrupted dismissively.

'That's three "I"s in one breath. Makes you sound a rather egotistical young lady!'

Confusion crossed Peri's face. The Doctor would never have spoken to her like that. But surely this *was* the Doctor – who else could it be? She tried again. 'What's happened?'

'Change, my dear.' The Doctor smiled, his thin lips pressed together in a rather self-satisfied manner. 'And, it seems, not a moment too soon!'

From *The Caves of Androzani* part four by Robert Holmes

As the swirling sea of colour dissipated and the burly figure of the new Doctor sat up abruptly on the TARDIS floor, the 21-year-old television series *Doctor Who* was – like its leading character – about to enter the most unsettled and difficult period of its history, which would see changes to its format, weekly slot and season length, as well as the eventual halving of its average viewing audience.

The sixth Doctor in the person of Colin Baker was introduced to the press on 20 August 1983. The event even made the BBC's own early evening news broadcast, which commented on the actor's earlier *Doctor Who* appearance as Maxil in the fifth Doctor story *Arc of Infinity*.

The press quizzed Baker as to how long he would like to play the role, and Baker replied – possibly with tongue in cheek – that as Tom Baker had played the role of the Doctor for seven years, he would have to play the character for at least eight years, as he could not bear the thought of anyone doing it for longer than him.

This statement was ultimately proved to be quite ironic, as events overtook Colin Baker's intentions, and the era of the sixth Doctor turned out to be the shortest of his television incarnations to that date, consisting of only eight individual stories over a period of a little under three years.

After three fairly successful seasons with Peter Davison in the title role, producer John Nathan-Turner found himself having to choose another actor to carry the programme into the second half of the decade. Davison had decided to leave the series in May 1983 after having asked for an extended period in which to consider whether or not he could accept the offer of a contract for a fourth season. In the meantime Nathan-Turner had been considering Colin Baker as a suitable replacement in case Davison did decide to leave. Baker's own vibrant and open personality was well suited to the role, and would prove an interesting contrast to Davison's more reserved nature.

Nathan-Turner telephoned Baker directly, asking him to come and see him. The actor assumed he was being asked to open a fête or some-such event, little guessing that he was actually being sounded out for the role which he himself had considered asking his agent to put him up for when the fourth Doctor, Tom Baker, had departed in 1981. Once offered the part Baker agreed without a moment's hesitation.

The new Doctor's era took place in a Britain in the middle of a prosperity boom. House prices were rocketing, and the personal phone had become the badge of a new social class nicknamed Yuppies. In the world at large, the threat of war had receded as the Soviet Union's new moderate president Mikail Gorbachev discussed the end of the nuclear arms race with US President Ronald Reagan. The Conservative Government was into its second term under the leadership of Mrs Thatcher, *Spitting Image* arrived on television and the Duke and Duchess of York were married.

During the mid-eighties the nature of broadcast television in Britain was entering a state of change. Competition for audience share was growing between the independent television companies and the BBC. Technology had altered the viewing habits of the British public. Instead of being slaves to the programme schedulers as to when they could watch their favourite series, they could choose what to watch and when to watch it by using the video recorders which were becoming common household items up and down the country. This meant that the often used ploy of scheduling two popular programmes at the same time on opposing channels, forcing the viewer to choose a channel and then stick with it, no longer worked, as one programme could be recorded whilst the other was being watched live. This fact also made a mockery of the audience viewing figures which all television channels used to judge the impact of their output, as no account was taken at that time of programmes watched on video.

The BBC needed to modernise its image, as well as increase its broadcasting activities into new areas such as breakfast television and daytime broadcasting, where they had not previously competed for viewers. Meanwhile the BBC was also taking its share of the government's obsession with bias against its policies in news and current affairs programmes. This led to a siege mentality developing amongst the top management of the Corporation.

On the face of it, none of these events would seem to have had any bearing on *Doctor Who,* yet indirectly they all played a part in the cancellation of the original Season 23, and to some extent the eventual replacement of Colin Baker in the lead role.

As with the other books in this series we have spoken to many different people involved in making *Doctor Who* during the period in question although regrettably the producer, John Nathan-Turner, de-clined to speak to us, explaining that, at the time we were researching it, he wanted to distance himself from *Doctor Who*. We also received help from many fans of the series and we hope that this volume presents a balanced and accurate record of perhaps the most turbulent and controversial period in *Doctor Who*'s long history. We look at the furore surrounding the postponement in 1985, we examine the scripts which might have been, investigate the development of one of the Doctor's most popular companions and look in detail at the production of *Revelation of the Daleks,* one of the highest rated adventures for the sixth Doctor.

Doctor Who in this period was adult in content, and yet featured a Doctor with a heart of gold – and a tasteless coat! Join us as we re-visit the era of the sixth Doctor.

PART ONE – THE DOCTOR

1: Colin Baker – In His Own Words

ON HIS EARLY LIFE:

'I was born in London – on Waterloo Bridge, which is quite a feat, isn't it? At the south end of Waterloo Bridge there is a hospital called the Royal Waterloo Lying-in Hospital, and in the summer of 1943 I was born in the maternity ward on the top floor of this hospital, during an air raid!'

Interviewed by David Banks in July 1989 for *The Ultimate Interview*, released by Silver Fist tapes.

'I spent the first two years of my life dodging bombs. I was oblivious of the fact, although I do still have a piece of shrapnel about the size of a key which apparently embedded itself in the back of my infant cot when the house opposite caught a direct hit. But for the six inches by which that missed my head, I wouldn't be sitting here today. Those are the little threads of circumstance which separate life and death. It's quite extraordinary, isn't it? Those little, tiny things.

'When I was two years old I met my father, who'd been away fighting in the war. He'd come home on leave a couple of times before, which I gather had been quite traumatic for me. At two, I didn't like the idea of this *man* who suddenly appeared and whom Mummy seemed to *like* quite a lot. At least, I've been told that. I don't remember it at all.

'I have an appallingly vague memory of my childhood. I think all of the information that I trot out on these occasions is stuff I've been *told*! Memory is half what you do actually remember and half what's been topped up by others through the years.

'When I was two or three years old, after my father came back, he was then moved from London up to Manchester for his work. He was managing director of an asbestos company. So I went up to live in the north of England when I was quite young, and lived there until I was 23. When I said that I wanted to be an actor, that was dismissed by my father as being an unworthy occupation for an intelligent young man, so I was despatched off to law college. I studied law for five years.

'About the time I was due to start practising as a solicitor, I decided I'd had *enough*. It just didn't work. I was anarchic, I'm afraid. I had too exaggerated a sense of justice to work in the law. It's quite interesting, but it does tie in with the Doctor actually. The Doctor isn't about the letter of the law at all – he's about *justice*. Natural justice, intergalactic justice or whatever you like. And I always felt that way. The company I worked for was a big company which always worked for the big man and was always crushing the little man, or so it seemed to me. So I used to be very *unethical*! I used to decide who I thought was in the right and structure the case accordingly! I used to tip people off! I'd ring 'em up and say, "Look, you're about to have a summons served on you – I should make myself scarce if I were you," and things like that.

'I've never regretted studying law though, because it does mean that, for instance, I can buy and sell my own house without having to hire a solicitor, I can make my own will and I can sue people.'

Interviewed by C. L. Crouch in 1985 for *Fantasy Empire* Issue 19.

ON HIS EARLY ACTING CAREER:

'I actually made one TV appearance as a child. This was around 1954. It was in a series called *My Wife's Sister*, starring Eleanor Summerfield, Martin Wyldeck and Helen Christie.

'In this particular story, Eleanor Summerfield has met a Frenchman who is very good looking, with a moustache and everything. She then has a dream that she is married to him, and she has three little boys. The viewer then sees the backs of these three little boys gathered around a Christmas tree. They all turn around, and they all have moustaches pencilled on.

The middle one, which was me, then says "*Jolie Noel* Papa."

'I got that part because I came top in French that year! The mother of one of the kids at the school was the casting director at Granada. They wanted three kids, and they asked who was good at French. "Oh, Colin is," came the reply. That set me on the slippery slope.'
Interviewed by Michael Sibley in May 1987 for *The Colin Baker Interview.*

'I was brought up in Rochdale and went to school in Manchester. Then, when I was twelve years old, at St Bede's College in Manchester, I was invited to take part in a production of *Yeoman of the Guard*. They did Gilbert and Sullivan each year at my school. So I was in the chorus for *Yeoman of the Guard*. Then, when I was thirteen, for some bizarre reason known only to themselves, they decided I ought to play the female lead. So I played Phyllis in *Iolanthe*.'
Interviewed by Trevor Ramsay in June 1989 for *Time Lord* **Issue 4.**

'I got a review in the school magazine which read "Colin Baker threw himself with verve into the part of Phyllis and rarely strayed more than half an octave from the notes." At the time I thought that was a good review! Thereafter I appeared in the Gilbert and Sullivan production every year at school.

'When I left school I went with my mother to see an amateur production of *The King and I* at the Palace Theatre, Manchester. I said to my mother, "I'd love to do that," and the man sitting in front of me turned around and said, "I'm the president of this society. If you'd like to join, come along next Friday night." So I joined the North Manchester Amateur Dramatic Society and I got really hooked on it. I was studying law at the time, and after five years I thought "Blow this for a game of soldiers. I'll have a go at doing what I want to do. I've only got one life, so I'll have a try." So I went to drama school and started acting.'
Interviewed by Paul Duncan in 1984 for *Arkensword* **Issue 11.**

'On 23 May 1969 I made my first professional appearance on the stage, in a play called *Plaintiff in a Pretty Hat* at the Arts Theatre in Cambridge. This was after completing three years' training at the London Academy of Music and Dramatic Art, or LAMDA for short, which I entered at the advanced age of 23, having already done five

years' training as a lawyer and deciding that the law wasn't for me.'
**Interviewed by Bob Furnell, Dean King and Janette Taylor in
March 1987 for *Time Meddlers of Vancouver*.**

'My career stared when I was 26. I did two or three years of repertory
theatre, in local theatres all over the country. Then I was quite lucky to
get my first television very early on, in a series called *Roads to
Freedom*. That set the ball rolling, because the next part I got was in the
BBC version of *War and Peace,* with Tony Hopkins as Pierre. It was
a 26-part series, but it was stunning. It was beautifully done, and I was
lucky enough to play Prince Anatol Kuragin. If you know the story,
he's the one who elopes with Natasha. The sort of villain of the piece.
That took about a year and a half to do. Then I played Count Wenceslas
Steinbock in a thing called *Cousin Bette,* which was a BBC serialisation
of the Balzac novel.

'I did a lot of those kind of "classics". Then I did a fair bit of theatre
again. I was at the Chichester Shakespeare Festival. I did *Macbeth* and
Hamlet, things like that. Around 1974, I got the part of a ruthless
tycoon, a J.R. type, in a series called *The Brothers*, which I suppose was
a kind of forerunner of soap operas like *Dallas* and *Dynasty*.'
Interviewed by C. L. Crouch in 1985 for *Fantasy Empire* Issue 19.

ON HIS ROLE AS PAUL MERRONEY IN *THE BROTHERS*:

'I was J.R. before J.R. was! In England I was the man you loved to hate,
which made me the most unpopular person, but at the same time the
most popular.

'It was a series that was on in England from about 1967 until 1976.
Halfway through the programme I came into it. It was about a haulage
company – truck driving – which was run by three brothers. And the
three brothers all had their own problems. It was a bit like the *Dallas*
set-up only it was set in London and they didn't sit by the pool freezing
to death pretending it was hot. Halfway through the series the company
had to expand so they had to borrow from the bank, and the bank put
in a chairman at the company. This young guy was Paul Merroney, a
whiz-kid banker. He was totally ruthless, totally unscrupulous, but
totally honest, unlike J.R. He never did anything anyone could send
him up for, he just ruined people's lives.

'He was a very interesting character and he made my name what it was in England, so much so that when the programme ended in 1976 I was out in the cold a bit. I couldn't do any television for about five years. I did stage work. That's the good thing in England; there's a very vital theatre network, and they're very anxious to get people they've seen on television out into the theatres. So you can earn a very good living working in the theatre. But I missed television so it's been quite nice to get back in again. It did rather typecast me. I've always got villain parts until now. They always cast me as the heartless, stone-blooded type.

'I enjoyed the success of *The Brothers* while it was happening. I went to Israel and was told that the Arabs would have stood a better chance during the Six Day War if they had attacked on the night *The Brothers* was on. I was at a party and I had a phone call from Moshe Dayan who said how very upset he was at not being invited and how much he enjoyed the programme. It had that kind of impact. It was the same in Sweden as well.'

Interviewed by Jean Airey in 1984 for *Fantasy Empire* Issue 12.

'I made Paul Merroney totally emotionless and without any sense of humour at all. He didn't drink or womanise, and was interested only in business. He was not an unpleasant person but if you got in his way he would utterly destroy you – legally, honestly and cleverly, which I thought was a little bit more interesting than the "J.R." type. Just by chance, another actor who was playing a pivotal role in the series left, and there was a kind of gap. They thought the character of Paul Merroney was a good one to write up, so they asked me to do the next series, and I stayed for about three series. This got me voted the most hated man on television!'

Interviewed by Michael Sibley in May 1987 for *The Colin Baker Interview*.

'*The Brothers* finished in 1976. We didn't *know* it had finished. What usually happened was that we went away for two or three months and did something else. Then the BBC would get in touch – "OK, we're starting again." This time, though, they didn't get in touch! That's the way they work. No one says, "We're cutting *The Brothers*." They just don't bother to do anything. That was the end of it.'

Interviewed by C. L. Crouch in 1985 for *Fantasy Empire* Issue 19.

ON HIS CAREER AFTER *THE BROTHERS*:

'I did very little TV for five years after *The Brothers*. That's the trouble with TV series: they tend to restrict your future employment. So I did a lot of touring. I went to Leicester and did *Macbeth* there, and I toured with productions of thrillers and comedies and all sorts of things. I was pretty constantly employed, I'm pleased to say.

'The first TV I did after *The Brothers* was, I think, an episode of *Blake's 7*, in which I played Bayban the Berserker, an intergalactic space pirate. He was the second most dangerous man in the galaxy, which caused him great annoyance because he wanted to be the *most* dangerous man. It was a great part, an over-the-top role.

'Then I did a series called *For Maddie with Love*, which was an afternoon weepie with Nyree Dawn Porter and Ian Hendry. I played a character a bit like the one in *The Brothers*; a kind of slightly mercenary but very articulate man. I must have done a couple of dozen episodes of that.'

Interviewed by Kevin Taylor in 1989 for *Timelines* Issue 3.

ON HIS ROLE AS MAXIL IN THE *DOCTOR WHO* STORY *ARC OF INFINITY*:

'After *For Maddie with Love*, I guested in three episodes of *Doctor Who* when Peter Davison played the Doctor. I played Maxil, who was chief of security on Gallifrey, and I got to shoot the Doctor. Many people suggested that that was my audition for the part – if you zap the incumbent, you get to be the next one!'

Interviewed by Kevin Taylor in 1989 for *Timelines* Issue 3.

'I played Maxil, aided and abetted by Esmerelda. For those of you who don't know who Esmerelda was, that was the name I gave to the hat that I dragged around with me in the story. It wouldn't go through any of the doors, so I couldn't wear it; I had to carry it.'

Interviewed on stage in 1985 at a convention in Texas, USA.

'I've never been one to regard a small part as a small part. So this guy Maxil struck me as the most important person in the show. I was doing a fair few things during the producer's run, and at the end of it John Nathan-Turner said to me, "Yes, that's fine, but . . . This isn't about

Maxil the guard, it's about the Doctor." And I replied, "Is it really? Good heavens, I didn't realise that. I thought it was called *The Maxil Show*." He said, "Could you tone down the reactions, please, and the acting in the background." Ha ha! But because of that, when Peter Davison said a few months later that he was going to leave, JN-T thought of me for the part of the Doctor. So it paid off in the end! Purely by chance.'

Interviewed by Kevin Taylor in 1989 for *Timelines* Issue 3.

'A little rider which is interesting is that they asked me to play Maxil again in *The Five Doctors,* but I couldn't because I was doing something else. If I had taken the part it would have been too recent, and perhaps I wouldn't be playing the Doctor.'

Interviewed by Paul Duncan in 1984 for *Arkensword* Issue 11.

ON WANTING TO BE CAST AS THE DOCTOR:

'The extraordinary thing is that when it was suggested that Tom Baker was finishing on the programme, I rang up my agent and said, "Look, I want to do that programme, get onto it." And before he could do anything Peter Davison was announced as the new Doctor. I was really annoyed. I didn't think I had much chance, but I thought it would be nice to have a go. And this time it happened the other way around. I didn't even know that Peter was leaving when John Nathan-Turner got in touch with me.'

Interviewed by Jean Airey in 1984 for *Fantasy Empire* Issue 12.

ON THE INITIAL SECRECY SURROUNDING HIS CASTING AS THE DOCTOR:

'It had to be hidden for a long time. In fact, John Nathan-Turner and I were having a sneaky drink at a pub one day when Peter Davison came in quite by chance, and we had to make up stories. He knew he was going but John didn't want anyone knowing who was taking over until the right moment. So I had to pretend I was there for another purpose. "I come to clean the windows." It's tough as an actor.'

Interviewed by Jean Airey in 1984 for *Fantasy Empire* Issue 12.

ON HIS INITIAL THOUGHTS ABOUT PLAYING THE DOCTOR:

'It's a bit like Biggles or *Just William* or Dan Dare, isn't it?

'I want to continue the tradition of making him as quirky and as eccentric as possible; to inject a little acid humour occasionally, perhaps. I think what the producers try to do with *Doctor Who* is to use as much of the actor's own personality as possible, because it's such a high-density rehearsal and performance rate that you don't have time to go out on a limb.

'Hopefully it'll be a combination of my ideas and their ideas . . . A lot of it depends on scripts, of course. People have to write the scripts before you can do it . . . An "edge" is a word that is useful to use.

'It's very exciting. There is no other part like it, because there are no other parts where you can actually play the same part as someone else in a television series which has already been created.

'Doctor Who must be nice. "Nice" doesn't mean, necessarily, soft! I think it's important that Doctor Who can be a bit spiky sometimes.

'It is one of those characters that has somehow got into . . . almost sort of current mythology. You do bracket him with the sort of great folk heroes of literature. And it was, I think, the first of the science fiction, if it can be so called, programmes on television. It transcends the age gap: children love it, adults love it.'

Interviewed in August 1983 for BBC1's *Breakfast Time* – his first ever *Doctor Who* interview.

ON HIS INTEREST IN SCIENCE FICTION:

'I think I have one advantage that perhaps none of the previous Doctors have had, which is that I have always been a sci-fi fan. Which means that there's more to it than just doing a job; it's something extra. So I think I'll enjoy doing it for as long as it's there.

'Obviously in a science fiction show you have to have some special effects, but I think special effects should serve the show rather than the show be a showcase for the special effects. Particularly in a show like *Doctor Who*. When you're making a big movie like *Star Wars*, the special effects play a much larger part, and quite rightly too. With a programme like *Doctor Who*, what matter most are the story and the characters and the interplay between the characters. Obviously if someone points a piece of twisted plastic at you, you can't just say

"Bang, you're dead." It's got to look as if something's happening, so the effect is put on electronically as an enhancement rather than as the whole.

'I love special effects. I can sit forever and watch that scene in *2001: A Space Odyssey* where the characters are running around inside the spacecraft, exercising. I adore that film, *2001: A Space Odyssey*. It's wonderful. I love all the *Star Wars* stuff. I love *Battlestar: Galactica*.'
Interviewed by Jean Airey in 1984 for *Fantasy Empire* Issue 12.

'I'm not mad keen, but science fiction is what I've read more of than anything else. There are some authors, like Ursula le Guin, Anne McCaffrey and Frank Herbert, whose every book I have got. I've just been reading the Thomas Covenant books.'
Interviewed by Paul Duncan in 1984 for *Arkensword* Issue 11.

ON WATCHING EARLIER ERAS OF *DOCTOR WHO*:

'I watched a lot of Hartnell and Troughton, and some Pertwee. Not so much Tom, and not so much Peter, because I was working.

'The ones I watched were in the days when I was younger, before I was an actor. But I've always watched it when I could. I've enjoyed the series and I have memories dotted all along its twenty-four years.'
Interviewed by Penny Holme in 1986 for *Doctor Who Magazine* No. 118.

ON HIS DOCTOR'S COSTUME

'John Nathan-Turner said to me, "What would you like to wear?" and I found that very difficult. My first instinct, which was wrong, was to wear something like the Master wears, all in black, something quite austere. It would have been wrong, I can see that ... it's just that I would like to wear slimming black!

'Nothing in Earth's history appealed to me, and you can't really use something futuristic for the Doctor, it's wrong. Then John said, "I think it should be very bad taste." I thought, "Yes, that is rather a good idea for my Doctor. He would just grab something and not care about it. Then, even though he may have realised that it's appalling, he would never admit it, and therefore he would be stuck with wearing it!

'We gave it to a designer, Pat Godfrey, and said "Give us something in bad taste," and she came back with an exquisitely tasteful design of lots of apparently clashing colours ... It's very hard for a designer to design something in bad taste. We said, "No, too good," and sent her away and away and away, until she came back with the present one, which she hated actually putting together because it was so appalling. But even so, when you get used to it, it has its own entity.

'The only thing I don't like about it is that it's so hot when we're out filming. When we were filming in Spain it was a hundred and ten degrees, and a couple of weeks ago on Brighton beach, there was no respite from the sun, and it was horrendous.

'But it's lovely on cold locations, when the companions in their skimpy costumes are all shivering and chattering their teeth. So you can't win 'em all.'

**Interviewed by Penny Holme in 1986 for *Doctor Who Magazine*
No. 118.**

'The only things which changed for Season 23 were the waistcoat and the ties; the trousers and the jacket were the same. We did have to have extra jackets made, because of scenes like the one where I had to be submerged in quicksand.

'I did keep saying that I wanted to change the costume, but it's a large expense unfortunately. John liked it as it was and so was not prepared to waste money, as he saw it. They did let me have new waistcoats and ties, just in order to make the timescale clear. I had a different tie and cat button in each of the different time zones.'

**Interviewed by Michael Sibley in May 1987 for *The Colin Baker
Interview*.**

ON RECORDING THE REGENERATION SCENE IN *THE CAVES OF ANDROZANI*:

'I'd met Peter Davison before on *Arc of Infinity*, but of course I didn't know then that I was going to be playing the Doctor. I was only slightly involved in *The Caves of Androzani*, because I just turned up on the studio day and did it.

'Peter and I didn't have much time to discuss the role, because he was very busy.

'After the recording, I went home, got out of my car, opened my front door, walked in to where my wife was sitting watching television, and stood there and said "*I am the Doctor*." She looked at me and said, "Oh yes? Could you take the rubbish out please." '

**Interviewed by Gary Levy in December 1984 for *Doctor Who
Bulletin* Issue 17/18.**

ON PLAYING THE DOCTOR:

'I've already found that, like all SF TV, *Doctor Who* is good fun off stage, very light hearted.

'Most of the work an actor does tends to be bread and butter, not *Hamlet*. This combines the best of working as it is so creative.

'As an actor it is marvellous in another way too, for every story has a new cast of guest stars. And, of course, as a devotee of *Doctor Who*, what could be better for me? A fair few years' employment in a role which goes round the world and which I've always wanted to do. Wonderful!

'It was exciting to get the role, not daunting. It's not like playing Hamlet. I used to get recognised from my time in *The Brothers* sometimes, but right from the announcement in August people have been recognising me as the Doctor, and I'm fully aware that I'm going to be unable to go anywhere without being looked at from now on.'

Interviewed by Wendy Graham in 1984 for *Space Voyager* No. 9.

'I believe that Tom Baker was quite right, that whoever plays the Doctor does have a responsibility never to cause any children ever to have the remotest worry about what they see him do in public. So I have no intention of breaking the senses of England as I amble through the streets. I think one does have to be very responsible, one's going into so many homes. To go into someone's home like that is a privilege. To be welcomed as the Doctor in this programme is an even greater privilege.

'I can't get over the fact that there are some actors who say "Oh, look, this is a real drag, all these people wanting autographs." My answer to that is, "Well, do something else then. Go be a bus driver." If you want to be an actor you want people to see your work. The more people who see your work, the better you're doing your job. The other side of that is that people are going to want you to sign bits of paper for them. If it makes them happy, why the hell not? It's lovely. What other job do you get where people come up to you and say "I really like what you do"? The majority of the people around the world never get any feedback on the work they do. They go and they do it nine to five. They go home and nobody says "You're doing well." It's wonderful, isn't it?

'I also love being the centre of attention. It's really nice. It suits me.'

Interviewed by Jean Airey in 1984 for *Fantasy Empire* Issue 12.

'I want everyone who watches *Doctor Who* not to be disappointed that I'm playing it. I think we all have our favourite Doctor and it is usually the one who was the Doctor when we started watching it. Each Doctor has left a block of loyalty behind him. There's a huge following for Tom Baker. A strong following for Peter. Maybe in ten years' time the fans will feel the same way about me. I hope so. That's nice, as long as nobody says "This is the *only* Doctor," and all the rest of it. That's silly, because they've all brought something to the part. They're all very good actors.'

Interviewed by Paul Duncan in 1984 for *Arkensword* Issue 11.

'The atmosphere is great – we have a good time. We always have the same camera crew in the studio, and I've known them from other programmes – we get on very well. I flatter myself that I'm a fairly easy person to get along with, and I'm not at all autocratic. There are people paid to do jobs: writers to write, directors to direct, producers to produce and actors to act. Of course, we discuss things, but I would hate to be in the position where my power was such that I could say "No, I want that cut, I want this line in," and all that, because I think when you're this closely connected with it, you are least qualified to know best.'

Interviewed by Gary Russell and Justin Richards in 1985 for *Doctor Who Magazine* Issue 97.

'At no stage does one ever really feel *au fait* with any part. There's always something one can learn and there are always further avenues to be explored. But if the question is do I feel happy in the role, then the answer is most emphatically yes. Right from the very beginning I felt that it was a part for which I – in all humility – was ideally suited, by chance rather than by any great skill on my part. And right from the beginning I've enjoyed doing it.

'I enjoy the totality of it. There isn't an individual aspect which overrides all the others; it's playing the role that I enjoy. I enjoy the day-to-day work in rehearsal with other actors, I enjoy the studio work and I enjoy the moment when the next script pops through the letter box and – a little ahead of the viewer – I find out what's going to happen next.'

Interviewed by Doug Smith in 1985 for *Fan Aid* Issue 2.

'Being associated with something which has such a grip on the imagination of several generations. It really is part of current mythology.

'It's like playing Robin Hood, or King Arthur. It's one of those characters . . .

'I was already sufficiently impressed with the fact that I was playing it, but I've had a great many very respected actors who've said to me, "You've got the best part in television." And in a sense they're right.

'It's given me a more secure life – or rather did give me a more secure life until Michael Grade's intervention last year, when the future of the programme seemed a little bleak. But that's beginning to turn over again, and I think everyone is now aware of the value of *Doctor Who* in people's lives.'

Interviewed by Penny Holme in 1986 for *Doctor Who Magazine* No. 118.

'I felt very positive about what I could add to the programme, and a kind of sense of responsibility. It's like when you take the baton and you've got the next 400 metres to run. You don't drop the baton, you don't throw it into the crowd, you don't stop and pick your nose. You actually do something worthwhile while you've got it; you do your best. I was always aware of that responsibility, and not just as a job; it was more than a job. I wanted to honour the tradition that those other five guys had upheld so marvellously before. I just wanted to add another cherry to the cake.'

Interviewed by Nick Briggs in 1990 for the *Myth Makers 19* video, released by Reeltime Pictures.

ON HIS MARRIAGE TO ACTRESS MARION WYATT:

'It was a pretty instant thing. I wasn't looking for a serious relationship at the time. I was having a jolly good time by myself doing all the things that chaps do when they're younger, like swilling beer, smoking too much and being a bit of a slob.

'The thing was that I'd hardly ever lived by myself. I'd shared flats, lived with girls, then married [to actress Liza Goddard]. So I took full advantage of the situation.

'At first I was hesitant about marriage again. Having had one failure I wanted to be sure I was doing the right thing. But then I knew this wasn't going to go wrong – and it hasn't. I don't think it's a problem being married to an actress either. There's extra pressure, of course. But it's people who go wrong, not their jobs.

'Marion isn't career crazy and she's not jealous of my current success either. She loves the country life we lead with our dogs and messing about in the home. She, like me now, knows what comes first.'

Interviewed by Ivan Waterman in 1984 for the *News of the World*, 29 April.

ON THE DEATH OF HIS SON JACK:

'It was like being hit in the stomach by a steam hammer. That's the only way I can explain it. Everything just stood still. It was totally numbing and draining. Marion and I will never, ever get over it. It's not something you *can* "get over".

'It took me twelve hours to get home [from working on *The Mousetrap* in Malmo, Sweden]. It was the longest night of my life. As I waited for a boat to catch the plane I was plagued by the appalling thought that Marion was having to cope on her own. I felt so awful that I wasn't there to support her. That I'd been out enjoying myself while our son was lying dead. I kept thinking: "I knew him only four weeks. I never saw my baby smile." I kept asking, "Would it have happened if I'd been at home? Was it something to do with the last time I held him? Were we feeding him right? Was the house too big, too small, too hot, too cold? Why? Why? Why?"

'He just stopped breathing. He wasn't in any discomfort. It was just as if the habit of breathing hadn't established itself firmly enough.'

Interviewed by Mary Peplow in 1984 for *Woman's Realm*, 1 September.

'Jack died almost a year ago this week, when I was about two weeks away from starting work on *Doctor Who*. I got in touch with the Foundation for the Study of Infant Deaths as soon as it happened, because I didn't know anything about cot death and I wanted to find out about it. Then a newspaper wanted to do an article about Jack's death, and the last thing I wanted to do at the time, about a week after it happened, was to talk to a newspaper, but suddenly I thought, "Maybe I can use this to help." Out of something dreadful like that, one can actually derive some good, and the good I could do was to make the newspaper pay an awful lot of money to the Foundation, which they did happily – it's terrifying what they'll just shell out, especially if it's for a charity, as they don't want to appear mean. Also the article publicised the cause of raising money for cot death research. I mean, 2,000 children a year in this country alone is a lot to go, and nobody knows why.

'The Foundation were, commendably, reticent to use me at the beginning. They said, "Look, give yourself a few months, you might change your mind." But I'm now on the fund-raising committee.

'When I do fêtes and things I get offered expenses and what have you, and I feel a bit embarrassed saying "Yes, it's £7.42 please," so I just ask them to make a donation to the Foundation.'

Interviewed by Dominic May, David Saunders and Robert Moubert in November 1984 for *TARDIS* Volume 9 Issue 3.

ON THE LENGTH OF HIS STAY IN *DOCTOR WHO*:

'I'm going to have a smashing time, and I'm going to have a long run!'

Interviewed by Wendy Graham in 1984 for *Space Voyager* No. 9.

'My thoughts are long term rather than short term. I am someone who likes to break records, and I understand that someone with a name not dissimilar to mine played the role for seven years. So I'd hate to be known as the second longest-running Doctor.'

Interviewed on stage in 1985 at a convention in Philadelphia, USA.

'I'd like to stay in the part as long as I'm enjoying it and the public want to see me playing it, which may be two years, three years, ten years . . . I've always stated publicly that it would be nice to equal Tom Baker's number of years and episodes, but that would be quite an achievement because he did seven years in the show, and made an awful lot of episodes.'

Interviewed by Chris Parnham in 1986 for *The Ribos Operation* Issue 2.

'I think it's probably in other people's hands, rather than my own.

'Say the choice was mine; when I started doing this, I said that Tom Baker's record of seven years was awfully attractive. I've done it for three years now, even though we've done only two seasons, and I'm enjoying it. So I see no desire on my part in the near future to stop. Also, I'd like to beat the episode tally! In order to do that at the present rate, I'd take about twenty years, because in Tom's day they were making 26 episodes a year, now we're down to fourteen.'

Interviewed by Penny Holme in 1986 for *Doctor Who Magazine* No. 118.

ON HIS FIRST *DOCTOR WHO* DIRECTOR, PETER MOFFATT:

'As he was directing the first story, *The Twin Dilemma*, he gave me a lot of room to experiment and try things out, and of course the first script was very strong. I'd never previously worked with Peter. We got on together well and very quickly. Altogether we had seven days' rehearsal in which we kicked certain ideas around, but it was a very pleasant process. It wasn't at all traumatic.'

Interviewed by Bill Baggs in 1984 for *Time Watcher*.

ON *THE TWIN DILEMMA*:

'*The Twin Dilemma* had the problem of establishing a new Doctor, and the difficulties of regeneration were the prime element of the story. In a sense, the plot of Mestor and Azmael and so on was subsidiary to that. Had the story been too strong it might have distracted from the main purpose of the first story – that is, to establish that the new Doctor was experiencing problems.'

Interviewed by Doug Smith in 1985 for *Fan Aid* Issue 2.

'When I did it, I had nothing to judge it against. I think first scripts are always very difficult. If you look back at any of the incoming Doctors' first scripts, they tend to be very hesitant, because neither the Doctor nor the writers – nor anybody – knows what is actually going to happen, on the basis that any kind of coming together of talents is an organic process.

'We had made certain decisions about what my Doctor was going to be, and I think they were very brave ones actually. They weren't just mine; we all agreed that we would go for making the Doctor inaccessible, so that people would think "This isn't my Doctor. Bring back that nice Peter Davison, who was kind and gentle. This awful man is going around strangling Peri, and being remote and arrogant and conceited!"

'The story itself may well have been a weak one. In retrospect I suspect it possibly was. In fact, it was one of the weaker stories of the time I was doing *Doctor Who*, and certainly didn't compare with the stories which I always remember from the past, such as the great Robert Holmes ones of the Tom Baker era. It wasn't in the same league. But that didn't necessarily matter because you could actually concentrate on what was happening with the Doctor and Peri, and the whole regeneration thing.'

Interviewed by Nick Briggs in 1990 for the *Myth Makers 19* video, released by Reeltime Pictures.

ON *VENGEANCE ON VAROS*:

'*Vengeance on Varos* is one of my favourite shows out of the first complete season. Like all successful plays – as well as *Doctor Who* stories – there are two elements involved. One is that it's on the surface a ripping good story. It's a good adventure, it's well told and the plot's well developed. It has humour in it and good characterisation. But at the same time it has an underlying theme which can quite simply be put as: violence corrupts, and violence as a form of entertainment in the media is not exempt from that corrupting effect.

'It's extraordinary that certain elements of criticism have been levelled at *Vengeance on Varos* because of its violence. That seems to me to have missed the whole point of the show. It's a bit like complaining about *Macbeth* because it glorifies regicide, murder and corruption. And – as a parallel – the whole point of *Vengeance on Varos* is that "video nasties" are not a good thing, any more than manipulation of the population is a good thing. For critics – I use a polite term to describe them – to complain because *Vengeance on Varos* portrayed the very scenes of violence it was condemning, strikes me as faintly ludicrous, quite honestly. It has been pointed out that *The A-Team*, which was shown opposite *Vengeance on Varos* on the other channel, was more successful than *Doctor Who* in terms of viewing figures. That illustrates the point that it's very difficult to cope with that kind of violence. *The A-Team* is surely gratuitous, spectacular aggression, and people find it easier to watch that kind of mindless violence. It's a shame that *Doctor Who* was criticised for making exactly that point.'

Interviewed by Doug Smith in 1985 for *Fan Aid* Issue 2.

ON *THE MARK OF THE RANI*:

'*The Mark of the Rani* was excellent. We had the writers, Pip and Jane Baker, with us most of the time on location. They had to do a lot of rewriting, usually because of the poor weather conditions. We had to kind of scrabble for the last few days, so a lot of cutting and changing went on. Pip and Jane went home of a night and produced another few pages to cope with what we'd had to lose or couldn't cope with the day before. I remember that very clearly.

'The thing I liked about Pip and Jane is that they wrote very well for my Doctor; they understood the sixth Doctor very well.'

Interviewed by Nick Briggs in 1990 for the *Myth Makers 19* video, released by Reeltime Pictures.

ON *THE TWO DOCTORS*:

'I'm afraid Patrick Troughton suffered rather badly at my and Frazer Hines' hands. Frazer is one of the quickest-witted, funniest people I've ever met. I mean, he has a repertoire of jokes that would make Bob Hope's card-carriers worry. A very funny man. I made the mistake of battling with Frazer the first two or three weeks of rehearsals, and then I gave up. I kept saying, "Frazer, I'm the Doctor, I do the jokes," but it was really he who did them. So we used to play practical jokes on poor old Patrick. For example, setting him off in his wheelchair. I don't mean that Patrick himself actually had a wheelchair, but there were scenes in the show where he was strapped into a wheelchair, and as soon as he was strapped into it he became very vulnerable. So we used to play chariot races with poor Patrick.'

Interviewed on stage in 1985 at a convention in Texas, USA.

ON THE CANCELLATION OF THE ORIGINAL SEASON 23:

'Michael Grade wanted very much to do things *his* way, and there's an old saying – "A new broom sweeps clean." The first thing he did was to cancel *Dallas*. This brought such a storm of protest that there was pressure put on from above (so I understand), and it went back on again. The *second* thing he did was to say, because the BBC is a bit short of money, "We've got to save money, so what we're going to do is *not* produce *Doctor Who* this year. That will save us money to do new drama, because we want to do new things and the only way we can do that is by cancelling some of the *old* things." That was his logic, and so *Doctor Who* fell under the axe. What then happened was another storm of protest – headlines in the national daily newspapers . . . "*Doctor Who* Axed!" *Thousands* of letters have been carried into Michael Grade's office . . . First from British fans and then, of course, once they got word of it, from the *American* fans.

'I was *shattered* by the cancellation. I was very upset. I mean, if you put it in the context of someone who had just taken over the part – and at the end of my first season, the programme's taken off! Now, I hope and pray – I think I *know* – that it's not because they think, "My God, he's dreadful! Let's take him off!" But none the less it could be *interpreted* that way. To someone who's not even slightly interested in *Doctor Who*, it reads: "Colin Baker's taken over the part. Oh, yeah, now they've taken it off . . ." The two things are linked together subconsciously in people's minds, and I don't like to be associated with that kind of failure!

'Also, I was enjoying *doing* it! I was geared up for it! I was ready to go on to the next series. We should have been starting next week on a superb story which I'd read and which I was really excited about – a really good one. It was harking back to something in the past, but a very clever story. So, yes, I'm very, very disappointed.'

Interviewed by C. L. Crouch in 1985 for *Fantasy Empire* Issue 19.

'I have been very busy during the suspension. I've been to America many times to conventions over there. My wife and I had a baby last March and I have been around home for the past few months, which has been very pleasant. I've had lots of work to do with the charity I'm involved with, the Foundation for the Study of Infant Deaths, to which the *Doctor Who* Appreciation Society have very kindly contributed quite a considerable amount over the last year. I've been very heartened by the way in which the members of DWAS have taken on the charity I'm involved with as their charity, and it's been marvellous to see the response from all the members.'

Interviewed by Chris Parnham in 1986 for *The Ribos Operation* Issue 2.

'Michael Grade came in as Controller of programmes, and he didn't single out *Doctor Who* as such. In the same breath that he axed *Doctor Who*, he summarily ended some other programmes. These included *Come Dancing* and *The Hot Shoe Show* and things like that, which had their own aficionados. For some reason, *Doctor Who* always seems to be able to attract the tabloid press to write headlines. It seems there is some knack the programme has of attracting those newspapers. So all the other programmes that were axed as part of the new Controller's clearout were not really mentioned, while *Doctor Who* was. I think –

and this is only my assumption – that probably Michael Grade was taken as much by surprise by that as by anything else.

'I saw him being interviewed on TV a long time before he came to the BBC. He was saying in response to a question that he thought the BBC had become very old fashioned and was producing anachronistic programmes which were driving viewers away. "For instance," he said, "that terrible, tired old format *Doctor Who*." I remember thinking – and this was before I played Maxil even – "I don't agree with that. I quite like *Doctor Who*." That's why it stuck in my brain.

'So he had a declared aversion to the show. He came along, presumably with far-reaching powers to reshape the BBC, and admittedly it did need it. To a certain extent he was right. It was becoming a sort of tired old machine, turning out tired old programmes. It's all part of the same attitude: "Right, we've got to go for change, so let's get rid of some dead wood. That's been on for a long time, so has that, and so has that, so let's get rid of them and get something new in." It does make a certain amount of sense. But not when you're dealing with a commodity like *Doctor Who*, which earns more money than it costs to make. For that reason alone, it's worth keeping, quite apart from the fact that it has a very strong adherence from a lot of people.

'Counting viewers is one thing, but you can count ten million viewers who sit and watch a quiz show in a sort of mild apathy, turn it off and never give it a thought again, or you can say that there are five million who watch *Doctor Who* and think about it non-stop, and who absolutely love the programme. I think the latter is the more worthwhile type of programme to be making.'

Interviewed by Gill Green and Dominic May in September 1987 for *TARDIS*, January 1988 edition.

ON MAKING SCRIPT SUGGESTIONS:

'I sometimes comment on something if I think that there is a better way of doing it, or if it is inconsistent with something that has previously been said, or if my Doctor – I feel – would not behave in precisely that fashion. But ultimately the producer and the director are the arbiters of what is best, and my attitude is purely that of an actor who is faced with a problem, sometimes, in bringing to the screen that which is written on the paper. On some occasions the producer and the director will agree with me, and on other occasions they will give a very good reason why my suggestion is not as good as the one of the author. The process of bringing a *Doctor Who* story to the screen is – like all acting – collaborative, so there's very little head-on confrontation. It's basically a question of getting together, working with the material we've got and coming up with the best result.'

Interviewed by Doug Smith in 1985 for *Fan Aid* Issue 2.

ON THE *DOCTOR WHO* RADIO SERIAL *SLIPBACK*:

'I think that *Doctor Who* is ideal for radio, given the fact that a major worry in the making of a series like this is the realisation of special effects and sets and costumes. It was wonderful to be in a situation where that was no longer a problem. We had the best sets, the best costumes, the best-looking actors. My costume was wonderful on the radio – it was a shame you couldn't see it!

'I'd been acting on radio for years. I did quite a lot around 1970 to 1972: several Shakespeare plays, poetry readings, all sorts of things. I do enjoy it. It has that wonderful joy that you don't have to learn the lines. You can have an awful lot of fun doing radio productions. They can be much more imaginative than television or theatre, in the sense that the audience – in this case, the listeners – are much more active participants in the play; they are supplying, with your help, all the things which have been taken away from them because it's not a visual production. Some of my most enjoyable experiences of plays have been plays that I've heard on the radio, in ideal circumstances, very often driving in a car, when you can get really involved in the story.'

Interviewed by Patrick White in 1988 for *Tranquil Repose* Issue 6.

ON HIS SENSE OF HUMOUR:

'There are some people who don't understand my sense of humour. I met someone at a convention recently who told me that I had been extremely rude to her at another convention. What it turned out had happened was that I had been walking through the foyer, seen her standing there wearing a huge Tom Baker scarf and said something along the lines of "Get rid of that scarf at once! How dare you wear that in my presence?" I think the mere fact of saying that indicates that it's not intended to be serious, but this woman had been distraught for weeks because I had told her to remove the scarf. I would say that was hypersensitivity rather than anything that was my fault.'

Interviewed by C. L. Crouch in 1985 for *Fantasy Empire* Issue 19.

'I don't think uproarious comedy is a good idea in *Doctor Who*, but I enjoy humour and I always try to put in moments of humour. Sometimes the directors like it, sometimes they don't. I think we have decided that the next season will have more of what you might call comedy in it.'

Interviewed by Chris Parnham in 1986 for *The Ribos Operation* Issue 2.

ON *THE TRIAL OF A TIME LORD*:

'I'm very excited by the new season. The trial has a great many twists. The three stories are all very different, and there are also interconnections between them. There are lots of layers, and it's very, very complicated, which I rather like.

'I like things you can't understand, like *Edge of Darkness*. What I loved about that series was what other people objected to, which was that the viewer hadn't got a clue what was going on. It stimulates your thoughts. It's like doing a crossword. I wanted to make the pieces fit before they told me, and I didn't, but it was all totally consistent.

'There is an awful tendency to let the "game show" mentality take over, which is reducing television to its lowest common denominator ... I think we have to get away from viewing figures. The BBC is about providing television for everyone, but not necessarily all at the same time. You can have seven million people watching one programme and then going off and doing something else, and a different seven million watching the next one. I think that is more important than having fourteen million sitting in apathy watching something with no contact, which only sinks them further into the stupor which we are encouraged to descend into. The BBC has stood for quality for so long, it would be a shame to allow it to be watered down.'

Interviewed by Penny Holme in 1986 for *Doctor Who Magazine* No. 118.

'It is very difficult when you're actually doing something on the inside to be objective about it. I read all the magazines sent to me, if I get the time. Some of the criticisms I think, "Well, that's fair, that's somebody's opinion." Others I think, "Oh, you stupid berk! That's just being petty and unpleasant, or you have missed the whole point of it!"

Sometimes I think people get it into their heads that whatever one does, they are not going to like it, and they will look for things not to like. I think that's a shame.

'I suppose I was naive when, before the season went out and after we had finished it, I said "I'm so confident of the new season that I think the future of *Doctor Who* is secure." I even thought my own job was secure, because the "buzz" when we were doing each separate story was really good. People I respected, like Michael Jayston, were all saying "This is good, this is working really well." Michael enjoyed doing it, and I thought it was excellent.'

Interviewed by Michael Sibley in May 1987 for *The Colin Baker Interview*.

'I thought it was a valiant attempt, a decision by Eric Saward and John Nathan-Turner to mirror what was actually going on – the series being on trial. Unfortunately, they fell out in the final analysis of the last episodes. Rightly or wrongly, I don't know. But I think Pip and Jane Baker did a brilliant job writing a replacement script.

'I loved all the stuff with the Valeyard. I thought that was very good. But it could equally have been the Master, and I know that Anthony Ainley was a little put out at being supplanted – he thought, "This is a part I could've played," and indeed he could.

'That's the sort of stuff I like: the good versus evil; opening doors and stepping out on to the beach; Popplewick and all that kind of weirdness in the Fantasy Factory.'

Interviewed by Guy Wainer, Greg Jones, Neil John and David Greenham in 1990 for *Skaro* Volume 5 Issue 2.

ON DOING HIS OWN STUNTS:

'One thing that I have insisted upon, as far as I can, is doing my own stunts. I always object when I'm watching something if I can see that it's a stuntman. In film it's easier to get away with, because they have more money and spend more time on it, so the double actually looks like the actor. But in television, you can see that it's a double; the head turns and you can see that it's not the actor.

'So far, everything that the Doctor has been seen to do, I've actually done. The most painful stunt was one in *The Mark of the Rani*, where I was dangling on a chain above a 150-foot drop – which, I'm happy to say, there was a board across, so that if I had dropped, I wouldn't have fallen 150 feet! It was a very cold day for filming, and my fingers were so numb that I couldn't actually feel them. I was still holding on to the chain while people were hitting me with poles, trying to make me lose my grip, and I got one of my fingers caught in the chain and ripped all the skin off. In fact, it's still bent, as you can see. That was . . . irritating.

'In the same story, there's a scene where I'm strapped on to a trolley on wheels. Peri supposedly pushes it in the wrong direction and lets go, and I go rolling down a hill. It's shot very well. Actually, everyone's saying it looked very frightening. I found it exhilarating! It was actually great, and I was really annoyed that they got it in the can the first time, because I wanted to go again!

'In *Vengeance on Varos* there's a hanging scene, and the platform on which I was standing collapsed! The rope around my neck tightened a little, but fortunately the bit which collapsed wasn't actually the bit on which I was standing, otherwise I wouldn't be here today.

'There was a lot more uncomfortable stuff, such as a couple of fights in *Revelation of the Daleks* in the snow – it was horrendous snow.'

Interviewed on stage in 1985 at a convention in Texas, USA.

'The scene in *The Trial of a Time Lord* where I had to be submerged in quicksand was brilliant! It was shot at Camber Sands in Kent. The prop boys got there a long time in advance and dug a huge pit. They made two chambers, so basically it was a pit with a wall across the middle. When we shot the scene we had a couple of guys standing in the first chamber with their arms protruding through a waterproof rubber roof, which was covered with water and had cork etc floated on top of it so that it looked just like sand. That was how the shot was done of the hands coming up through the sand and grabbing my ankles. In the second chamber, which was about six feet deep and filled with water, was a hydraulic lift, with a central pole and a platform at the top. All I had to do was to fall onto the platform, which again was covered with the cork etc to make it look like part of the beach. The lift was then lowered so that it looked as though I was sinking into quicksand. Once my hands had gone under I had to grab the sides and force my own head down, otherwise I would just have floated. I had to hold myself under for about ten seconds, then come out and do it all over again for a retake. In fact, I had to do it three times, I think.

'The funny thing was, the pit was so well concealed that the sound man fell into it! He was walking around checking the sound with his microphone and the poor chap fell straight into this thing!'

Interviewed by Michael Sibley in May 1987 for *The Colin Baker Interview*.

ON HIS FAVOURITE *DOCTOR WHO* WRITERS AND DIRECTORS:

'My favourite writer was Robert Holmes, because over the years he contributed more in terms of imagination and depth of writing than did many other writers. All his stories worked on several levels. They worked on the superficial level of a ripping good yarn, but also he always wrote a story which had an underlying, very significant message. He didn't shirk the more thorny problems of violence, or indeed of cannibalism in *The Two Doctors*. That was a fairly nasty subject to tackle, but he tackled it.

'I liked very much working with an awful lot of directors. Matthew Robinson was very good. He directed *Attack of the Cybermen*. Peter Moffatt, who directed my first and *The Two Doctors*, is a lovely director. Graeme Harper, who did *Revelation of the Daleks*, was a great favourite of mine. He had an enormous amount of energy and was a smashing director.'

Interviewed by Patrick White in 1988 for *Tranquil Repose* Issue 6.

ON HIS FAVOURITE ADVERSARIES:

'I have a liking for the Autons from Jon Pertwee's time. They've only ever had two stories. I enjoyed them. They provoked, I gather, a reaction from Mary Whitehouse, who didn't like telephone lines and daffodils killing people, because it made children frightened of every-day objects. I loved their smooth faces. I find the humanoid monsters more frightening than the totally alien ones – the bug-eyed monster syndrome. That's why the Master is so effective, because he's another Time Lord. There are all sorts of things that can go on between the two. There's almost a pleasure at the confrontation. One thing that I see in my Doctor is that even though the defence of the weak and the championship of right against wrong is uppermost, there is a certain enjoyment of conflict. I want him to think, "Hello, there's something going on here. I'd like to get stuck in and see what it is!"

'What other monsters? There are the old classics. It would be nice

to meet the Ice Warriors. They haven't been around for a long while, have they? Oh, and Davros. I must meet Davros.'
Interviewed by Bill Baggs in 1984 for *Time Watcher*.

'My favourite enemy is the Master, because Sherlock Holmes has his Moriarty, and while most monsters have no particular desire to destroy the Doctor – they want to get on with whatever it is they are doing that's particularly evil, and the Doctor gets in the way – the good thing about the Master is that it's a personal matter. So there is a great opportunity for confrontation. I would like, and haven't yet had, a really thundering good Master story.

'I would also love to work with the Rani again. She was a wonderful adversary. But after the Master and the Rani, I would say the Daleks and the Cybermen come joint second, along with Sil.'
Interviewed by Penny Holme in 1986 for *Doctor Who Magazine* No. 118.

'I rather enjoyed working with Sil, particularly because the actor, Nabil Shaban, is such a nice bloke and such a very good actor. I also thought it was a smashing character and the relationship between Sil and the Doctor developed quite nicely.'
Interviewed by Michael Sibley in May 1987 for *The Colin Baker Interview*.

'My favourite enemy is the Master. I think he's been underused very much in the last few years, and it's a great shame because the one-to-one Holmes–Moriarty syndrome is a lot of what *Doctor Who* should be about. The Daleks, they're kind of silly, but they're there and they work, and they terrify everybody! The sad thing about *Revelation of the Daleks* was that there wasn't a lot of contact between the Doctor and the Daleks. It wasn't a full-blown Dalek story because there was so much going on with Davros, the city and all that. I do like the Cybermen as well. I think it's a shame that they have been reduced in their abilities to an extent over the seasons. I have a slight predisposition towards continuity, wanting it to be good, and once or twice it has slipped.'
Interviewed by Guy Wainer, Greg Jones, Neil John and David Greenham in 1990 for *Skaro* Volume 5 Issue 2.

ON THE LACK OF HANKY-PANKY IN THE TARDIS:

'I don't think the world is ready for Doctor number six and Perpugilliam Brown and hanky-panky! The rule is that there should be absolutely no possibility of any kind of love interest between the Doctor and his companion. The companion is there for the viewer to identify with, so younger people, children, can imagine what it's like for them to be flying in the TARDIS with the Doctor. The one thing we don't want them imagining is . . . well . . . It's the way the show is structured; that's the way it is and has always been. Mind you . . . I could make an exception for Leela!'

Interviewed on stage in 1985 at a convention in Texas, USA.

ON HIS TWO TV COMPANIONS:

'One problem with Peri is that the scriptwriters think that they're writing authentic American dialogue, but they're not. Nicola tries to get them to change the script, but bear in mind that it's her first job, and in your first job you don't go around trying to tell scriptwriters how to write scripts! She does say, "This is not the way an American would say it; I'd rather say so-and-so," and they reply, "Could you please say the script as it's written." So don't blame her. Also, bear in mind that the programme is made by the BBC initially for showing on British TV. If you have too many words like "faucet" and "sidewalk" you'll confuse the British viewer.'

Interviewed on stage in 1985 at a convention in Texas, USA.

'I think Nicola encountered the problem that an awful lot of companions have, which is that the character isn't ever properly developed by the writers. All they ever do with her is make her say "Oh Doctor!" and fall over. Then they separate her from the Doctor – have her carried off by the monster or something – so that they can get two different story strands going. It's very, very difficult, and considering that this was Nicola's first proper job out of drama school – she'd not even had any theatre experience when she played *Doctor Who* – I think she did wonderfully. She didn't want to do all the whining; it was imposed upon her by the nature of the scripts. Had she been an actress with fifteen years' experience behind her she might have been able to stand up and say, "Look, I won't have this," but like any newcomer she basically did just what she was asked to do. She was great to work with; I am very fond of Nicola.

'Bonnie was lucky, because she was a known personality. She's been in the theatre longer than I have! The character of Melanie was very quickly made very specific – she had an interest in keep-fit, she was spunky, she was enthusiastic. The idea was that I would be the one who was always saying "Hey, let's be careful," because she would always be rushing out and doing things. That's a good, positive thing to grab hold of when you're starting in a role.'

Interviewed on stage in 1987 during a convention at the University of Western Washington, USA.

ON HIS FAVOURITE STORY:

'From the point of view of watching them, I think my favourite would be either *Vengeance on Varos* or *Revelation of the Daleks*, because as complete stories they stood up extremely well and were different. The one I enjoyed doing most was probably *The Two Doctors*, mainly because of working with Patrick Troughton and Frazer Hines, both of whom are now very good friends of mine. I have a particular regard for Patrick Troughton's Doctor, so it was a great honour for me to work with someone who I believe is a very gifted and versatile actor.'

Interviewed by Doug Smith in 1985 for *Fan Aid* Issue 2.

'Pat I've adored for many years, and I've known him for a long time. I was best man at his son David's wedding, and I shared a flat with David for ten years, so I've known Pat off and on, and always admired his acting, and adored his Doctor, so actually to work with him was a special treat.

'I was a bit in awe actually, but that was dispelled in a couple of days, and Frazer also is a delight. Frazer and I got on extremely well. We larked around a lot, and Pat treated us like an affectionate . . . I'd say father, but he'd be offended. No, I'll say father anyway, because he calls me Miss Piggy at the moment (a reference to my weight); I call him Gonzo (which is a reference to his physical appearance)!'

Interviewed by Penny Holme in 1986 for *Doctor Who Magazine* No. 118.

'I think in retrospect I was unlucky in that I never really had any great stories; there weren't any that stood out. I think *Vengeance on Varos* was the nearest in that it was very different. Yes, and that was the one that got all the criticism in Britain. It was violent and it was dark and it was gloomy. I liked that. I enjoyed that a lot. I thought it was a good story, and I enjoyed doing it.'

> **Interviewed by Bob Furnell, Dean King and Janette Taylor in March 1987 for *Time Meddlers of Vancouver*.**

ON HIS LEAST FAVOURITE STORY:

'I suppose it was *Timelash*, which never quite gelled for me.

'It was actually much better than I thought it was going to be. Pennant Roberts did a good job directing it. There was nothing intrinsically wrong with it, it's just that, of that particular series, it was the one that didn't work for me. I don't think that the Doctor's element was as strong as I'd have liked.'

> **Interviewed by Penny Holme in 1986 for *Doctor Who Magazine* No. 118.**

ON SCRIPT EDITOR ERIC SAWARD'S RESIGNATION:

'We had a hiccup towards the end of *The Trial of a Time Lord*. I suppose, like all of us, Eric's a complex man. He used to ring me up late at night and moan on about John Nathan-Turner. I would spend an hour and a half or two hours talking on the phone with him – and he'd ring about midnight, so at two in the morning I would say "Look Eric, I have to go to bed, I'm tired." I would calm him down and say "Look, Eric, I think you are being paranoid. I don't think John is trying to do you down. I think all he's doing is disagreeing with you, which he is entitled to do as producer of the programme." Then suddenly I read the interview that Eric did for *Starburst*, most of which he spent slagging off John. Most of it was unfair, and some of it just his opinion. Some of it I don't know about as I wasn't present.

'What had happened was that dear old Robert Holmes had died before completing his script for the final episode of the season. Eric had been very close to him. He wanted to stick to the spirit of what Robert Holmes had wanted to do. John asked Eric to write it, even after they had fallen out. I've got a copy of the actual script that he wrote. He seemed to be venting his anger in the writing, and he wrote a very strange ending. John turned it down for many reasons.

'Pip and Jane Baker then had to write a new version of the last episode over a weekend, and I thought they did it brilliantly. I think episodes thirteen and fourteen were the best; the characters of Glitz, Popplewick and the Valeyard were wonderful.'

Interviewed by Michael Sibley in May 1987 for *The Colin Baker Interview.*

'The truth is an awful lot of things: there are no absolute villains, there are no absolute good guys. It's certainly true that JN-T and Saward were chalk and cheese, but in the early days that worked extremely well, because they complemented each other. It's only as both of them – and John will admit this himself – have become a bit jaded doing the programme . . . JN-T wanted to leave the show. He announced that he was leaving, he told all the fans this. Then suddenly the BBC said, "We want you to carry on and do more." He replied, "I don't want to. I want to go and do something else, please." And they said, "Either you do more or you pack your bags." Obviously he wanted to stay at the BBC – he's got a living to make – so he had to do what they told him. I mean, all I know is what he's told me. There may be things going on behind the scenes. But it does strike me as ludicrous that when you have an actor who wants to carry on playing the part and a producer who wants to go, you do exactly the reverse: you keep the guy who doesn't want to do it and get rid of the guy who does!'

Interviewed by Bob Furnell, Dean King and Janette Taylor in March 1987 for *Time Meddlers of Vancouver.*

ON THE SERIES' SCRIPTS:

'Actually, I found there was an awful lot of casual script-writing went on during my time in the series. I had terrible trouble with *The Trial of a Time Lord* in particular. I remember that the worst part was the segment written by Philip Martin. I would ask the director, "Is this the Matrix lying, is the Doctor under the influence of the process he's been subjected to, or is he lying for some reason of his own that we'll later discover?" "I don't know," came the reply, "you'd better ask Philip Martin." So I asked Philip Martin, and he said, "I don't know. Eric Saward put that bit in. You'll have to ask him." I asked Eric, and Eric said, "Oh, I don't know. Philip Martin wrote that bit!" I told him, "Look, I need to know, in order to play this scene. When I'm chaining Peri to the rock, is that a Matrix lie or am I behaving like that because I'm being watched?" "Oh, whichever suits you!" The thing is that no one had ever bothered to work it out. In the end, I decided that most of it was a Matrix/Valeyard lie.

'Small continuity points don't bother me: what bother me are basic mistakes like that, which usually come from a total lack of caring. I wouldn't normally accuse an individual, but because Eric was later so vociferously critical of the programme and of me, I will say this: make sure your own slate is clean before you start criticising other people's dirty slates! He really was very casual about it. You can't blame the writers, because they get given a brief.'

Interviewed by Stephen James Walker, David J. Howe, Mark Stammers and Gordon Roxburgh in August 1989 for *The Frame* Issue 13.

ON THE SERIES' RATINGS:

'Michael Grade said publicly that the ratings for Season 23 were very disappointing. I wrote him a letter in which I said, "Given the fact that you had cancelled us for eighteen months, and given that we were again opposite *The A-Team*, which pulls in 30 million viewers and is the kind of whiz-bang violent programme that you don't want to make . . . We came on immediately after *Roland Rat – The Series*, which sadly pulled in only two million viewers. Then, halfway through *Roland Rat – The Series, The A-Team* started. To get the five million viewers that we did get, I actually thought was bloody good."

'I suppose we did also go out in the hours of daylight, with good weather. These of course are not the factors that people mention when they say that the ratings are poor. So – scapegoat – change the Doctor!

'I would never dream of wishing my successor any ill, but I hope that if he is successful, it's because the programme deserves it, not because of the schedule. I would feel well peeved if the series was put opposite something kind of flabby, and put out at seven o'clock at night, and therefore doubled its figures. Of course, they would say, "Ah, there you are, told you so! Get rid of Colin Baker and you get 10 million viewers!" '

Interviewed by Michael Sibley in May 1987 for *The Colin Baker Interview.*

ON HIS OUSTING FROM *DOCTOR WHO*:

'At the end of *The Trial of a Time Lord* we left the studio with a party, I had a nice time and we all said "See you next year." I kept in close contact with John Nathan-Turner because, as you know, we did the conventions and things together. Then when the time came for the option on my contract to be taken up by the BBC, which was the end of October, he rang up and said, "I don't even know if we're doing the programme. They haven't even told me if I'm producing it next year, so I can't take up the option at the moment." So the option lapsed. Then, at the beginning of November, he rang me up and said, "Look, I've got a bit of bad news. The programme is going ahead but Michael Grade has instructed me to replace the Doctor."

'I was quite surprised by this! You know that sort of blood-draining-from-your-veins kind of feeling? John said he had told them that he thought it was a dreadful mistake and he wanted me to play the Doctor, but they were adamant. "Grade says three years is quite enough. He's said nothing derogatory about your performance, he thinks you are fine, but he thinks a new Doctor will give the programme a boost. I have pointed out that you have not done three years, and that you have done only one and a half seasons, but he remains adamant that that is long enough and it's time for a change." So there was nothing much I could do about it.

'Three days later I got a phone call from the BBC asking me to go to America with Grade to publicise *Doctor Who*. I thought that was rather odd, but I agreed to do it on the basis that I might be able to find out some more. However, Grade avoided me very cleverly throughout the whole time I was there. All I've ever got from anybody – and I've seen Jonathan Powell, who is Head of Series and Serials – is that they were happy with my performance but that they had decided that three years was enough.

'It goes against what I was asked to do, when I started the show, by David Reid – Powell's predecessor. He asked me if I was prepared to commit myself to the programme for *four* years. Having said yes in 1983 to four years of 26 episodes a year, I actually did one year of 26 episodes (or the equivalent), nothing at all the next year, and just fourteen episodes the next. Then I was unceremoniously bundled out. So I felt fairly aggrieved.'

Interviewed by Robert Cope in September 1987 for *Doctor Who Bulletin* Issue 48.

'How do I feel about it as we sit here now? As we sit here now, I feel quite calm and unbothered about it. I suppose if I thought about it for a few minutes I could work myself up into a bit of a lather again, but I think that's rather a waste of time. When it happened I got cross. I felt I had been treated unfairly and badly. I thought I was a pawn in a game of publicity and power politics, played by Michael Grade. I thought that he had got to a point where he had criticised the show so much that he had to be seen to do something, and the most overt thing he could do was to change the Doctor, because that's the one thing that would get all the publicity. It seems perverse that the Doctor wanted to stay, so he had to go, but the producer wanted to go, so he had to stay. John Nathan-Turner was very keen to move on to something else and wasn't allowed to. That strikes me as the action of someone who doesn't have the programme's best interests at heart.

'Having said all that, this all happened six months ago now. I had had a career for fifteen years before I became involved in *Doctor Who*, and I hope most sincerely that I will have one for another fifteen years afterwards. I am enjoying the play I am doing now.

'Yes, I shall miss the programme. But my connection with it will remain as long as people like you and all the other smashing people I have met through *Doctor Who* maintain an interest.'

Interviewed by Michael Sibley in May 1987 for *The Colin Baker Interview*.

'I would be dishonest if I was to pretend that suddenly it wasn't the best job on television, because it was. I had a brief spell when I was allowed to play with the best toy there was. And like any little child that has had his biggest and best toy snatched away from him before he is finished with it, I was a little bit *cross*. But my life goes on. I suppose my feelings about *Doctor Who* remain as they were. I loved doing it. I had a great time. Perhaps it is just as well that it was taken away from me. I have done far better than I thought I would this year with the play I am doing. Maybe somebody's done me a favour in some way. I miss it, though.

'I was very irritated about the treatment I received. I could have done what was suggested, which was to pretend that I was leaving for personal reasons, but I don't like to tell lies. I like to tell the truth. It may have been a mistake, I suppose, as I have to talk about it now.'

Interviewed on stage in September 1987 at the *Doctor Who* Appreciation Society's PanoptiCon 8 convention in London.

'I feel that "unlucky" is the word that sums up my tenure, really. A combination of Michael Grade – who changed the schedules, changed the length of the programme, cancelled it in the middle, then put it on after *Roland Rat – The Series* and opposite *The A-Team* – together with the whole Eric Saward business, the upheaval that the BBC itself was going through at that time . . . all those things conspired to make it very difficult. In a way, it was more frustrating than anything else. If someone had said, "Look, we think you're awful and we're replacing you," I would have had to live with that. But when I know it was just a combination of circumstances, and I was powerless to do anything about it . . .

'You know, if someone else had been cast as the Doctor in 1984 and I was doing it *now*, I'd still be in that part for years to come.'

Interviewed by Stephen James Walker, David J. Howe, Mark Stammers and Gordon Roxburgh in August 1989 for *The Frame* Issue 13.

ON HIS CAREER AFTER *DOCTOR WHO*:

'The first thing I was offered was a tour of a play called *Corpse* – a brilliant play, set at the turn of the century, in which I got to play murderous twin brothers. It meant a number of quick changes, in that I exited through one door as one brother and, as the set changed, returned as the other. Chaotic at first. That went into the West End for five months and covered the full year after *Doctor Who*.

'Then I did panto at Wimbledon with Dennis Waterman and Rula Lenska. Immediately after that I did another play, *Deathtrap*, with Anita Harris. Then I did 65 programmes for the Children's Channel, a satellite station. These were co-produced by Longmans, the book publishers, and were scholarly in a *Sesame Street* style, which was great fun. I loved doing that.

'I then did four months of *Run for Your Wife* with Terry Scott, following which I directed a play called *Bazaar and Rummage*. Then it was straight into the *Doctor Who* stage show. So I've been busy!'

Interviewed by Kevin Taylor in 1989 for *Timelines* Issue 3.

ON THE STAGE PLAY *DOCTOR WHO – THE ULTIMATE ADVENTURE*:

'Everyone says it must be pretty painful going back as the Doctor after my untimely removal, but it's not, as I never really took personal umbrage at what happened. It was just an irritant in the same way as if a headmaster at school was to say that one's half-holiday was cancelled. One feels a bit cross about it.

'My decision to take the part was based on exactly the same criteria as any other work on offer. What else is available? What would be the enjoyment factor therein? What would be the financial rewards thereof? This role had the advantage of my already knowing the character. I'd seen Jon Pertwee in the show and thought it would be fun to do, because the cast were all enthusiastic and inventive. I've been proved right; it is great fun.

'I think my new costume is very successful. I wanted a complete break from the previous image and to have something that was going to be cool on stage *and* say something different: add another layer to the Doctor if you like. But for very understandable reasons, Mark Furness, the producer, said he wanted a costume as close as possible to the essence, if not the actuality, of the original. They borrowed the BBC costume for the brochure photographs as they hadn't made the new one at that point.

'The only brief I gave the designer was that it must be lightweight, because of my being two hours on stage under heavy lights. Even now it's still heavier than I'd have liked, but I think Yvonne Milnes, the costume designer, did an excellent job. The trousers are similar to the ones I wore on TV. I've got red shoes instead of green, and another jazzy waistcoat, this time with pineapple buttons. But the *tour de force* is the coat, which I think is much better than the TV one. It's got blue in it, which I couldn't have for television because of the electronic effects, and I think the colours blend rather nicely. Worth seeing, folks!'

Interviewed by Dominic May in June 1989 for *Doctor Who Magazine* tenth-anniversary special.

'Jon Pertwee had been playing the part for ten weeks before I took over, and Terrance Dicks, who wrote the script, wrote it specifically with Jon in mind. So he sent me a copy of the script and asked me what kind of changes I thought I'd want. When I'd read it, I rang him up and – to his great relief, I think – said that there were very few changes I would make. Basically, the Doctor is the Doctor, and it's the mere fact that I'm saying the lines instead of Jon that makes it different. The voices are very different.

'The lines that have been changed are about one or two per cent of the script. "Reverse the polarity of the neutron flow," which is a Jon Pertwee trademark line, has been changed, and there are things that've been added in, some by me and some by Terrance Dicks, in consultation with each other. It's a shift of emphasis rather than a change of dialogue. I mean, I'm my usual kind of bumptious, arrogant self, and he was his usual kind of dignified, courteous self, but we're saying more or less the same lines.'

Interviewed by Trevor Ramsay in June 1989 for *Time Lord* Issue 4.

'I saw the show in Wimbledon, shortly after it opened, and I wasn't particularly impressed. Then I saw it again four or five weeks later, in Bristol, and it was much, much better. Even when I saw it the first time, though, when it was a bit of a shambles, I realised – with no disrespect whatsoever to Jon – that it was particularly suited to my Doctor. That's because my Doctor is a "stage" Doctor – he's flamboyant and over the top. Jon's dignified portrayal was brilliant on television, but as the centre of a busy show he had a problem, and the script didn't serve him as well as perhaps it ought to have done. My Doctor, on the other hand, can rush around and do a few things, and I thought, "Maybe I can contribute something to this." So that was one reason why I decided to do it. Obviously the negotiations came into it too – the fact that I was well paid for it. And it fitted in with all the other things that I wasn't doing!

'When I was rehearsing, we took the opportunity to make a few changes to the script. In the swordfight, for example, I wanted to have the Doctor saying, "Now, if you go over there . . . " – and as he pointed over there with his sword he deflected one blow – "Or is it over that way?" – and he deflected another one – so that he was totally oblivious that he was actually having a swordfight. Unfortunately, there wasn't enough time to work that out, so in the end we played it as if I was such an expert swordsman that I could actually have a conversation with somebody while fighting behind my back. I mean, it's a terrible gag, but it was a compromise.

'The other scene I particularly wanted to change was the one with the flying ant creatures. When I watched it, I couldn't believe that the Doctor just walked off, consigning these things to a grisly death at the hands of the Cybermen. So now I play it as if I'm trying to stop them from sacrificing themselves, saying, "No, no." And then, as I run off,

I say, "Thank you." Otherwise, it made the Doctor look totally callous, actually asking them to fly down and get themselves killed!

'Since rehearsals, we haven't changed anything, apart from the small variations I put in nightly, which keep the rest of the cast on their toes! I see myself, in a show like this, a bit like a soloist in an orchestra. I mean, I've got to play the tune – I've got to say the words – but I'm allowed a little licence. I think the part, and the show, benefit if the Doctor's slightly unpredictable and does something different every now and again. For instance, the business with Zog has grown tremendously since I started doing it.

'The audiences have varied enormously. Usually, if you open to a certain advance booking at a theatre, you can gauge from that how you're going to do during the week, because you know a certain proportion of people will just turn up on the night. With this show, though, it seems we always open quite low, then gradually build and build and build. By the end of the week we're doing quite well, because the word's got round, but then we go on somewhere else. We just haven't been able to sell it properly in advance, and I don't know why. The hot summer might have had a lot to do with it, or perhaps people have the wrong impression of what *Doctor Who* will be like on stage.

'I learnt quite quickly that I either spend twenty minutes signing autographs at the stage door, uncomfortably jammed against a brick wall, or I formalise it. So I formalise it, and sit at a table in the foyer to sign a few autographs after each performance. Mums, dads and children come up, and the comment I've had consistently from parents is, "Well, we only came because, you know, little Jason wanted to see the show, but we've had a wonderful time, we've loved it."

'Funnily enough, doing this tour has helped to redress the balance. I've had young kids hugging me, in tears, saying, "Why can't you come back on TV? You'll always be my Doctor." I expect every other Doctor has had the same thing, but I personally had never experienced it before. Families, too, have come up and said, "You will always be our Doctor." OK, that's probably because I just happened to be the one who was in it when they started watching, I realise that. But it's nice to know there are people out there who feel that way.'

Interviewed by Stephen James Walker, David J. Howe, Mark Stammers and Gordon Roxburgh in August 1989 for *The Frame* Issue 12.

2: The Sixth Doctor

'The light that burns twice as bright burns half as long, and you have burned so very, very brightly . . .'

So says Doctor Eldon Tyrell to his android creation Roy Batty in the classic Ridley Scott film *Blade Runner*. Looking back, it seems that the analogy could apply equally well to Colin Baker's Doctor – the most incandescent of the first seven incarnations, but also the shortest-lived.

Peter Davison, the fifth Doctor, had decided in May 1983 that he would not wish to renew his contract when it expired toward the end of production on the following season of stories, the 21st in *Doctor Who*'s history. Thus the producer, John Nathan-Turner, was again faced with the difficult task of finding a new leading man. His first instinct was to go for a contrast – a sixth Doctor who would be as different from the fifth as the fifth had been from the fourth – and he was quoted in the press as saying that he was looking for someone older and more obviously eccentric. 'We do want to make the next one a little more eccentric than Peter's been,' he confirmed at a November 1983 convention in Chicago, USA. 'To make him a little more crotchety and perhaps give him a kind of acid wit, which we think would make a nice change.'

He had in fact had Colin Baker in mind since the previous summer, as he later explained in an interview with Peter Haining:

'I got to know Colin during the time he played Maxil, a Gallifreyan guard captain, in a Davison-era story called *Arc of Infinity*. Then we met up again later when we were invited to the wedding reception of my assistant floor manager, Lynn Richards, with whom Colin and his wife Marion had become very friendly. The *Doctor Who* crowd were sitting together on the grass, having a good time, and for the whole afternoon Colin kept us thoroughly entertained. Even though I wasn't actively looking for a new Doctor then, I thought that if he could hold the attention of fifteen hard-bitten showbusiness professionals for hours, then he could do the same with a television audience.'

Strangely enough, even though she was unaware that Peter Davison was planning to leave the series, Lynn Richards later went to see Nathan-Turner to suggest that Baker would make an ideal candidate for the next Doctor. Little did she know that he was already the hot favourite for the role!

In an August 1989 interview for *The Frame*, Baker recalled how he had first been approached to play the part of the sixth Doctor, and how the character had then been developed:

'John Nathan-Turner rang me up one afternoon and said he'd like to see me. I went in to the office, thinking that he was going to try to talk me into opening a fête or something, and he said, "I'm not offering you the part, but Peter Davison is leaving and I wondered if you would be interested in playing the Doctor?" So I replied, very casually, "Oh, yeah, I wouldn't mind." He said, "Well, I'm going to give you a few tapes and ask you to go away and watch some of the earlier Doctors. We'll meet again in a week's time and you can tell me how you think *you'd* like to play him." And that's what we did.

'I can't remember all the stories I was given, but they included *The Space Museum, The War Games, Carnival of Monsters, Pyramids of Mars* and *Warriors of the Deep*. Anyway, I watched them all several times, then I went back to see John. He asked me what I thought and I said, "Well, I would obviously play the part as a kind of distillation of myself, as all the others have done, but one thing I would like to bring out is the fact that the Doctor is an alien – he's not a human being, even though he looks like one."

'I thought it would be quite nice if sometimes he didn't behave in the way we would expect him to behave. So, on one day, if a person was mown down in front of him he might just step over them and ask somebody the time; on another day, he might go into terrible paroxysms of grief about a sparrow falling out of a tree. Obviously we'd have to be able to explain why, and what it was that was concerning the Doctor; I just didn't want him to behave in an obvious, sentimental, approachable way. I wanted him to be a little bit unapproachable. He could get extremely angry about something – a build-up followed by a sudden explosion, so that the rage might seem to be about one thing when it was actually about something which had happened two episodes ago, perhaps. I think there's a danger with this kind of programme that it's all too pat, all too obvious.

'Now, John liked this idea, and in the end he pushed it further than probably I would have had the courage to do, by making the Doctor *so* unapproachable in my first story, *The Twin Dilemma*. You had to wait for four episodes before finding out if this person had anything remotely *likeable* in him, and I think that was very brave, especially as it was the end of a season. I like that kind of bravery in television. It's all too easy to play safe all the time.

'So that was one thing I wanted. I also saw the Doctor as being rather austere, dressed in black. I wanted a black velvet costume, but it was pointed out to me that the Master had got in there first, so I couldn't have it. And the one aspect of my Doctor which I suppose I do regret is the costume. It works for me now, but I would have liked it to have been something different. Really, though, the costume was, to me, a very unimportant part of the whole enterprise. This was partly because I was inside it looking out – everybody else had to look at it, therefore it meant a lot to them!

'I also suggested that the Doctor should tell excruciatingly bad jokes – you know, the puns. The idea of using quotes was mine, as well. I wanted to use quotes from the English language – obviously, as we were making the programme in English! – but also I wanted to make things up that sounded like quotes from other cultures. So it might be a Venusian quote, or a quote from Aldarberan 4. I thought that was a nice idea.

'There was another thing, too. I have a little bee in my bonnet about the English language. It's the richest language in the world in terms of the amount of words available, but gradually we're losing most of them. I wanted there to be at least half a dozen words in each episode that viewers would have to rush off and look up, because they didn't know the meaning. If you are really hooked on a character and he uses a long word that you don't understand, then you'll go and find out what it means: it's extending people's vocabularies, which I think is nice.

'All these ideas John Nathan-Turner liked, and we both went upstairs to see David Reid, who was then the Controller in charge of BBC1. Fortunately he was watching a Test Match on TV at the time, and I asked, "How's Botham doing?", or something. He said, "Oh, do you like cricket?" and we chatted about cricket for twenty minutes – to JN-T's total perplexity, because he knew nothing about cricket! After that, we talked about the role of the Doctor for a minute or two, and David Reid said, "Well, I think that's great, excellent." Apparently the fact that I liked cricket did it for me!

'I was then asked if I would sign a four-year option, because Peter had left after three years and they wanted to get a bit more continuity. I said "I'd like that very much!" – I was thinking, "Four years, 26 episodes a year, wonderful!"

'And that's really how it all happened!'

As is apparent from this account, *Doctor Who*'s then script editor, Eric Saward, made relatively little contribution during the meetings when the sixth Doctor's character was being conceived. He now explains that he did not feel inspired to come up with ideas as he was unhappy with the casting of Colin Baker as the Doctor, considering that although he was a competent character actor he lacked the screen presence required.

Saward recalls that he took on board Nathan-Turner's idea of making the new Doctor more crochety and more at odds with the world than the previous one, and also that an attempt was made to reintroduce more humour into the part. Again, however, he considers that Baker lacked the lightness of touch required to bring the humour across on screen.

'The other thing that we were going to try to introduce,' explains Saward, 'which just didn't work, was a sort of Holmesian ability to make extraordinary deductions. Just as Sherlock Holmes might say something like "I see that you came via Marylebone Road," and then explain that he had deduced this from the distinctive clay on the person's boots, the Doctor would have this wonderful ability to make sense out of highly improbable things. In the real world, of course, it just wouldn't work – the whole of London happens to be built on clay! But that's the sort of thing we were going to try to do. Unfortunately, because of problems with scripts and so on, there were aspects which just got left behind. It takes quite a lot of time to work that sort of thing out; ideally it should be firmly locked into the story.'

When asked by *The Frame* if he felt that he had been given an unusually large say in the development of his Doctor's character, Baker replied:

'Well, in terms of the shape of my character at the beginning, it's not that I had any say as such, it's just that they asked me how I would play it, I told them, and they liked it. I think you'd have to do that with any Doctor. There's no point in hiring an actor for that part and then telling him to play it in a way which is different from how he would naturally approach it. He's got to play it his way.

'After that, though, I certainly wasn't consulted by Eric Saward about scripts, and if ever I made any suggestions about scripts he didn't respond very warmly to that. He was of the "writers write, directors direct and actors act" school, which to a certain extent I am myself, but I think that when you've got a long-running programme with a central actor, eventually he's going to have more input potential than new people coming in from outside. I could never make any headway with that, though.'

The sixth Doctor's 'unapproachable' debut in *The Twin Dilemma* came as a shock to many of the series' viewers, who had grown accustomed to Peter Davison's sensitive, charming portrayal. Following his regeneration, the Time Lord was seen to suffer a number of violent fits – at one point actually attempting to strangle his companion, Peri – and even during his more lucid periods he appeared to experience a rapid succession of different moods, ranging from disconsolate self-pity through cringing cowardice to narcissistic bravado. Viewers were left uncertain as to whether these bewildering switches of temperament were simply after-effects of the regeneration itself or whether they would continue to be apparent in later stories.

The sheer unpredictability of the sixth Doctor was, indeed, the quality which Colin Baker often chose to emphasise in his earliest *Doctor Who* interviews. 'He has many facets to his personality,' he told the fanzine *Arkensword* in 1984, 'and, bearing in mind that he is an alien, some are difficult for humans to understand. When he's a little bit curt to his assistant. Impatient. Irascible. I think that these are very important aspects for the Doctor to have. For him to behave exactly the same way as a human behaves would be a shame. It would be wasting the character . . . He's not a slavish follower of anybody. He is prone to reacting very differently to exactly the same situation, according to the way he feels. The one thing he'll always do is to champion the cause of the weak. In casual conversation he won't always be polite. That's an Earthly concept. He can't be bothered with the social graces.'

Talking to the magazine *Space Voyager* shortly before starting work on *Attack of the Cybermen*, the opening story of the 22nd season, the actor drew a contrast between this alien unpredictability and the comparatively staid behaviour of more conventional heroes: 'My Doctor will be insatiably curious, intolerant, waspish, and kind but cruel . . . Many times he won't react with the emotions expected. As a rule the baddies are the more interesting parts. The Doctor is the great exception to that. He is a hero but not in the bland mould. Baddies generally are best because the writers have found it more interesting to write about people who break the rules, but the Doctor makes and breaks his own rules. He is a galactic buccaneer. Neither good nor bad. A bit of a meddler.'

Not for this Doctor the role of a passive observer, staying quietly in the background until forced to act. On the contrary, as signalled by the garish, tasteless costume which John Nathan-Turner decreed he should wear, he seemed actively to court attention; and the overblown, oratorical way in which he often expressed himself was indicative of an ostentatious, self-important personality.

The mood changes he experienced immediately after his regeneration became less violent and erratic as time went by but never abated entirely, making him a highly capricious character. Flamboyant, pretentious, grandiloquent, overbearing, petulant and egotistical: all these adjectives could reasonably be used to describe typical aspects of his behaviour. With these traits in mind, some critics have ventured the assessment that he was 'unpleasant' and 'unlikeable', but this overlooks the fact that on many occasions he also displayed such admirable qualities as kindness, compassion, humour, courage and moral outrage at the many injustices he encountered. Following the events of *The Two Doctors*, he even became a vegetarian! It could be seen as a tribute to Colin Baker's abilities as an actor that he was able to assimilate so many diverse and apparently contradictory idiosyncrasies and mould them together into a three-dimensional (or should that be four-dimensional?), consistent and believable character.

Another common criticism made of the sixth Doctor is that, particularly during Season 22, he appeared to possess a rather violent streak, frequently resorting to the use of force to resolve problematic situations

– for example, shooting Cybermen with a gun in *Attack of the Cybermen*, causing some of his opponents to be killed with poisonous vines in *Vengeance on Varos* and physically tackling and suffocating the character Shockeye in *The Two Doctors*. The introduction of a running thread of black humour was also thought by some commentators to have misfired when the Doctor was seen to crack jokes over the bodies of dead and injured adversaries. Rather than fostering an air of alien aloofness, it was argued, this merely made him appear callous.

Colin Baker was generally unmoved by such objections. 'I personally would probably go a bit further myself,' he said in a 1984 interview for the fanzine *Time Watcher*. 'I'm undecided, to be honest. John Nathan-Turner is very keen that the Doctor should not be a violent person, and of course I agree with that. But I think that it's sometimes naive to expect that one can get out of every situation without being placed in a position where one might have to be violent, or to use violence.

'I think that if one sanitises violence, if one cleans it up too much, it has the effect of conditioning people to it. They become so used to seeing people being shot and falling over and nothing messy happening that it makes violence seem acceptable. Whereas, despite what the critics say, directors who show blood pumping out and severed organs dragging across the ground, things which are horrific and unpleasant to look at, are at least showing what violence really is. Violence is horrible. But it's maybe true that in *Doctor Who* we're dealing in an area which is a bit removed from first-degree naturalism, so it's better if we stay away from showing that kind of direct effect of violence. I think it's always better if the Doctor can get himself out of a situation by using the mind.'

On other occasions, the actor was rather less equivocal. 'I am quite fond of violence,' he told the audience at a US *Doctor Who* convention in 1985. 'I like it a lot. Some people were appalled at the vicious way in which I disposed of the Cyber Controller in *Attack of the Cybermen*. I wanted to go much further, but they wouldn't let me. I wanted to stand over him pumping machine gun bullets into him for hours . . . green stuff all over the walls. But they said, "No, that's going too far; three or four will do quite nicely, thank you." '

While remarks like this were made partly tongue-in-cheek, Baker clearly relished the more physical aspects of the role. This was something on which he had commented when discussing his interpretation of the Doctor's character in a 1984 interview for the magazine *Fantasy Empire*:

'Doctor Who is neither a good guy nor a bad guy. He's an apart guy. He has a very strict code. He's always on the side of goodness in the universe, but you couldn't say he was being saintly. He's very rude to people and apparently quite heartless, although he's not really.

'I think in order to play the Doctor an actor has to draw on himself very largely. I think the reason John Nathan-Turner asked me to play the part is that he saw things in me which he thought I could usefully bring to it . . . An interest in cats, a sense of the ridiculous, a sense of chivalry. I believe in a lot of the great values of chivalry, like a sort of a cross between the Dragonriders of Pern and William Tell . . . I hope my Doctor will be cerebral. I certainly want him to be the brightest there is around.

'When John Nathan-Turner spoke to me he asked me how I felt about the physical stuff and I said I loved doing it. I've done stage fighting in Shakespeare and all that. There's not a lot of swordplay in *Doctor Who*. I think it might be nice to have a fight between the Master and the Doctor. I'd like to get involved in one of those. I love the physical stuff and I want to climb the walls and fight the villains.'

Season 22 was, for *Doctor Who*, unusually grim and downbeat in tone, and the depiction of a somewhat harder Doctor can be seen as merely symptomatic of this more general shift in the series' emphasis, the responsibility for which must rest primarily with the production team. The on-screen realisation of a character such as the Doctor is inevitably a fusion of the actor's own qualities with the writers' conception as reflected in the action and dialogue laid down in the scripts. As Baker put it in his interview for *Fantasy Empire*, this synthesis of performer and script is 'a sort of marriage, if you like. Your own personality plus the page in front of you which tells you what the Doctor says and what he does. All somehow gradually combining over a period of time into something different.'

It should also be noted that the Time Lord's earlier incarnations had been by no means averse to becoming involved in direct physical action: the first Doctor had gleefully indulged in a bout of 'fisticuffs' with the mute assassin Ascaris in *The Romans*; the third had frequently overpowered assailants using Venusian karate; the fourth had launched violent assaults on a number of opponents in stories such as *The Seeds of Doom* and *The Deadly Assassin*; and there are many other examples which could be quoted. So it can be argued that the sixth Doctor's use of force was not an entirely unprecedented departure from established characterisation. The issue was really one of degree.

Having initially studied a number of his predecessors' stories on video, Colin Baker did make a conscious effort to include some of their traits in his own performance, as he told *Arkensword* in 1984:

'It's a lot made up with ingredients of the previous Doctors. Pertwee's adventure sense. I like that, the derring-do, swinging from ropes, and I want Eric Saward to write in things like that because I enjoy it. Hartnell's irascibility. Tom Baker's irreverence, up to a point. The one thing I don't want to do is belittle the monsters. I think that if you start joking and clowning around when being threatened by a Cyberman or a Dalek it's so easy to make them look as though they are not very threatening. When analysed, a Dalek is a very difficult thing to be frightened of because it can't even climb a flight of stairs. And once you start sticking jelly babies in the end of their nozzles then it makes life difficult, because it has to work for the audience.'

Another influence was Baker's love of cats. He adopted the cat as the symbol of the sixth Doctor's persona, as reflected in various badges which he wore on his coat lapel, and often quoted Rudyard Kipling: 'I am the cat that walks by himself, and all places are the same to me.' (This is actually a paraphrasing of lines from the poem *The Cat that Walked by Himself*: 'The Cat. He walked by himself, and all places were alike to him.') 'Cats', said the actor in a 1985 interview for the *Doctor Who* Appreciation Society's magazine *TARDIS*, 'do what *they* want to do, *when* they want to do it, and it may fit in sometimes with what you want to do, but that's never a consideration, and I think that's a bit like the Doctor.'

In another 1985 interview, for the fanzine *Fan Aid 2*, Baker was asked how he saw the character of the sixth Doctor developing in future stories. 'I'm afraid it sounds like a cop-out,' he replied, 'but there is no answer to that question. I see it developing, full stop. I wouldn't wish to prejudice that development by saying how I think it should go, because that would imply that the job of the writer and the producer is merely that of a cipher – which is not the case. We work together in a kind of symbiotic way. Very rarely are conscious decisions about development made. It comes out of ideas and developments of ideas.'

In later years, however, the actor asserted that there *had* been a long-term plan for development of the sixth Doctor's character. Talking to the 1989 fanzine *Kroton* about the irritation he had felt at his premature expulsion from the series, he said:

'It was very frustrating because we had envisaged an overall plan over a few years of how we could learn more about this Doctor, and didn't want to give too much away in the first few seasons. We wanted people to be a little unsure about this person and then gradually find out "Ah, he's not really like that, that's because of this." All sorts of things and clever nuances that we never had a chance to explore. That's life though.'

In a 1990 interview for the *Myth Makers 19* video, released by Reeltime Pictures, the actor again spoke of his long-term plan for the development of the character, and gave the following literary analogy:

'I always like to compare the idea to that of the character Darcy in *Pride and Prejudice*. For the first 35 per cent of the book you hate him, then you grudgingly come to like him, and then by the end of the book you think he is the best person in it. That's sort of what we wanted to do with the Doctor.'

A degree of progression in the Doctor's character was certainly apparent between the end of the 22nd season and the beginning of the 23rd, when the series returned after the 1985/86 production hiatus with the fourteen-part story *The Trial of a Time Lord*. Apart from during a short period when his sanity was called into question for the purposes of a sub-plot, the Doctor as seen in this season was noticeably mellower and less aggressive than before, again reflecting a more general shift in the series' emphasis (and incidentally providing an effective contrast to the season's major villain, the Valeyard – a character intended literally to personify the dark side of the Doctor's nature).

To a casual observer the sixth Doctor might still have appeared to be little more than a rather egotistical adventurer with a poor taste in clothes and a tendency towards over-reaction and brash theatricality. Beneath this facade, however, Colin Baker had by this time succeeded in establishing a deeper level to the character, making him more interesting and agreeable. He was now clearly capable of compassion whilst outwardly continuing to appear off-hand and detached, as illustrated by his habit of offering allusive quotations rather than making direct statements. A distinction was drawn between his superficial image as perceived by others and his true underlying qualities, which were gentler and more concerned. 'I am known as the Doctor,' he would often announce, whereas his predecessors had been content to say simply 'I am the Doctor.'

This softening of the sixth Doctor's demeanour was very evident in his relationship with his companion, Peri. Up until this point, their conversations had been characterised by ill-tempered bickering and petty point-scoring, Peri displaying a distinct tendency to whinge and whine – a situation which John Nathan-Turner attributed to a lack of ingenuity on the writers' part, as he told *Doctor Who Magazine* in an interview published in May 1986:

'There is a problem that writers face in terms of the show, which is that the initial TARDIS scene between the companion and the Doctor is inevitably preoccupied with its position in setting out where you're going and why you're going there and so forth, in order to lay the foundations for a particular story. One obvious way of getting out of that is by conflict, and often a writer will lapse into unnecessary conflict in order to get that information over. That is just a dramatic device, and one that I would like to see less of.'

In *The Trial of a Time Lord* this wish was fulfilled, as the Doctor and Peri appeared to be on much friendlier terms. Interviewed for *Doctor Who Magazine* some years later, actress Nicola Bryant explained how she and Colin Baker had modified their performances, sometimes playing scenes against the way they had been written, to help achieve this effect:

'When we came back after so long we felt we couldn't have the same relationship. We would have parted company on bad terms – either I would have left or he would have dropped me off. The relationship settled down and we had to establish that although they may have their differences they still cared for each other. Looking back, I think the constant bickering and fighting was taken too far.'

A further change occurred partway through *The Trial of a Time Lord* when Peri was written out of the series and Bonnie Langford was introduced as her successor, Melanie. Interviewed during a March 1987 convention at the University of Western Washington, USA, Colin Baker spoke of the Doctor's more demonstrative behaviour towards this new companion:

'One change, which was rather nice, was that I was able to be much more openly affectionate towards Mel than I had been towards Peri. This was because Bonnie was very young-looking and wasn't as voluptuous as Nicola, so nobody could misconstrue my actions as having a sexual connotation. If I had put my arm around Nicola and said, "Come on darling," people would have been very taken aback. Bonnie, though, had a kind of asexuality about her in the character of Melanie. As I'm much older than she is and she's so very girlish, the relationship was obviously paternal or avuncular. So I was able, especially the way it was written, to give her the odd cuddle. That was always very difficult with Nicola's character, and I was constantly being asked by the directors to tone it down; there might have been some suggestion of hanky-panky in the TARDIS, and we couldn't have that! I think the relationship between Melanie and the sixth Doctor would have worked out very nicely, but sadly it was thwarted in its progression.'

It is perhaps ironic that just as Baker had refined his interpretation of the Doctor and succeeded in winning over many of the viewers who had been uncomfortable with his initial, rather more abrasive characterisation, any further development was abruptly forestalled by the BBC management's decision not to renew his contract. As he recalled in his interview for *The Frame*, he was asked to stay on for just the first four episodes of Season 24 to record a regeneration story, but declined to do so: 'I was offered the chance to do the first four episodes of the following season – that was actually a concession won by John – but I said, "Quite honestly, if I've got to leave, I want to leave now and start making a career." The analogy I've always used is that it's like your girlfriend giving you the push and saying, "But you can come back and spend a night with me next year!" It's just not on.'

This was not quite the end of the road for Colin Baker's portrayal of the sixth Doctor, however, as he returned in 1989 in the Mark Furness Ltd touring stage play *Doctor Who – The Ultimate Adventure*.

Many commentators felt that it was in this production that Baker was at his most assured and engaging in his portrayal of the Doctor. As one reviewer put it, 'He gives a great performance, which leaves you yearning for more.' This reflected the actor's own satisfaction with his return to the role, as he explained in his interview for *The Frame*:

'Doing this show has been like putting on a pair of comfy old slippers. I was a little alarmed at how easily I slipped into it again, and how much I enjoyed it, although it's rekindled old sadnesses as well. I won't feel particularly sad when it finishes, mind you, because I've done nearly a hundred performances, and that's enough. But it's been nice to play the part again. In a way, it's laid a ghost, it's added a coda. It's made me believe that my Doctor has a part in the scheme of things.'

In a 1990 interview for the fanzine *Skaro*, Baker looked back on his time in *Doctor Who* and offered the following summation of the sixth Doctor's character:

'I would describe him as embodying all the Doctor's traditional virtues – compassion, kindness, high principles, a crusading spirit and a desire to relieve oppression and deal with the oppressor – but at the same time tinged with arrogance, irritability and impatience, which I got a little bit from the first Doctor. He enjoyed the pursuit of the mind and did not find it necessary to display what he was feeling, and could therefore appear to the Earthling observer to be a little unfeeling. That doesn't mean he *was* unfeeling; he just didn't feel the necessity to display it.'

Controversial though it had been, the era of the sixth Doctor finished all too soon for the many viewers who had come to savour his effulgent, larger-than-life personality – truly a light burning bright.

PART TWO – FICTION

3: The Stories

'What's happened?'

'Change my dear. And, it seems, not a moment too soon!'

As the new, rather arrogant sixth Doctor sits up in his TARDIS after his near-fatal adventure on Androzani Minor, it seems that he has rejected totally the affable persona of his previous incarnation. Viewers have little indication of what lies in store, or of what the new incarnation of the Doctor will ultimately be like. Picking himself up off the floor, the Doctor heads for the TARDIS wardrobe . . .

Note: In the following listings, the technical details are as follows: 'Time' refers to the starting time, rounded to the nearest minute, of the original transmission of an episode in England; 'Durn' indicates the exact duration of the episode on the master tape; 'Viewers' gives the official viewing figure in millions; 'Chart Pos' is the position of the episode in the top 200 programmes for that week. Where a dash appears in the 'Viewers' or 'Chart Pos' column, this signifies that no information was collected by the BBC for the transmission in question. 'OB' stands for Outside Broadcast recording.

SEASON TWENTY-ONE

The Twin Dilemma (6S)

EP	DATE	TIME	DURN	VIEWERS	CHART POS
1	22.03.84	18.41	24'42"	7.6	66
2	23.03.84	18.41	25'09"	7.4	71
3	29.03.84	18.41	24'27"	7.0	59
4	30.03.84	18.43	25'04"	6.3	67

PRODUCTION DETAILS

Location filming: 07.02.84–08.02.84

Studio: 24.01.84–26.01.84 in TC8, 14.02.84–16.02.84 in TC3

The Doctor's regeneration has left him mentally unstable. He changes his cricket attire for an outfit of clashing colours, including a multicoloured patchwork frock coat. After almost killing Peri during a fit of instability he decides to live as a hermit to avoid putting others at risk.

On Earth, mathematical genius twin brothers Romulus (Paul Conrad) and Remus (Andrew Conrad) are kidnapped by Professor Edgeworth (Maurice Denham). The kidnapping is discovered – tell-tale traces of a material called zanium are found on the floor – and a squadron of space fighters under the command of Lieutenant Hugo Lang (Kevin McNally) is sent to pursue the X.V.773 Space Hopper Mk III Freighter on which Edgeworth is escaping with the twins. The fighters are attacked, leaving Lang as the sole survivor when his ship crashes on the asteroid Titan 3. The TARDIS lands here too, and the Doctor and Peri find Lang in the wreckage. The Doctor reluctantly agrees to investigate a distant dome, which is in fact where Edgeworth has taken the twins as a halfway safe house on his journey back to the planet Joconda.

The Doctor and Peri arrive at the dome only to be captured by Edgeworth's two Jocondan guards, Noma (Barry Stanton) and Drak (Oliver Smith). Edgeworth is recognised by the Doctor as a retired Time Lord whose real name is Azmael. Azmael had ruled Joconda since his retirement, but the planet has now fallen under the control of a race of giant Gastropods – slug-like creatures from Jocondan mythology – led by Mestor (Edwin Richfield), who is now forcing Azmael to do his bidding.

The Doctor and Peri are left sealed in the dome as Azmael and the others leave for Joconda. When they are alone, they discover that the dome has been set to self-destruct – an action taken by Noma without Azmael's knowledge. The Doctor hastily adapts a Revitalising Modulator to transmit his and Peri's molecules back in time to the TARDIS and thus escape the destruction of the dome. To his amazement, it works.

Together with Lang, who had been left behind in the TARDIS to recuperate while they explored the asteroid, the Doctor and Peri journey to Joconda, where they are soon captured and imprisoned with Azmael. Mestor claims to need the twins' mathematical prowess to provide the energy equations required to realise his plan of placing the Jocondan sun's outer two planets into orbit around Joconda, thus providing a ready-made larder facility. To balance the gravitational forces, Mestor wants all three planets to occupy the same space, but in different time periods, one Jocondan day apart. The Doctor realises that as the outer planets are small, the gravitational differences will pull them into the sun and cause a massive explosion. This is Mestor's real plan, as the explosion will activate millions of his eggs and send them out into space to fall on to other worlds, thus populating the whole of space with the giant slugs.

The Doctor tries to destroy Mestor by throwing at him a vial of corrosive chemicals from Azmael's laboratory, but the attempt is thwarted when the creature raises a force shield around itself. Mestor now wants to possess the Doctor's body, and to prove that he is capable of doing so he attempts to mind-link with Azmael. While Mestor is distracted, the Doctor hurls a second vial of chemicals at him, and this time strikes the target. Azmael triggers his thirteenth and last regeneration, and Mestor's mind, having nowhere to flee now that his body has been destroyed, dissipates into nothingness. Unfortunately Azmael dies too. The threat from the Gastropods is lifted and the Doctor prepares to return the twins to Earth. Hugo elects to stay on Joconda to help the Jocondans rebuild their planet.

WHO FAX

- Novelised as *Doctor Who – The Twin Dilemma* by Eric Saward in 1986.
- Story released on BBC Home Video in 1992.
- Locations: Gerrards Cross Quarry, Bucks; Harefield Quarry,

Rickmansworth, Bucks.

- For the first time since 1966, the Doctor's regeneration takes place mid-season, leaving Colin Baker to close Season 21 as the Doctor after only one story.
- A new opening and closing title sequence was used, featuring the sixth Doctor's face.
- Eric Saward extensively re-wrote Anthony Steven's original script.
- Actor Edwin Richfield (Mestor) had previously appeared in *Doctor Who* playing Captain Hart in the 1972 story *The Sea Devils*.
- Denis Chinnery, who played Albert C. Richardson in the 1965 story *The Chase* and Gharman in the 1975 story *Genesis of the Daleks*, appears in a cameo role as Professor Sylvest, the twins' father.
- The Doctor uses the TARDIS's wardrobe room to look for a new set of clothes. Among the garments he picks up are the voluminous fur coat worn by the second Doctor in *The Five Doctors*, and a velvet jacket similar to those favoured by his third incarnation.
- There is a musical cue for Tegan when the Doctor recalls her in part two.
- Romulus and Remus were played by twins Gavin and Andrew Conrad. For the programme, Gavin's name was changed to Paul as there was already an actor by the name of Gavin Conrad.
- One of the two Gastropods seen as extras in part three was played by actor Steve Wickham, who went on to become Coordinator of the *Doctor Who* Appreciation Society.
- The cat badge worn by the Doctor in his lapel for this story was hand-made and painted by Suzie Trevor, and purchased for the programme from a specialist badge shop in central London.
- Production of *The Twin Dilemma* was affected by industrial action at the BBC. It eventually went into the studio about a month later than intended and, unusually, the location filming was done not in advance of but between the two blocks of studio work.
- Three Gastropod costumes were made for the story by Richard Gregory of the freelance effects firm Imagineering. The one for Mestor was more sophisticated than the other two, featuring an animated mouthpiece, and the mask was designed to be easily removable as the actor, Edwin Richfield, suffered from claustrophobia.

QUOTES

- 'The whole behavioural aspect of the Doctor in *The Twin Dilemma* was quite deliberate – I wanted to explore what happened after the regeneration. With this in mind we wanted a writer who was very experienced and who could write the sort of dialogue to make this sort of bizarre situation believable. The whole thing needed expert handling. Now Anthony Steven is a tremendously successful and experienced prize-winning writer. He had worked with John Nathan-Turner on some episodes of *All Creatures Great and Small* and on this basis I approached him. He agreed, and from his basic ideas and a lot of long discussion we got *The Twin Dilemma* as we wanted it.' Script editor Eric Saward interviewed by Richard Marson for *Doctor Who Magazine* Issue 94.

- 'Because we were shooting in February we had only about five hours of each day with enough light to shoot. On top of that it was cold and very muddy – everyone wore plastic bags to protect their costumes between takes!' Director Peter Moffatt interviewed by Richard Marson for *Doctor Who Magazine* Winter Special 1985.

- 'Edwin Richfield, who played Mestor, could hardly move – it was very restricting. He had to use his arms like fins because he couldn't use his elbows. The difficult thing was that, in rehearsal, actors playing monsters give a beautiful facial performance and you have to keep reminding them that they won't be visible in the studio. I chose Edwin for his voice – he had so much to express and it was recorded naturally on the boom mike, coming out slightly distorted from behind the mask and then treated in sypher dub.' Director Peter Moffatt interviewed by Richard Marson for *Doctor Who Magazine* Winter Special 1985.

- 'I thought it was going to be impossible to find twins for the roles of Romulus and Remus. I suggested to John opting for a boy and a girl so it wouldn't be noticeable that they weren't identical. I'd interviewed a lot of actors and actresses with this in mind when suddenly an agent rang up out of the blue and said "We've got some real twins." They read well, although they were not experienced, and so I took them on.' Director Peter Moffatt interviewed by Richard Marson for *Doctor Who Magazine* Winter Special 1985.

COMMENT

DJH: *At the time of transmission I hated* The Twin Dilemma. *The problem lies both in the script – which is ill conceived and confusing – and in the acting – which is almost universally bad. The character of the Doctor comes over as unpredictable and unlikeable, which is not a good way to start off a new Doctor. I found that I didn't know who the Doctor was any more, and, worse, that I didn't like him. However, looking back on the story now, one can see the eventual character of the Doctor quite clearly, and the manic unpredictable aspects are concentrated in selected sequences. Colin Baker's performance is much better in retrospect than I thought at the time, and this just reinforces my opinion that* The Twin Dilemma *should never have been his debut adventure, and certainly should not have closed a season. (1/10)*

MS: *After the highly dramatic* The Caves of Androzani, The Twin Dilemma *is a very disappointing and lightweight story. To introduce the new Doctor to the public in a story which saw him acting deranged and out of character was a mistake which was to haunt the programme throughout the Colin Baker era. The whole production has a very garish feel to it which matches the Doctor's new tasteless outfit. The plot of the story is extremely disjointed and barely manages to hang together at all. Colin Baker has a difficult job to achieve in acting the role of the manic and unstable sixth Doctor before he has had the chance to work out the finer points of his character. The result is a rather over-the-top performance. Nicola Bryant has little chance to shine, Peri being rather overshadowed by the new, larger-than-life Doctor. The acting of the supporting cast is also uninspired, with the exception of Maurice Denham, who brings to Azmael a believability missing from the rest of the story. Overall, a rather inauspicious start for the new Doctor. (2/10)*

SJW: *The idea of making the new Doctor dangerously unstable was a brave attempt at a different approach. Sadly, however, his bizarre behaviour and violent mood-swings come across as being rather forced and artificial, and succeed only in alienating the viewer. It doesn't help that the story itself has little to recommend it, being clichéd, flimsy and undramatic. Peter Moffatt's direction is flat and uninteresting, and the whole production has a rather tacky, B-movie feel to it. The Gastropods must be one of the series' most uninspired* creations, although – on the plus side – the bird-like Jocondans are quite effective, due in large part to Denise Baron's excellent make-up design. The performances are equally varied, ranging from the praiseworthy – Maurice Denham as Azmael and Seymour Green as the Jocondan Chamberlain – to the lamentable – Paul and Andrew Conrad as the twins and, truly cringe-inducing, Helen Blatch as Fabian. In summary, this is the least appealing of any of the Doctors' debuts, and one of the weakest entries in Doctor Who's entire canon. (2/10)

SEASON TWENTY-TWO

Attack of the Cybermen (6T)

EP	DATE	TIME	DURN	VIEWERS	CHART POS
1	05.01.85	17.23	44'17"	8.9	71
2	12.01.85	17.23	44'29"	7.2	104

PRODUCTION DETAILS

Location filming: 29.05.84–01.06.84

Model filming: 07.06.84, 08.06.84

Studio: 21.06.84, 22.06.84, 05.07.84–07.07.84, all in TC6

Whilst travelling alongside Halley's Comet, the TARDIS picks up an alien distress call from Earth.

In the sewers below London's Fleet Street, a small gang of petty criminals – Griffiths (Brian Glover), Payne (James Beckett) and Russell (Terry Molloy), with their boss Lytton (Maurice Colbourne), ex-commander of the Dalek task force [*Resurrection of the Daleks*] – are apparently attempting to pull off a jewellery robbery.

The Doctor and Peri arrive in London, the TARDIS materialising at 76 Totter's Lane [*100,000 BC*]. As the Doctor had been trying to repair the chameleon circuits, the TARDIS takes a few seconds to adjust and then transforms into a large, decorated cupboard. The Doctor and Peri track the distress signal to a deserted house, but the Time Lord then realises that it is being relayed from elsewhere. They return to the TARDIS to follow the signal back to source, unaware that they are under surveillance by the two policeman-disguised androids (Mike Braben, Michael Jeffries) who also escaped from the Dalek spacecraft with Lytton.

The travellers arrive at a scrap metal yard and investigate a car-inspection pit through which Lytton's gang has gained access to the sewers. They are confronted by the policemen, but the Doctor manages to disarm them. They then enter the sewers to investigate further.

Lytton has contrived to get his unwitting gang into the sewers to bring them to the Cybermen, who have established a secret base there. Payne is killed by a Cyber Scout in the tunnels and Lytton and Griffiths are captured by the Cybermen. Russell – in reality an undercover policeman – runs back through the sewers and encounters the Doctor and Peri. Lytton has meanwhile offered his help to the Cybermen and the Cyber Leader (David Banks) has agreed to transport him to Telos to meet the Cyber Controller (Michael Kilgarriff).

On returning to the TARDIS – which is now 'disguised' as a pipe-organ – the Doctor, Peri and Russell are captured by the Cybermen, who have already found and entered the ship. Russell is killed and the Cyber Leader forces the Doctor to transport them all to Telos.

Telos is being mined by the Cybermen using slave labour – a group of partially cybernised humans who were found to be unsuitable for complete conversion. Three of these workers make a bid for freedom, but only two, Stratton (Jonathan David) and Bates (Michael Attwell), manage to escape. They intend to steal back their time ship which the Cybermen had captured, but unfortunately it requires three pilots.

Thanks to the Doctor interfering with the guidance systems, the TARDIS materialises, in the form of a gateway, in the lower levels of the tombs on Telos, slightly off course. On emerging, the occupants are attacked by a rogue Cyberman and, in the confusion, Peri, Lytton and Griffiths manage to escape. Peri is found and captured by Rost (Sarah Berger) and Varne (Sarah Greene), two of the Cryon race who were the original inhabitants of Telos, and taken to their base. The Doctor, meanwhile, is taken up to Cyber Control.

Peri discovers that Lytton is in fact working for the Cryons to try to thwart the Cybermen's plan of knocking Halley's Comet off course in 1985 and crashing it into the Earth, thus preventing the destruction of the Cybermen's original planet Mondas in 1986 [*The Tenth Planet*].

Lytton and Griffiths find their way to the Cryon base and from there make their way to hijack the time ship.

The Doctor has been taken before the Cyber Controller, who apparently survived his earlier attempt to destroy him [*The Tomb of the Cybermen*]. The Controller orders that the Doctor be imprisoned in a sub-zero store room. There the Doctor meets Flast (Faith Brown), the Cryon leader.

Flast tells the Doctor of the Cybermen's plan and he guesses that he has been manoeuvred by the Time Lords into being their agent to prevent the alteration of history. Flast explains to the Doctor that they are being held in a refrigerated chamber which also contains many crates of vastial, a mineral found in the coldest areas of Telos which becomes extremely volatile in temperatures above ten degrees and self-ignites at fifteen degrees. The Cybermen intend to destroy Telos with this when they leave, as an experiment to see what it will do to the planet's atmosphere. The Doctor uses a small amount of vastial to despatch their guard and then leaves Flast with a sonic lance which should have sufficient power remaining to ignite the rest of the mineral. Flast activates the lance and hides it in a box of vastial.

Lytton and Griffiths locate Stratton and Bates on the Telosian surface and the four of them join forces to capture the time ship. They are almost there when Lytton is re-captured by the Cybermen. He is tortured until he reveals his plan and the Cybermen then set up an ambush at the time ship. Bates is electrocuted when he touches the door to the ship, and Griffiths and Stratton are gunned down by Cybermen waiting inside.

Discovering that the Doctor has escaped from the store room, the Cybermen investigate. They kill Flast by dragging her out of the cold storage room into the warm corridor – Cryons being able to exist only in sub-zero temperatures – and then start to check the vastial in case the Doctor has interfered with it.

With arrangements made for Lytton to steal the time ship, the Cryons take Peri to the TARDIS with the intention of forcing her to move it, leaving the Cybermen with no means of carrying out their plan. The Cybermen guarding the TARDIS are killed and the Doctor and Peri reunited. Peri explains the Cryons' plan to the Doctor and he attempts to rescue Lytton from Cyber Control.

Lytton has already been partially cybernised. The Doctor attempts to remove him from the machinery, but is interrupted by the arrival of the Cyber Controller. The weakened Lytton manages to stab the Controller, who rains down blows upon him before turning his attention to the Doctor. Two Cybermen arrive but kill each other in the confusion and the Doctor finally manages to destroy the Controller with a Cybergun. He is too late to save Lytton, however, who dies from his injuries.

The Doctor and Peri leave Telos in the TARDIS just before a huge explosion, caused by the vastial reaching its ignition point, destroys the Cyber Control centre. The Doctor, safe in the TARDIS, ponders on how he could have so misjudged Lytton.

WHO FAX

- Novelised as *Doctor Who – Attack of the Cybermen* by Eric Saward in 1989.
- Locations: Wapsey's Wood, Gerrards Cross, Bucks; junkyard, Birkbeck Road, Acton, London; scrapyard, Becklow Road, Acton, London; Davis Road and alley, Acton, London; Glenthorne Road, Hammersmith, London.
- For this season all the stories were broadcast as 45-minute episodes.
- Maurice Colbourne reprised his role of Lytton from *Resurrection of the Daleks*.
- Michael Kilgarriff reprised his role as the Cyber Controller from *The Tomb of the Cybermen*. He had also appeared as an Ogron in the 1973 story *Frontier in Space* and as the Robot in the 1974 story *Robot*.
- At the end of the story, the TARDIS reverts to the familiar form of a London police box. One is left to presume that either the chameleon circuit has failed or the Doctor has fixed it in that form once again.
- A version of part of Ron Grainer's *Steptoe and Son* theme is used when the TARDIS arrives in the junkyard. When the ship converts into its pipe organ form, an arrangement of Bach's *Toccata and Fugue* is heard.
- Lytton is revealed to originate from the planet Riften 5, the fifteenth satellite in orbit around Vita in Star System 690.
- Writer Paula Moore (real name reported to be Paula Woolsey) had previously worked in radio and was a friend of script editor Eric Saward. The final scripts, which were completely rewritten by Saward, also incorporated some ideas from *Doctor Who* fan Ian Levine.
- Actress and celebrity Koo Stark was originally to have appeared in this story as one of the Cryons but pulled out after a disagreement with the production team over publicity.

QUOTES

● 'With the Bates, Stratton and Griffiths characters, the narrative was that as they developed and finished their contribution they were killed. The idea behind that was to create a separate theme. We had the Doctor locked up in most of episode two and this was the second story strand – of people struggling to get out. It was the resistance bit that the Doctor was unable to do. It was quite a positive element. Being pretentious about it, it showed the energy and effort that people put in to avoid death. They don't just sit there. They were being very determined about trying to escape from Telos and, although they died in the attempt, I think the way they went about it lifted the story dramatically.' Script editor Eric Saward interviewed by Richard Marson for *Doctor Who Magazine* Issue 104.

COMMENT

DJH: Although it is very complex, and demands a lot from the viewer, Attack of the Cybermen *is very enjoyable. Whereas* The Twin Dilemma *failed in the quality of the acting, this is an area of great strength here. The only disappointments are the Cyber Controller and his Lieutenant, who do not have the presence on screen that David Banks brings to his Cyber Leader. Kilgarriff plays the Controller with very jerky, robotic movements which are at odds with the smooth fluidity of most of the rest of the Cybermen. The location work is excellent, with Gerrards Cross Quarry again becoming the Telosian surface, and the model effects are also of a very high standard. The Cryons are well conceived and directed. Their constant delicate movements and translucent costumes and masks make them quite eerie, and – with the possible exception of Sarah Greene, whose voice seems wrong for the character and whose movements seem forced rather than natural – the actresses are very successful in conveying the unearthly qualities of the creatures. The interleaving of different aspects of* Doctor Who *history works well, although the tombs look nothing like those in* The Tomb of the Cybermen, *and 76 Totter's Lane has undergone a major facelift. Overall this is one of the better Cyberman adventures, and would have made a far superior debut for the sixth Doctor. (8/10)*

MS: Attack of the Cybermen *features the interweaving of plot elements from a number of previous stories, including* The Tenth Planet, The Tomb of the Cybermen *and* Resurrection of the Daleks. *These make the story a treat for regular fans, but perhaps a little alienating for more casual viewers. Strong performances from the majority of the cast add much to the atmosphere, with Maurice Colbourne as Lytton and Jonathan David and Michael Attwell as Stratton and Bates worthy of special praise. The only problem is that, with many different plot threads taking place at the same time, it can be confusing. (6/10)*

SJW: *Unlike earlier Cyberman stories,* Attack of the Cybermen *is an all-out action adventure – a move no doubt partly inspired by the acclaim accorded the 'Cyber massacre' scenes in* The Five Doctors. *As such it is reasonably successful, although the convolution of the plot detracts from its overall impact, as does the excessive reliance on the series' own mythology. What makes matters worse in this regard is that the continuity points are often inaccurate, particularly from a visual standpoint. Not only do the Cybermen's tombs look completely dissimilar to those seen in* The Tomb of the Cybermen, *they are nowhere near as impressive. Even worse is the Cyber Controller who, although played by the same actor, is far removed from the sleek, menacing figure of his debut story. One consequence of all these deficiencies is that the only viewers who could appreciate the many continuity references, namely the series' fans, instead tend to find them irritating.*

There is, however, much to enjoy in this story. The sewer scenes featuring the camouflaged Cyber Scout are tense and effective, as are those in which various humans are shown being converted into Cybermen – a process often referred to in previous stories but never really depicted. It's good, too, to see Maurice Colbourne making a return appearance as Lytton, although the mercenary's sudden repentance of his past wrongs is, it must be said, rather unconvincing. All in all, not a bad start to the season. (5/10)

Vengeance on Varos (6V)

EP	DATE	TIME	DURN	VIEWERS	CHART POS
1	19.01.85	17.22	44'42"	7.2	110
2	26.01.85	17.21	44'43"	7.0	108

PRODUCTION DETAILS

Studio: 18.07.84–20.07.84, 31.07.84–02.08.84 in TC6

The TARDIS becomes stranded in space after its transitional elements lose their ability to generate orbital energy. There is a small residue of power remaining, however, and this enables the Doctor to direct the ship to the planet Varos in the constellation of Cetes, where he hopes to obtain some zeiton 7 with which to reline the trans/power system.

Varos is a bleak world, formerly a penal mining colony for the criminally insane. The descendants of the original guards still rule, while the people, like Arak (Stephen Yardley) and his wife Etta (Sheila Reid), live and work in hunger and squalor, entertained by continuous television transmissions from the Punishment Dome, a labyrinth of traps and deadly games where enemies of the state are tortured and executed in a variety of imaginative ways.

The Doctor is not the only visitor to Varos. Sil (Nabil Shaban), the representative of the Galatron Mining Corporation, is here for negotiations with the current Governor (Martin Jarvis) to try to fix a new price for the planet's zeiton ore. The Governor wishes to raise the price to pay for a better lifestyle for his people, but Sil threatens that unless the price is cut he will refuse to buy any at all, leaving the Varosians unable to afford essential supplies.

The TARDIS materialises inside the Punishment Dome, where the Doctor and Peri prevent the execution of the rebel leader Jondar (Jason Connery). They are chased by the guards into the tunnels where they are helped by Jondar's wife Areta (Geraldine Alexander) and Rondel (Keith Skinner), one of the guards and a friend of Jondar. Rondel is killed and the Doctor, Peri, Jondar and Areta head deeper into the Dome's tunnels in order to shake off the guards. They enter the Purple Zone, where they are confronted by a giant gee-jee fly. The Doctor realises it is an illusion and, by shutting their eyes, they pass it. They make their way back to where the TARDIS was left but it has been taken away. They are again chased by guards and the Doctor becomes separated from Peri, Areta and Jondar, who are recaptured.

The Governor makes a television broadcast to explain to his people his decision to hold out for a better price for the ore, arguing that there would otherwise have to be further food rationing. The people of Varos vote on the Governor's plan and he is defeated, causing him to submit to a short bombardment of human cell-disintegrator rays. He manages to survive the bombardment – his third – but next time the effects will be fatal.

Sil believes the Doctor to be a rival negotiator from AMORB

Prospect Division and demands that he be killed. Peri and Areta, meanwhile, are placed in the custody of the sadistic head of the Punishment Dome, Mr Quillam (Nicholas Chagrin), who wears a half-mask to cover his disfigured face.

The Doctor wanders into a No-Options Kill Centre in the Dome and suffers an hallucination, believing himself to be dying of thirst in a desert. He collapses, apparently dead. His body is carried away by two Varosian mortuary attendants (Gareth Milne, Roy Alon), who prepare to tip it into a vat of acid. He comes round, however, and surprises the workers, one of whom accidentally falls into the acid and then pulls the other in after him. The Doctor leaves to find his friends but is recaptured.

Quillam uses a transmogrifier to alter the physical appearance of Areta and Peri so that they come to resemble the creatures that they subconsciously aspire to be. Areta starts to change into a scaly lizard-like creature, Peri into a feathered bird. The Doctor, having piqued the Governor's interest with hints about what he may have to offer, insists that Peri and Areta are freed before he will say more. Quillam refuses to help and so the Doctor destroys the control panel before forcing a guard, Maldak (Owen Teale), to take him to the girls. With the transmogrifying power switched off, the girls' metabolism resets itself, the change not having had time to become permanent.

Sil has been getting nowhere in his negotiations and so makes arrangements for an armed force from his home planet of Thoros-Beta to invade Varos.

The Chief Officer (Forbes Collins) forces the Governor to a final poll. The people again vote against him and the cell-disintegrator bombardment begins. Maldak, who is on guard, destroys the equipment before the process is completed – the Governor has convinced him that Varos's future prosperity lies with the knowledge possessed by the Doctor.

The Doctor and the rebels re-enter the Punishment Dome closely pursued by Quillam and the Chief Officer, both of whom are secretly in the pay of the Galatron Mining Corporation and are desperate to stop the Doctor revealing the true worth of zeiton 7 to the Governor.

Arriving in the Dome's End Zone, the Doctor and his friends are attacked by two cannibals (Jack McGuire, Alan Troy) and enter a forest-like area to escape. The Doctor notes that there are poisonous tendrils in amongst the foliage and lays a trap for their pursuers. As

Quillam, the Chief Officer and a guard approach, Jondar releases a cluster of the tendrils and they are killed.

Sil is still awaiting his invasion force when the Doctor and the Governor return to the control room. He brags to the Governor of the impending arrival of his troops, but the Doctor then draws his attention to an incoming message from the Galatron invasion force: the invasion is cancelled due to the discovery of traces of zeiton 7 on the asteroid Bio Sculptor, and Sil is ordered to secure supplies of the ore from Varos at whatever price the Governor wants.

The Governor thanks the Doctor and Peri for their help, and the Doctor requests a small amount of the ore for his own use.

WHO FAX

- Novelised as *Doctor Who – Vengeance on Varos* by Philip Martin in 1988
- Story released on BBC Home Video in 1993
- Locations: none.
- The story originally intended for this slot was *Space Whale* by comics writer Patrick Mills.
- *Vengeance on Varos* started life as a four-part storyline entitled *Domain*, featuring the fifth Doctor, Tegan and Nyssa. A later working title was *Planet of Fear*, which was ruled out as being too similar to the previous season's *Planet of Fire*. The final title was devised by writer Philip Martin from the "V" logo that he had suggested in his scripts.
- The script dates this story to the latter half of the 23rd century, although this is not confirmed on screen.
- Jason Connery, who played Jondar, is the son of film actor Sean Connery.
- For the sequence when the Doctor imagines himself to be dying in a desert, stock footage was obtained from the EMI picture library. Footage of a bluebottle was obtained from Oxford Scientific Films to represent the giant gee-jee fly.
- The characters of Arak and Etta were late additions. Philip Martin had conceived them as silent observers, but Eric Saward decided that they should comment on the action, rather like a Greek chorus.
- Nabil Shaban was cast as Sil after director Ron Jones interviewed a number of dwarves and midgets for the role. Shaban suffers from a disease called osteogenesis imperfecta, as a result of which his legs

are underdeveloped and he is confined to a wheelchair.
- It was originally intended that Sil would be partly submerged in his tank. This was too difficult to realise in the studio, however, so it was decided that he should instead be perched on a platform above it.
- Sil's costume was designed and made by effects designer Charles Jeanes.
- The marsh minnows that Sil habitually munches during the story were chopped peaches dyed green.
- Martin Jarvis, who played the Varosian Governor, had made two previous appearances in *Doctor Who*, as Hilio in *The Web Planet* and as Butler in *Invasion of the Dinosaurs*.
- The story had to be slightly edited for timing reasons, with the result that a number of scenes were lost. As some of these were humorous in nature, the finished story ended up being rather bleaker than Philip Martin had intended.

QUOTES
- 'When I started writing it, the series was on mid-week in 25-minute segments. Then it changed to 45-minute episodes, then I was told that Tegan and Nyssa were leaving, then that the Doctor was leaving. In fact, I remember doing one draft when we didn't know who the new Doctor was going to be, we didn't know who the companions were, and we weren't even sure of the timeslot! I had a track record of four scripts before *Varos* was ready to record – I felt as if I'd been writing it for a long time . . .' Writer Philip Martin interviewed by Paul Cornell for *Doctor Who Magazine* Issue 125.
- 'The original idea for the story was that I wondered what the entertainment business of the future would be. Then I got another idea; I wondered how a prison planet would develop. The two ideas collided, as they often do when you're creating things. I began to get the idea that the original officers of the prison planet had become the ruling elite, and that the original prisoners and their descendants had become the masses who would need to be entertained by violence.' Writer Philip Martin interviewed by Paul Cornell for *Doctor Who Magazine* Issue 125.
- 'When I was thinking about having an alien on Varos, I read something of Asimov's, which said that you never seemed to see water-based creatures. (This is partly because they don't like water in TV studios – you drop it on the floor and the paint, for some

reason, immediately blisters.) If he's in water he's probably an amphibian, a mutant. The designer came up with that. Then we had a real stroke of fortune, in that we had Nabil Shaban, who made the character of Sil his own, in terms not only of acting but also of intensity and motivation.' Writer Philip Martin interviewed by Paul Cornell for *Doctor Who Magazine* Issue 125.

● 'I read the script and thought at once "This is very exciting." If you remember *Gangsters*, it was in the same way a mix of toughness and humour. *Vengeance* fitted quite comfortably in the studio and I was quite happy for it to be that way. I thought the sets were most effective, and they were fairly flexible. For the mortuary fight scene we had to construct an entire water tank in the corner of the studio.' Director Ron Jones interviewed by Richard Marson for *Doctor Who Magazine* Issue 101.

● 'We were very lucky in our cast. Jason Connery, who played Jondar, is very up-and-coming, for instance, and Nabil Shaban was exactly right as Sil. I wanted him to appear as slimy as possible, and Nabil gave a lovely performance of the right kind of eye-rolling evil. The voice was designed to be quite sinister as well.' Director Ron Jones interviewed by Richard Marson for *Doctor Who Magazine* Issue 101.

COMMENT

DJH: Vengeance on Varos *proves again that there is nothing like a good story well told, but it is in the acting that it really shines. Only Geraldine Alexander (Areta) is weak, but any shortcomings are well compensated for by Nabil Shaban and Martin Jarvis. It is a thoroughly enjoyable adventure, which, like all good drama, can be enjoyed on several levels. (8/10)*

MS: Vengeance on Varos *is by far the best story of the sixth Doctor's era. The plot is based on the very clever idea of exploring people's fascination with video nasties. The viewer is presented with a society based around the production of this type of entertainment, the difference being that the torture shown on their video screens is for real. With such a controversial theme, the story was perhaps bound to attract attention from watchdog bodies like the National Viewers' and Listeners' Association, who accused the programme of promoting the kinds of violence that it was actually trying to parody.*

The story's greatest asset is its leading villain, Sil, who is superbly portrayed by the very talented Nabil Shaban. It is the character of Sil, part con-man part megalomaniac, and the inclusion of Arak and Etta – two Varosians who watch the unfolding drama of the story on their video screen – which lift Vengeance on Varos *from being a typical run-around adventure into something much more memorable. Colin Baker and Nicola Bryant both turn in fine performances, and are ably assisted by a good supporting cast which includes Martin Jarvis as the Governor and Jason Connery as the rebel leader Jondar. Stephen Yardley (Arak) and Sheila Reid (Etta) are also worthy of special praise. (8/10)*

SJW: Vengeance on Varos *is, in the best traditions of* Doctor Who, *a story which works on more than one level. At its simplest it is a tense and mildly horrific monster story which can be enjoyed as a piece of pure escapism, but at the other end of the spectrum it is an intelligent and thought-provoking discourse on such weighty issues as video nasties, torture and the responsibilities of leadership. Philip Martin's script is excellent – the stylised, almost Shakespearean dialogue of the Varosian characters being particularly noteworthy – and Ron Jones's direction is appropriately moody and atmospheric. Colin Baker gives a very strong performance as the Doctor and is backed up by a fine cast of supporting players, only Jason Connery as Jondar falling slightly short of expectations.*

Sil is an unusual and amusing character, excellently brought to life by the ideally cast Nabil Shaban. With his fractured speech, excitable manner and deliciously evil laugh he easily qualifies as the best original villain created during the sixth Doctor's era. (8/10)

The Mark of the Rani (6X)

EP	DATE	TIME	DURN	VIEWERS	CHART POS
1	02.02.85	17.22	45'01"	6.3	111
2	09.02.85	17.22	44'32"	7.3	84

PRODUCTION DETAILS

Location filming: 22.10.84–02.11.84 and one other day, date unknown

Studio: 18.11.84–20.11.84 in TC1

Deflected off course, the TARDIS materialises in the north of England at the dawn of the industrial revolution, a critical period in Earth's history. The introduction of machinery has met with much opposition from working people, some of whom have begun attacking and destroying it; and in the rural backwater where the Doctor and Peri have arrived, these Luddites are more violent and active than anywhere else in the country.

The Doctor is not the only alien visitor here, nor is he the only Time Lord. The Master (Anthony Ainley) is plotting to use Earth as a base for his operations, and it is he who is responsible for diverting the TARDIS here. There is also another Time Lord at work in the village. This is the Rani (Kate O'Mara), an exile from Gallifrey and a brilliant biochemist.

Cast out from Gallifrey because of her dangerous and callous experiments, having caused mice to be turned into monsters which ate the President's pet cat and bit the President himself, the Rani has now become dictator of a planet called Miasimia Goria. There, she has altered the metabolism of the populace, heightening their awareness but also, as an unfortunate side-effect, lowering their ability to sleep. In order to correct this defect, she has been extracting a chemical from the brains of humans, unconcerned by the fact that this leaves the humans aggressive and unable to sleep themselves. She has been conducting this operation at various points throughout Earth's history, some of her previous visits having aggravated the Trojan Wars, the Dark Ages and the American War of Independence. Now she is adding to the unrest caused by the Luddites.

When the Rani discovers that both the Master and the Doctor have arrived, she is less than happy. She initially refuses the Master's pleas to help him in his continuing attempts to kill his adversary but is forced to change her mind when he steals a vial of precious brain fluid from her and uses it for blackmail.

Lord Ravensworth (Terence Alexander), the owner of the mine in the village, has invited a number of the finest engineering geniuses – including Humphrey Davy, Thomas Telford, Michael Faraday, Mark Brunell and George Stephenson – to a meeting where they are to view Stephenson's latest steam engine. The Master realises that, with the aid of some maggots which the Rani has chemically impregnated with an obedience-inducing drug, he can control these key figures in Earth's history and thereby change the future, ensuring that the Industrial

Revolution never happens. But first he has to deal with the Doctor.

The TARDIS is pushed down a mineshaft by a group of aggressive miners directed by the Master, and the Doctor nearly goes the same way. He is rescued by George Stephenson (Gawn Grainger), who is preparing for his meeting. Using one of the Rani's maggots, the Master takes over Stephenson's apprentice, Luke (Gary Cady), and uses him to spy on the Doctor and Stephenson. The Doctor meanwhile investigates the bath house which is being used by the Rani as a base and, after escaping from a dichlorodiethyl sulphide – mustard gas – volcano trap, enters her TARDIS.

Operating her ship using a Stattenheim remote control, the Rani brings it into a mine shaft where she and the Master are waiting. Unaware that the Doctor is hiding on board and can overhear them, they plot to set a trap for Stephenson in Redfern Dell. When they have gone, the Doctor sabotages her TARDIS's navigational system and velocity regulator.

Peri has gone to the Dell looking for the herb valerian with which to brew a sleeping draft for the afflicted miners. The Doctor arrives just in time to prevent her from suffering the same fate as Luke, who has stumbled on to one of the Rani's chemical land mines and been converted into a tree. The Doctor forces the Rani to lead Peri out of danger. However, once Peri has left to escort the Rani and the Master as prisoners back to the Rani's TARDIS, the Doctor is again captured by the Luddite miners. He is tied hand and foot to a pole, but manages to escape when the two miners who are carrying it simultaneously step on to landmines and become trees.

Following Peri to the mine, the Doctor finds that her prisoners have outwitted her and escaped. The Master fires his tissue compression eliminator at the Doctor but hits a support beam instead, causing the mine roof to collapse. The Doctor and Peri head for the exit while the Rani and the Master leave in the Rani's TARDIS.

Affected by the Doctor's sabotage, the Rani's ship crashes out of control through the vortex. The resultant time spillage causes a tyrannosaurus rex embryo, collected by the Rani on an earlier visit to Earth, to crash to the floor and begin to grow. The Master and the Rani are trapped against the TARDIS walls by G-force and can only look on in horror.

Stephenson arranges for a group of forty men to get the Doctor's TARDIS out of the pit, and the Doctor and Peri leave after giving

Ravensworth the vial of brain fluid which the Doctor had retrieved from the Master.

WHO FAX
- Novelised as *Doctor Who – The Mark of the Rani* by Pip and Jane Baker in 1986.
- Working titles: *Too Clever by Far, Enter the Rani*
- Locations: Blists Hill Open Air Museum, Ironbridge Gorge, Shropshire; Coalport China Works, Coalport, Telford, Shropshire; Granville Colliery spoil heaps, Lodge Road, Donnington Wood, Donnington, Telford, Shropshire; Queen Elizabeth Woods, nr Harefield Hospital, Hants.
- First appearance of the Rani, played by Kate O'Mara.
- When discussing the time distortion at the start of the story, the Doctor mentions that it could be the work of the Daleks.
- In this adventure viewers see the inside of the Doctor's patchwork coat, revealing the presence of three cat silhouettes sewn into the lining. Baker had arranged for this to be done – one cat for each story of the season so far.
- Nicola Bryant hurt her neck while on location for this story and had to wear a brace to hold it steady between takes.
- The story was regarded as being set in 1830 by those who worked on it, but this is not stated in the televised programme.
- The Rani's chemically impregnated maggots were realised both with real maggots (for the shots of them squirming) and with marzipan (for scenes where they had to be eaten by actors.)
- The incidental music for this story was originally to have been provided by freelance composer John Lewis, but he died while working on it. His estate was paid a fee for the 12 minutes' worth of music he had already completed for part one, and for the 20.5 minutes' worth he had completed for part two. None of this music was used on the transmitted story.

QUOTES
- 'It was at about Christmas 1983 that John Nathan-Turner asked me to direct it. I had popped in to see him about a month earlier and said "I'd love to direct a *Doctor Who*, particularly if you've got any period ones," because I'm a great *Doctor Who* fan and the ones I've always liked best are the ones where they've gone back in time. He

said "Oh, yes, maybe" and later on telephoned my agent and suggested it. I didn't know what I was going to do, and I suppose the scripts came in late spring and then I saw!' Director Sarah Hellings interviewed by Gary Russell for *Doctor Who Magazine* Issue 103.

● 'I wouldn't say it was a planning *error* exactly, because it worked in our favour, but there was some kind of hiccup in the regular planned facilities so that John found himself with a story into which he could slip a bit more film than normal. I was absolutely thrilled, because I prefer film to studio work. I suppose because I'm trained as a film editor, I feel very much at home with film and I find it more exciting. I enjoyed *The Mark of the Rani* not just as a *Doctor Who* story but as a good drama, and I feel that the film went a long way to help that feeling.' Director Sarah Hellings interviewed by Gary Russell for *Doctor Who Magazine* Issue 103.

● 'We were filming in October and the days were very short. So it was a very tight schedule, and I think what came as a great blow to everybody was the fact that the last day was rained off. It rained so hard that we got in only three shots, which in the end proved unusable. We had to do a re-shoot a little way outside London in an area called Queen Elizabeth Woods, which looked very similar to Blists Hill. It is very unusual to do a re-shoot because it involves a lot of time and money, but it was an element – the scene where the Doctor is tied up and carried off by the miners, who are then turned into trees – which was very filmic and just would not have worked in the studio.' Director Sarah Hellings interviewed by Gary Russell for *Doctor Who Magazine* Issue 103.

● 'It was one of those things where director and producer both decided at the same time that I would be right for this part. I adored the Rani when I first read *The Mark of the Rani*, because it really is a lovely part. I love the clothes, too; it's dressing up, all butch with boots and padded shoulders and lots of hair!' Actress Kate O'Mara interviewed by Richard Marson for *Doctor Who Magazine* Issue 128.

● 'I was given guidance on the design of the Rani's TARDIS by the director, Sarah Hellings, and by John Nathan-Turner. I'm told there's a basic similarity between TARDISes, so I based it on the same floor area as the Doctor's one, but made it a lot heavier and more satanic. The Doctor's is all white and cheerful, so I made the Rani's metallic and dark. I felt the steps leading down from the door gave it a nice feeling of entering a chamber rather than just walking in. You are going down into an inner sanctum, a control area at the very heart of the vessel. I designed the overall control console unit, but all the workings, including the magnificent gyroscope, were the work of Dave Barton of Visual Effects.' Designer Paul Trerise interviewed by Gary Russell and Justin Richards for *Doctor Who Magazine* Issue 103.

COMMENT

DJH: It is hard to see why The Mark of the Rani *fails, but fail it does, as watching it invariably induces abject boredom. The acting is again of a very high calibre, with Kate O'Mara as the Rani, Terence Alexander as Ravensworth and Gawn Grainger as Stephenson turning in exceptionally believable performances. The effects are all well realised (with the sole exception of the quite dreadful 'living tree'), and the story is very firmly grounded in history, making superb use of the Ironbridge Gorge location.*

What lets it all down is the lack of any believable motivation on the part of either the Master or the Rani and the glossing over of several unexplained points. We never learn how the Master escaped from the numismatic flames on Sarn (Planet of Fire), in which we heard him being burnt to a crisp, so his reappearance here is something of a mystery. It is also unclear why the Rani has visited so many different points in Earth's history to collect her brain fluid, and why she so readily enters into an alliance with the Master when blackmailed over just a very small vial of the chemical.

Ultimately it is the script which lets the production down. It is very nice to look at, but there is no substance to the plot, and the action drags interminably over each of the 45-minute segments. Not one of the better stories. (3/10)

MS: The Mark of the Rani *is an interesting story which boasts some excellent location work at the Ironbridge Gorge museum, the site of the world's first all-metal bridge. The plot threads seem to become very muddled, however, as the Master's schemes overlap those of the Rani. It would have been much better had the Master not been included, as the Rani is quite strong enough to be the sole villain of the piece.*

Perhaps the worst aspect of the story are the scenes where several characters are transformed into trees by the Rani's chemical mines. The resultant, rather fake-looking, trees which can move on cue are unintentionally very comical.

The story also suffers from the get-caught-and-escape-only-to-be-recaptured syndrome. This trait is apparent in many of the sixth Doctor's adventures, especially the 45-minute episode ones of Season 22.

Most of The Mark of the Rani's *problems are merely minor niggles which could have been sorted out at the script-editing stage. (6/10)*

SJW: I have always found The Mark of the Rani *a very enjoyable story. The historical setting – something of a rarity in eighties* Doctor Who *– is very well realised, with some excellent location filming, and makes a nice contrast to the futuristic locales in which the other sixth Doctor stories take place. The plot is a relatively leisurely and straightforward one, which makes a refreshing change. The most entertaining aspect for me, though, is the amusing interplay between the three outcast Time Lords – the Doctor, the Master and the Rani – who seem at times almost to forget the momentous events going on around them as they indulge in their own private feud. The production is also excellent, with some notably good sets, such as the stylish interior of the Rani's TARDIS. I don't even mind the animated tree, which everyone else seems to hate! All in all, a fine story. (8/10)*

The Two Doctors (6W)

EP	DATE	TIME	DURN	VIEWERS	CHART POS
1	16.02.85	17.22	44'22"	6.6	92
2	23.02.85	17.21	44'49"	6.0	90
3	02.03.85	17.23	44'45"	6.9	66

PRODUCTION DETAILS

Location filming: 08.08.84–15.08.84

Studio: 30.08.84, 31.08.84 in TC1, 13.09.84, 14.09.84 in TC6, 27.09.84, 28.09.84 (studio unknown)

The second Doctor and Jamie – having left Victoria behind to study Graphology – visit Joinson Dastari (Laurence Payne), Head of Projects on space station Camera, Third Zone. On a mission for the Time Lords, they question him about the time travel experiments of Professors Kartz and Reimer. Whilst in Dastari's office they meet Chessene o' the

Franzine Grig (Jacqueline Pearce), an Androgum. The Androgums are a race of voracious gourmands who serve as cooks and menials, but Chessene has been technologically augmented nine times by Dastari, giving her an increased intelligence.

Chessene has used her expanded intelligence to betray the scientists on the space station to the Sontarans. She has offered the commander of the ninth Sontaran Battle Group, Group Marshal Stike (Clinton Greyn), the Kartz–Reimer time module to help his race in their continuing war against the Rutan Host. Chessene drugs the scientists on the space station with calgesic and sabotages the station's defences so that the Sontarans can raid it, killing almost everyone aboard and capturing the second Doctor, whom they intend to dissect in the hope of discovering the Time Lord secret of successful time travel.

One of Chessene's fellow Androgums, Shockeye o' the Quawncing Grig (John Stratton), suggests that the conspirators then head for Earth, where he might savour the delicacy of human flesh. Chessene agrees, as Stike has also suggested that planet – the Sontarans are planning an attack in the Madillon Cluster and Earth is within convenient range.

Chessene, Shockeye, Dastari, the second Doctor and Sontaran Major Varl (Tim Raynham) travel to Earth ahead of Stike and land four km from the Spanish city of Seville, where they occupy a large hacienda owned by an old lady, the Dona Arana (Aimee Delamain), who becomes Shockeye's first human victim. They set up their equipment unaware that their arrival has been observed by Oscar Botcherby (James Saxon), an unemployed English actor, and Anita (Carmen Gomez), his Spanish girlfriend, who were out collecting moths.

In the TARDIS, the sixth Doctor undergoes a strange fainting spell – caused by his second incarnation being tortured by the Sontarans – and decides to visit his old friend Dastari. Arriving at the space station, he and Peri discover the carnage left by the Sontarans twelve days earlier. It has been made to look as if the Time Lords were responsible for the attack, a scenario which the Doctor is reluctant to accept. The station computer (Laurence Payne) has its defences up, so the Doctor and Peri must find some way of getting into the control room and disabling it. They climb through the station's infrastructure, where Peri is attacked by a wild creature – which turns out to be Jamie, deranged after his narrow escape from the Sontarans' attack and his subsequent abandonment in isolation on the station – and the Doctor is temporarily stunned by a defensive blast of vorum gas.

Recovering, the Doctor hypnotises Jamie and, restoring his sanity, learns what really happened in the attack on the station. The Doctor then attempts to communicate telepathically with his second incarnation across space. He hears a tolling bell, identifies it as Santa Maria, the largest bell of the 25 in the Cathedral at Seville on Earth, and determines that his former self is about three miles away from it.

Materialising near to the hacienda, the sixth Doctor, Peri and Jamie meet Oscar and Anita, who assume that they are plain-clothes policemen. Oscar tells them what he and Anita have seen. The Doctor and his companions then attempt to rescue his other incarnation, who has been drugged with siralanomode, but each in turn is captured when Dastari, who had at first appeared to be a prisoner of Chessene, turns out to be a willing conspirator.

Eager to discover the secrets of the Time Lords' immunity to the dangers of time travel, Chessene threatens the Doctor's companions until the sixth Doctor is forced to reveal that all members of his race have a symbiotic print contained within their genes. In the hope that it will enable him to activate the Kartz–Reimer time module, which Stike has now brought to Earth in his ship, Dastari begins a series of operations on the second Doctor to discern this code. He is interrupted, however, as Chessene changes her plan: she now wants the second Doctor implanted with Androgum genes, to turn him into a consort for herself. When Dastari performs the first stage of this operation, the Doctor begins to transform into an Androgum with a huge appetite.

Chessene has intended all along to double-cross the Sontarans, and she attacks them with coronic acid. Varl is killed but a wounded Stike, mistakenly believing the briode-nebuliser within the Kartz–Reimer module to have been primed by the Doctor's Rassilon Imprimatur, attempts to use the device to rejoin his troops in battle. He is badly injured as a result of this and tries to return to his ship, but it has been set to self-destruct by Varl and he is killed in the blast. The sixth Doctor, Peri and Jamie escape from the hacienda and follow the second Doctor and Shockeye into Seville, where they have gone to find a restaurant in which to sate their gargantuan appetites.

Chessene and Dastari are also searching Seville for the Androgums, but the sixth Doctor finds them first as he is led to the restaurant by virtue of the effect which the alien genes in his former body are beginning to have on him. The restaurant, Las Cadenas, is being run by

Oscar, who is stabbed to death by Shockeye when he won't accept a twenty-narg note in payment for the meal. The second Doctor collapses at the table, his body finally rejecting the Androgum genes as Dastari has not been able to perform the stabilising operation. As they leave the restaurant, both Doctors, Peri and Jamie are recaptured by Chessene and Dastari.

Back at the hacienda, the sixth Doctor tricks Chessene into believing that the briode-nebuliser has been correctly primed. He then attempts to escape, but is pursued by a cleaver-wielding Shockeye. He is forced to kill his attacker, using a cyanide-soaked pad from Oscar's moth-collecting kit, which he finds by a tree. Dastari releases the second Doctor, Peri and Jamie, but Chessene kills Dastari as her bestial nature resurfaces. She then attempts to escape in the time module and is herself killed by molecular disintegration.

The now-recovered second Doctor summons his TARDIS with a Stattenheim remote control and he and Jamie depart. The sixth Doctor and Peri are left to consider the merits of becoming vegetarians.

WHO FAX

- Novelised as *Doctor Who – The Two Doctors* by Robert Holmes in 1985.
- Story released on BBC Home Video in 1993.
- Working titles: *The Kraglon Inheritance, The Androgum Inheritance*. Other rumoured working titles are *Parallax, The Seventh Augmentment* and *Creation*, but these do not appear in any known BBC documentation.
- Locations: the following areas of Seville, Spain: Santa Cruz streets; *Restaurant del Laurel*; villa near Gerena; stream; roadside.
- Director Peter Moffatt and costume designer Jan Wright are seen as customers sitting outside the *Bar Hosteria del Laurel* in part three.
- The opening shots of part one, with the second Doctor and Jamie in the TARDIS, were transmitted in black and white.
- 'Dastari' is an anagram of 'A TARDIS.'
- Producer John Nathan-Turner carried out some script editing duties on this story while Eric Saward was off-contract writing *Revelation of the Daleks*.
- The original location planned for *The Two Doctors* was New Orleans, USA, but this proved financially impossible. John Nathan-Turner then suggested Venice, Italy, but this was ruled out as it was

felt that there would be too many tourists who would disrupt filming.

● The extremely high temperatures in Spain caused problems during location filming, particularly for actors Clinton Greyn and Tim Raynham in their heavy Sontaran costumes and make-up.

● Laurence Payne, who portrayed Dastari, had appeared in *Doctor Who* twice before: as Johnny Ringo in *The Gunfighters* and as Morix in *The Leisure Hive*.

● The role of Chessene was originally to have been played by character actress Elisabeth Spriggs, but she had to pull out shortly before production. The part then went to Jacqueline Pearce, best known as Servalan in *Blake's 7*.

● The BBC Radio 4 schools' programme *Wavelength* on 20 September 1984 ran a feature on the making of this story, including recorded interviews with Colin Baker, Patrick Troughton, Nicola Bryant and members of the production team.

● Complementing Peter Howell's radiophonic incidental music were a number of pieces played on Spanish guitar by Les Thatcher.

QUOTES

● 'Apparently Patrick Troughton and Frazer Hines so enjoyed *The Five Doctors* that they asked if they could come back and do another one. We were moving from to the 45-minute time slot and this was going to be the season "biggie". Eric Saward wanted someone with experience of writing what is virtually an old six-parter and asked if I'd mind writing it. Then they said "Can we have Sontarans?" I don't really like bringing back old monsters but I don't think the Sontarans were really well used in their last appearances so I was glad to redress the balance.' Writer Robert Holmes interviewed by Gary Russell for *Doctor Who Magazine* Issue 100.

● 'I had written the script to be set in New Orleans, not Seville. I couldn't think of any reason why aliens should visit New Orleans. I recalled it was a jazz place, but not even I could envisage a race of aliens obsessed with jazz. Then I remembered that New Orleans is the culinary centre of America, with lots of restaurants. So I invented the Androgums, who are obsessed with food – an anagram of gourmand. They went to New Orleans for the food. They stayed in the script however when it shifted to Seville because I couldn't think of anything else.' Robert Holmes interviewed by Gary Russell for *Doctor Who Magazine* Issue 100.

● 'Peter Moffatt, our director, was wonderful. He had a saying about our locations: "Does it say Spain?" So there's a lot of Spain. We were mostly out in a beautiful farmhouse, out of the way for five or six days. It was only when we went into Seville to film that it became difficult – mostly because of American tourists! People will keep quiet for one shot, but by take two they are bored and start whispering to each other, which can easily be picked up on sound. The Spanish were very friendly to us – we had two policemen who went everywhere with us and made sure things were okay.' Actress Nicola Bryant interviewed by Gary Russell for *Doctor Who Magazine* Issue 96.

COMMENT

DJH: Like many Doctor Who *stories in the eighties,* The Two Doctors *works best if viewed only once and if the viewer doesn't think about it too much. It is rich in visual impact, heightened by the Spanish locations. The cast is uniformly good, with John Stratton's superb Shockeye stealing the show. Unfortunately, if one watches it several times, and tries to work out what the plot is, one quickly realises that the characters change their minds and motivations each episode, and that there is very little depth to it at all.*

The story is absolutely typical of John Nathan-Turner's 'dot-to-dot' approach to Doctor Who. *The writer, Robert Holmes, was presented with all the elements – a New Orleans setting (originally); Sontarans; two Doctors with their respective companions – and then had the somewhat unenviable task of weaving a plot around them. That the story works, even on a first showing, is remarkable; but it definitely suffers from a convoluted and incomprehensible plot. (7/10)*

MS: At first sight this story has a lot going for it: the return of the second Doctor and his longest serving companion, Jamie; popular monsters in the form of the Sontarans; a foreign location; and a supporting cast which includes actors of the calibre of John Stratton (who gives a brilliant performance as Shockeye) and Jacqueline Pearce (Chessene).

The most successful element of The Two Doctors *is the renewed partnership between Patrick Troughton as the second Doctor and Frazer Hines as Jamie. Both actors slip effortlessly back into their respective roles and almost return the viewer to the era of the second Doctor.*

Where the story falls down is in its plot. This contains many gaping holes and is in places quite nonsensical; unusual shortcomings for a tale from the pen of Robert Holmes, although it is possible that they arose from the fact that extensive re-writes were required when the original idea of setting the story in America fell through. Despite these drawbacks, though, the overall impression is of a fun story to watch. (7/10)

SJW: *Another good story, this one, although perhaps not quite as strong as the previous two. The script is very entertaining – as one might expect from Robert Holmes,* Doctor Who*'s most highly acclaimed writer – and sustains the viewer's interest over the whole length of the three parts. It is great, too, to see the second Doctor and Jamie making return appearances, teaming up very successfully with the sixth Doctor and Peri. What lets the production down slightly is Peter Moffatt's indifferent direction – his undramatic long-shot revelation of the Sontarans has been rightly cited as an extraordinary error – and some occasional shortcomings in the production, such as the loose-fitting collars on the Sontarans' costumes, which rather spoil the illusion that the creatures have thick necks. The location filming in Seville, although nicely done, comes across as being gratuitous, making one wonder if the money could not have been better spent on something else. On the whole, though, any quibbles are minor ones. (7/10)*

Timelash (6Y)

EP	DATE	TIME	DURN	VIEWERS	CHART POS
1	09.03.85	17.23	45'00"	6.7	69
2	16.03.85	17.21	44'36"	7.4	79

PRODUCTION DETAILS

Studio: 04.12.84–06.12.84, 19.12.84–21.12.84 (studios unknown), 30.01.85 in TC8

The once prosperous and peaceful planet Karfel stands on the brink of destruction. It is ruled by a ruthless dictator, the Borad (Robert Ashby), whose insane leadership has brought the Karfelons to the edge of a war they cannot win against their former allies, the Bandrils.

Some of the citizens within the Citadel cannot understand why their mysterious leader, whom they only ever see on the video screens, should want to provoke a war. Any spark of unrest amongst the people is however quickly crushed by the blue-faced androids which do the bidding of their cruel ruler.

When Maylin Renis (Neil Hallett), the current second-in-command to the Borad, is killed for insubordination, his daughter Vena (Jeananne Crowley) is horrified. Her fiancé, Mykros (Eric Deacon), tells her that the Borad's power lies in the symbolic amulet worn by the Maylin. When Tekker (Paul Darrow) announces himself as Renis's successor, Vena rips the amulet from his neck and, in doing so, accidentally falls into the Timelash. This is a kontron tunnel – a time corridor – into which the Borad banishes those who would fight his will, and which the Karfelons fear more than death itself.

The TARDIS has been caught in the Timelash and Vena passes through it as she travels down the time corridor. The corridor originally terminated in the year 1179, but the TARDIS's presence has the effect of diverting her to 1885.

The Doctor materialises on Karfel to see what is going on and is warmly welcomed by Tekker. He is remembered with affection here from a visit he made during his third incarnation, when he saved the Karfelons from a disaster. While she and the Doctor are being entertained by Tekker, Peri is surreptitiously given a cryptic message: 'Sezon at the Falchan Rocks.' Tekker, unaware of this, suggests that she take a look around. When she has gone, he uses threats against her in order to blackmail the Doctor into going in search of Vena in the TARDIS.

Vena arrives safely at the end of the time corridor and finds herself in a small cottage in the Scottish highlands near Inverness. The cottage is currently the residence of a young writer called Herbert (David Chandler) who, although startled by her sudden appearance, is enough of a gentleman to try to help her when she collapses. The Doctor then arrives in the TARDIS, scaring the writer even more, and persuades Vena to return to Karfel with him. Having noticed that there are no reflective surfaces in the Citadel, he also appropriates a hand-mirror.

Peri meanwhile is chased by Guardoliers – the Borad's force of guards – and finds herself in the caves under the city. She is rescued from a Morlox – a reptilian creature with a long, snake-like neck – by Katz (Tracy Louise Ward) and Sezon (Dicken Ashworth), rebels who explain that the Borad plans to wipe out all the Karfelons by instigating a war with the Bandrils. If the Bandrils strike the planet with a benalypse warhead, all life with a nervous system will be destroyed, although the buildings will remain intact, as will the Morlox. The rebels are attacked by Guardoliers and taken prisoner. Peri is confined in a cell while the others are sentenced to death by Timelash.

The Doctor returns to Karfel with Vena, the amulet and also Herbert, who stowed away on board the TARDIS. Once Tekker has the amulet he orders that the Doctor be thrown into the Timelash. The Doctor, however, uses the hand-mirror to distract the android guard (Dean Hollingsworth) and the rebels attack the Guardoliers, seizing and securing the Timelash control room. The Borad orders an attack using the power from his time-web.

The Doctor determines that he needs some kontron crystals and, attached to a rope, enters the Timelash to obtain them. He gets two crystals and converts one into a ten-second time break: it slips the Doctor ten seconds into the future while projecting an image of him in the present. The other he uses to create a device which will reflect any weapon's power back to its source.

The control room comes under attack from the Guardoliers and from the Borad's android, but the android is destroyed and the Doctor's power reflecting device sends it into the past. During the battle, a section of wall panelling is smashed, revealing underneath it a large painting of the Doctor in his third incarnation.

The Bandrils have meanwhile launched an attack on Karfel.

The Doctor goes to confront the Borad and discovers that he is the mutated form of a scientist named Megelen, whom he had previously reported to the inner sanctum for unethical experimentation on the Morlox. Megelen admits that he had been experimenting further when he was accidentally sprayed with a substance called Mustakozene 80; this excited a Morlox into attacking him and resulted in spontaneous tissue amalgamation, forming the combined mutant creature which he has now become. The Borad explains that he now intends to wipe out all mammalian life on Karfel. When Tekker, who has been listening, objects, the Borad kills him.

Peri has been tied to a stake within the tunnel system with a canister of Mustakozene 80 strapped to her, to await the approach of a Morlox.

The Borad reveals Peri's fate to the Doctor – she is to be transformed into a Morlox mutant like him and become his mate. The Doctor uses the kontron crystal first to avoid the Borad's ageing time-web ray, then to reflect it back at the Borad, killing him. Herbert, who was left by the Doctor to watch the confrontation from a nearby window, is told to go and rescue Peri. He arrives just in time to frighten off a Morlox with a burning torch.

Karfel still faces destruction as the Bandrils have fired a missile at it. The Doctor leaves in the TARDIS, with Herbert as an uninvited passenger, and positions the ship in the missile's path, thereby saving the planet.

The Karfelons, who believe the Doctor and Herbert to have been killed, contact the Bandrils and start peace negotiations. The Bandrils agree to send an ambassador to Karfel. While everyone is indulging in mutual congratulations, Peri is suddenly grabbed by the Borad. The Doctor had not killed him after all, but merely disposed of one of his clones.

The Borad wants the Bandril ship captured but is distracted when the Doctor and Herbert return, having survived the missile attack un-scathed. The Doctor smashes the painting of himself on the wall, revealing a mirror beneath it, and the Borad recoils in horror at the sight of his own reflection, causing him to release his grip on Peri. The Doctor then quickly activates the Timelash and pushes the Borad into it, surmising that he will arrive on Earth in the twelfth century and live for a thousand years or so in Loch Ness. The Doctor tosses his kontron crystal into the Timelash, which blows itself up.

With Karfel safe, the Doctor prepares to return Herbert to Earth. He shows Peri one of Herbert's calling cards. It reads 'Herbert George Wells.'

WHO FAX
- Novelised as *Doctor Who – Timelash* by Glen McCoy in 1986.
- Locations: none.
- A Bandril is seen only on a communications screen. The creature was realised as a hand-operated puppet.
- The image of the third Doctor seen on the wall behind the smashed panelling was painted by American fan artist Gail Bennett.
- Tekker was played by Paul Darrow, better known for his role as Avon in *Blake's 7*.
- A photograph of Jo Grant (Katy Manning) is seen in a locket owned by Katz.

- Several aspects of this story parallel the writing of the real H. G. Wells: Vena and the Morlox become Weena and the Morlocks (*The Time Machine*); the Borad is a hybrid creature (*The Island of Doctor Moreau*); and the Doctor becomes invisible when using the kontron crystal (*The Invisible Man*).
- Writer Glen McCoy also worked as an ambulance driver.
- In early draft scripts, the Bandrils were called Gurdels and the character Aram was male rather than female.
- This story came bottom in the *Doctor Who* Appreciation Society's season poll.

QUOTES

- 'I was a bit disappointed when I read the script. I remember Eric Saward was a bit defensive about it. He said "It's really quite good – Glen McCoy is quite a good writer." I disagreed and persuaded Eric to do a complete rewrite on it, to make it more lucid.' Director Pennant Roberts interviewed by Richard Marson for *Doctor Who Magazine* Issue 122.
- 'Our original set designs kept getting sent back and pared down because of lack of money, and that scaling down was, in itself, time-consuming. We'd taken the time on the first draft, so the last one – which the viewers saw – was a bit slapdash.' Director Pennant Roberts interviewed by Richard Marson for *Doctor Who Magazine* Issue 122.
- 'We were short of material for the second episode, so we had to go into one of the next story's studio sessions and record an extra scene in the TARDIS to fill it out. This was written by Eric as padding, a complete deviation from the story. I don't think *Who* was built for 45-minute episodes, with its emphasis on a kind of adventure shorthand, and rapid pace.' Director Pennant Roberts interviewed by Richard Marson for *Doctor Who Magazine* Issue 122.
- 'I think Paul Darrow faced a problem playing Tekker, in that he wanted to get away from the role of Avon in *Blake's 7* and so his ideas for the part never coincided with what John Nathan-Turner or I felt would be right. I spent quite a lot of time watering Paul's input down – he came to me and said, "Why don't I play it with a hump?" I thought, "He can't be serious." But at the beginning I think he was *completely* serious! Elements of that came back and encouraged the same kind of playing from Colin, for example.' Director Pennant

Roberts interviewed by Richard Marson for *Doctor Who Magazine* Issue 122.

COMMENT

DJH: One of the great things about Doctor Who *is that every story has something of value. In the case of* Timelash, *the simplicity of the plot is wonderfully refreshing after the tortuous complexity of* The Mark of the Rani *and* The Two Doctors; *and the Borad, boasting one of the most chilling voices* Doctor Who *has ever presented, is a return to the out-and-out monsters of old.*

Where the story fails is in its non-existent production values. It is obvious that very little money was spent on it – perhaps the series' budget had been exhausted by the expensive excursion to Spain for The Two Doctors *– and it suffers as a result. Almost every area of the production can be criticised, and yet I would still rather watch this than* The Twin Dilemma *or* The Mark of the Rani! *(4/10)*

MS: In a close race with The Twin Dilemma, Timelash *just wins the title of the worst sixth Doctor story. The plot is weak and turgid, and the supporting cast are as wooden as a pine forest. Paul Darrow hams up his role for all he is worth.*

Timelash's *plot would barely be sufficient to sustain a two-part story in the more traditional 25-minute format, and yet here it has to stretch to twice that length, the result being that large sections of padding are evident. The Karfelons themselves appear to be so morose that it is difficult to care much about their fate.*

The story also suffers from poor production values. The inside of the Timelash itself looks like a piece of scenery left over from a Christmas light entertainment show, and the corridors of the Citadel are just drab grey, looking as if they have been made up straight from stock flats. (1/10)

SJW: Colin Baker again gives a strong performance as the Doctor, and Nicola Bryant struggles gamely against the severe limitations which the story imposes upon her as Peri, but Timelash *is easily the worst material with which either of them ever had to work on* Doctor Who. *Weakly scripted, poorly designed, atrociously directed and appallingly acted by the guest cast, this is a production I find it painful to watch. Quite possibly the least appealing* Doctor Who *story of all time. (1/10)*

Revelation of the Daleks (6Z)

EP	DATE	TIME	DURN	VIEWERS	CHART POS
1	23.03.85	17.22	44'31"	7.4	65
2	30.03.85	17.22	45'26"	7.7	58

Repeat (BBC2 – Chart Pos refers to BBC2 programmes only)

1	19.03.93	19.15	24'04"	1.7	28
2	26.03.93	19.15	23'22"	1.8	unplaced
3	02.04.93	19.15	24'28"	1.6	30
4	09.04.93	19.15	24'13"	1.2	unplaced

PRODUCTION DETAILS

Location filming: 07.01.85–10.01.85
Studio: 17.01.85, 18.01.85 in TC1, 30.01.85–01.02.85 in TC8

The Doctor and Peri arrive on the planet Necros where, in a facility called Tranquil Repose, the wealthy can have their newly deceased bodies cryogenically frozen until such time as medical science can cure whatever killed them. The Doctor wishes to pay his last respects to Professor Arthur Stengos, and also to assuage some nagging suspicions about the reports of the man's death. The Time Lord's suspicions prove justified, as it turns out that the scientist's death is just a ruse by one of the Doctor's old adversaries to lure him into a trap.

Tranquil Repose is run by the Great Healer, in reality none other than Davros, creator of the Daleks. Davros is using the organic material surrounding him in the cryogenic storage units to create a whole new army of Daleks with which he intends to take control of the universe.

WHO FAX

● See Chapter 6 on the making of this story for a full synopsis and details of how a *Doctor Who* adventure was brought to the screen during Colin Baker's era.
● Locations: IBM UK HQ, Southampton, Hants; airfield near Poole, Dorset; Goodwood horse racing track; Queen Elizabeth Park, Nr Cosham, Portsmouth, Hants.
● The Tranquil Repose DJ played his captive, and largely unaware, audience the following tunes: 'Good Vibrations' (The Surfers),

'Whiter Shade of Pale' (Procul Harum), 'Hound Dog' (cover of Presley version), 'Blue Suede Shoes' (cover of Presley version), 'In the Mood' (The Ted Heath Orchestra), 'Moonlight Serenade' (The Ted Heath Orchestra) and 'Fire' (Jimi Hendrix Experience).

● The story was originally planned to end with the Doctor promising to take Peri to Blackpool, where the action would pick up in the first story of the new season. However, with the announcement of the postponement of the 23rd season, plans for the Blackpool story were dropped, and *Revelation of the Daleks* ends with a freeze frame of the Doctor's face, cutting the word 'Blackpool'. [See Chapter 7 for information on the original plans for Season 23.]

● A ten-second stock shot of factory complexes used in part one came from World Backgrounds.

● This story came top in the *Doctor Who* Appreciation Society's season poll.

COMMENT

DJH: I remember that when Revelation of the Daleks *was originally transmitted, I watched the first episode with some friends. I turned to them about halfway through and commented that if I wasn't a fan, I would have turned the television off or over by this point. Like* The Mark of the Rani, *it bored me.*

I have never been fascinated or excited by the Daleks, or by Davros, and while Genesis of the Daleks *and* Resurrection of the Daleks *are two of the best adventures to feature them, this is one of the worst.*

The problem is that there are too many characters vying for centre stage: the Doctor and Peri; Jobel and Tasambeker; Orcini and Bostock; Kara and Vogel; Grigory and Natasha; Takis and Lilt; the DJ; Davros; and of course the Daleks. To keep all these elements interesting while at the same time advancing the plot is an extremely difficult task which Saward and Harper just about manage. Unfortunately, the result is that many characters slip into the background for periods and then step forward once more, making it hard for the viewer to follow the threads of the plot. I also feel that the virtual exclusion of the Doctor and Peri from the main plot until about 50 minutes in was a definite mistake.

Graeme Harper makes it look great and keeps the action moving along, and the cast are again superb – with the exception of Jenny Tomasin (Tasambeker), who is so dreadful that she defies description

—but overall it falls flat, lacking the climax on which the season should perhaps have ended. (5/10)

MS: *The return of the Daleks to* Doctor Who *is always something of an event, yet in* Revelation of the Daleks *the evil mobile dustbins have to take second billing to their creator, Davros. Even Davros appears to be a little diminished, as only his head can be seen for much of the story.*

In terms of atmosphere, the story is a rather morbid black comedy, populated by somewhat ridiculous characters like Jobel, the DJ, Kara and the professional assassin Orcini, who is more interested in his personal honour than in the events taking place around him. The plot contains many interesting ideas, particularly the creation of a new race of Daleks, loyal only to Davros, out of the remains of the rich customers of Tranquil Repose. But it seems to come to an anticlimax as the grey Daleks simply sweep in and whisk Davros away to Skaro. A more effective ending could have turned a good story into a great one. (7/10)

SJW: *The frustrating thing about mid-eighties* Doctor Who *is its inconsistency. For every classic like* The Caves of Androzani *there is a clunker like* The Twin Dilemma, *for every triumph like* Vengeance on Varos *a travesty like* Timelash. Revelation of the Daleks *is a story so superior in every way to the one which immediately preceded it on screen that it is difficult to believe that they were both part of the same series, let alone the same season. Graeme Harper's stylish and atmospheric direction is superb, while Eric Saward's script is full of tension, excitement, perception and pathos. The two regulars, Colin Baker and Nicola Bryant, give outstanding performances, and the guest cast are uniformly excellent. This is certainly the best sixth Doctor story, as well as being one of the strongest Dalek adventures ever. An all-time* Doctor Who *classic. (9/10)*

Note: *A gap of eighteen months, rather than the usual six, separated the end of transmission of Season 22 and the beginning of transmission of Season 23. During the break in production of the TV series, a radio adventure starring Colin Baker as the Doctor and Nicola Bryant as Peri was broadcast on Radio 4 within a programme entitled* Pirate Radio 4. *The serial,* Slipback, *consisted of six ten-minute episodes written by series script editor Eric Saward. [See the appendix following this chapter for further information.]*

SEASON TWENTY-THREE
The Trial of a Time Lord

Note: Season 23 took the form of a single fourteen-part story called *The Trial of a Time Lord*. For production purposes, however, it was divided into four separate segments, the final working titles of which were *The Mysterious Planet, Mindwarp, The Ultimate Foe* and *Time Inc*. These working titles did not appear on screen and there has subsequently been some confusion over them – see Who Fax below for further details, and also Chapter 7 for information about the development of the season.

EP	DATE	TIME	DURN	VIEWERS	CHART POS
1	06.09.86	17.47	24'57"	4.9	69
2	13.09.86	17.47	24'44"	4.9	75
3	20.09.86	17.48	24'18"	3.9	98
4	27.09.86	17.46	24'20"	3.7	97
5	04.10.86	17.47	24'42"	4.8	76
6	11.10.86	17.46	24'45"	4.6	87
7	18.10.86	17.47	24'33"	5.1	87
8	25.10.86	17.48	24'44"	5.0	84
9	01.11.86	17.47	24'56"	5.2	85
10	08.11.86	17.46	24'18"	4.6	93
11	15.11.86	17.47	24'07"	5.3	86
12	22.11.86	17.46	24'45"	5.2	89
13	29.11.86	17.20	24'42"	4.4	98
14	06.12.86	17.46	29'30"	5.6	80

Parts One–Four (7A)
PRODUCTION DETAILS

OB: 08.04.06–11.04.86
Studio: 24.04.86, 25.04.86 in TC6, 10.05.86–12.05.86 in TC3

The TARDIS is drawn down into a large space station, where the Doctor, appearing rather dazed, exits alone from his ship. His memory of recent events has apparently gone, along with his companion Peri. He steps through a doorway to find himself in a courtroom. Opposite him is the Valeyard (Michael Jayston), who chides the Doctor for being late. The court stands as the Inquisitor (Lynda Bellingham) enters and takes her place.

The Valeyard, the prosecuting Time Lord, explains that this is an impartial inquiry into the Doctor's behaviour, which, he hopes to prove, is unbecoming of a Time Lord. Furthermore, he intends to prove that the First Law of Time has been broken.

The Valeyard draws on information from the Matrix to show the Inquisitor and the Time Lord jurors a series of events from the Doctor's recent past. On a large screen set in the back wall of the courtroom, the Doctor sees himself and Peri walking on the surface of the planet Ravolox in the Stellian galaxy.

Ravolox was supposed to have been destroyed by a solar fireball five centuries ago, but the lush vegetation belies this fact. It seems that the Gallifreyan records are wrong. The Doctor also notes that Ravolox is almost identical to Earth – a fact which puzzles him. The mystery deepens as Peri affirms that the planet feels just like Earth. The Doctor finds a necklace in the undergrowth, proving that they are not alone here.

The travellers' progress is observed by the mercenary Sabalom Glitz (Tony Selby) and his sidekick Dibber (Glen Murphy), who are attempting to destroy a Magnum Mark 7 Light Converter – a black light collection aerial – which is supplying energy to an L3 robot. They decide to kill the Doctor and Peri, but the attempt is foiled when the pair duck out of sight.

The Doctor and Peri have entered an old building which turns out to be the remains of Marble Arch station in the London Underground – apparent proof that Ravolox is in fact the Earth, two billion years or so after Peri's time. However, the planet and its constellation have been shifted two light years across space.

Finding a hermetically sealed door which leads further down into the building, the Doctor resolves to explore. Peri, upset at the fate of her planet, opts to stay on the surface, but soon regrets her decision as she is captured by a group of primitive-looking humanoids.

Down in the brightly lit tunnels, the Doctor picks up a carafe of water and is immediately arrested for being a water thief. Balazar (Adam Blackwood), keeper of the three Books of Knowledge – *Moby Dick, The Water Babies* and *UK Habitats of the Canadian Goose* – orders that the Doctor be stoned to death. The Doctor's presence has also been noted by the Immortal – the L3 robot – and it sends the train guard leader Merdeen (Tom Chadbon) to investigate. Meanwhile, the stoning commences and the Doctor is knocked unconscious.

The Valeyard now suggests that the inquiry be turned into a trial. If the Doctor is found guilty, then his life will be terminated.

Glitz and Dibber encounter a group of the primitive-looking natives, members of the Tribe of the Free, and are taken to their leader, Queen Katryca (Joan Sims). The matriarch explains that the black light collection aerial is a totem to the earth-god Haldron, worshipped by the Tribe, and that many others have come before, all with different stories as to why it should be destroyed. She orders that Glitz and Dibber be held in a guarded hut along with Peri.

The Immortal orders that the Doctor be brought to him. The Doctor discovers that the robot is called Drathro (voiced by Roger Brierley), and that its purpose is to guard three Sleepers from Andromeda, along with the secrets in their possession, until such time as they can be returned to Andromeda. The black light converter has now developed a fault, however, and without power the Sleepers will die. Drathro wants the Doctor to repair the converter. The Doctor tricks Drathro and his helpers, Humker (Billy McColl) and Tandrell (Siôn Tudor Owen), and manages to escape from the control room. Drathro sends an L1 service robot after him.

The Doctor discovers that Merdeen has been smuggling people out of the city so that they can avoid the regular culling which takes place to keep down their population's numbers. It is generally believed amongst the city-dwellers that the planet's surface is uninhabitable, but Merdeen knows this to be untrue. The Doctor and Balazar head for the surface.

Glitz, Dibber and Peri escape from their make-shift cell, and Dibber destroys the collection aerial. They meet up with the Doctor and Balazar at Marb Station but become trapped between the pursuing Tribe and the service robot. One of the Tribe, Broken Tooth (David Rodigan), recognises Balazar as an old friend and attacks the robot, temporarily halting it. Everyone then returns to the Tribe's village, where Katryca orders that Glitz, Dibber and Peri be taken back to the prison hut, this time joined by the Doctor.

The reactivated service robot subsequently crashes through the hut wall and seizes the Doctor, but the Tribe attack and disable it. Mistakenly assuming that it was the Immortal, the emboldened Katryca mounts an attack on the station with her warriors. She and Broken

Tooth are both killed by Drathro, while Glitz and Dibber make their way into the station to try to obtain the Sleepers' stolen secrets.

A section of the evidence is bleeped out at this point, and the Inquisitor wants to know why. The Valeyard explains that it is because the information is sensitive and has no bearing on the Doctor's trial. The affected portion concerns the origin of the secrets.

The Doctor gains access to Drathro's control room and is soon joined by Peri, Merdeen, Glitz and Dibber. Glitz manages to persuade Drathro to accompany him to his ship with the secrets, claiming that he will return them to Andromeda. When they have gone, the Doctor tries to shut down the converter and thereby prevent a chain reaction which would result in the destruction of the universe. He succeeds in his main aim, but the control room is wrecked in an explosion. *En route* to Glitz's ship, Drathro is affected by the blast and collapses, burnt out from inside. The heat also destroys the secrets. Dibber consoles the disappointed Glitz by pointing out that the black light aerial was made from siligtone, the hardest and most expensive metal in the galaxy, which means that he can still come away with a sizeable profit.

In the courtroom, the Doctor insists that his interference was justified in order to save the universe from destruction. Yet many questions remain unanswered. Who were the mysterious Sleepers, and what secrets had they stolen? Who had moved Earth through space and changed Gallifrey's records to make it appear that the planet was Ravolox? The Doctor determines to find out.

WHO FAX

- Working title: *The Mysterious Planet*.
- Episodes released as part of *The Trial of a Time Lord* boxed set on BBC Home Video in 1993.
- Novelised as *Doctor Who – The Mysterious Planet* by Terrance Dicks in 1988.
- Locations: Butser Ancient Farm Project, Pidham Hill, Hants; Queen Elizabeth Country Park, Gravel Hill, Horndean, Hants.
- Merdeen was played by Tom Chadbon, who had previously appeared in *Doctor Who* as the detective Duggan in the 1979 story *City of Death*.
- Katryca was played by Joan Sims, better known for her comedy roles in the *Carry On* series of films.
- The train guards' helmets were originally created for the troopers in

the Cyberman adventure *Earthshock* during the fifth Doctor's era.

- The Doctor states in this adventure that he is 900 years old.
- It is revealed that Sabalom Glitz comes from Salostophus in Andromeda.
- The food sludge in which Balazar gets covered in part four was made from mashed potato, water and food colouring.
- Part three featured a pre-credit narrative, spoken by the BBC continuity announcer over a colour slide from the story, giving a brief summary of events so far. This format was repeated for all subsequent episodes in the season.
- In part three, when the Doctor is recovering from being captured by the service robot, he does an impression of the fourth Doctor and calls Peri 'Sarah Jane'.
- The opening model shot of the Time Lord space station was filmed at Peerless Studios using a computer-controlled camera rig. The 45-second scene took a week to set up and shoot, working from 9 a.m. to 11 p.m., and another week to edit. The model itself was built by Visual Effects Department assistants working to designer Mike Kelt's drawings. It was six feet in diameter and assembled from six fibreglass sections, then embellished with detailed plastic components and dozens of lights.
- Actor Roger Brierley, who supplied the voice of Drathro, was originally to have been inside the costume as well, but he backed out at the last minute and a Visual Effects Department assistant had to take over. The costume was made of very thin fibreglass, held together by internal steel joints, and the operator saw out through the chest panel. A tube was regularly inserted at the rear to allow air to circulate.
- The L1 robot was also operated by an Effects Department assistant. Its main shell was made of aluminium and steel, and it had a fibreglass casing.
- Both Drathro and the L1 robot appeared (along with Sil) on the BBC children's programme *Blue Peter* to publicise the season.
- Parts one to four were voted the least favourite segment of the story in the *Doctor Who* Appreciation Society's season poll, and part three the least favourite individual episode.

QUOTES

- 'I felt that it was a very good piece of drama, showing various shades of light and dark, and I think John Nathan-Turner felt I could give it the sensitivity it needed. What appealed most was establishing the life outside the city and comparing the lives above and below ground.' Director Nick Mallett interviewed by Richard Marson for *Doctor Who Magazine* Issue 132.

● 'One had to be terribly gentle with stuff like Peri realising that this was Earth – her home. And when I first read the scripts I found the characters of Glitz, Dibber and Katryca particularly appealing. I liked that element of a lot of comedy, but wanted to be very careful not to overstate it. I think John felt I would be good at the real-life human drama, and at containing the heights of the comedy present.' Director Nick Mallett interviewed by Richard Marson for *Doctor Who Magazine* Issue 132.

● 'Joan Sims actually came to my mind for the part of Katryca right from the start, but then I had to be very careful with the balance of the rest of the casting. John had mentioned Tony Selby for Glitz from day one, and as a producer he's very good because he allows you complete freedom and he'll discuss things with you – he'll encourage you to take a slight risk.' Director Nick Mallett interviewed by Richard Marson for *Doctor Who Magazine* Issue 132.

Parts Five–Eight (7B)

PRODUCTION DETAILS

OB: 15.06.86–16.06.86

Studio: 27.05.86–29.05.86 in TC1, 11.06.86–13.06.86 (studio unknown)

The Valeyard's evidence against the Doctor continues with an account of his adventure on the planet Thoros-Beta in the 24th century, last quarter, fourth year, seventh month, third day.

The Doctor and Peri arrive on a coastal beach on Thoros-Beta, the Doctor having decided to investigate after learning from the dying words of a Warlord of Thordon that phasers – technologically advanced and highly dangerous weapons – are being supplied from this planet. Exploring a tidal cave, the travellers are attacked by a squid-like creature, the Raak, which has apparently been stationed there to operate machinery extracting energy from the sea water. The Doctor kills the Raak with the phaser which he acquired from the dying Warlord.

This act is cited as proof by the Valeyard of the Doctor's inherently violent nature. The Doctor protests that the death was an accident.

The Doctor and Peri are captured by humanoid guards and taken to the laboratory of a scientist named Crozier, whom the guard leader had assumed they were here to see. They escape before the mistake is discovered and, in some nearby tunnels, find a wolf-creature, the Lukoser (Thomas Branch), chained to the wall. A procession of Mentors, natives of Thoros-Beta, then passes by, and amongst their number is Sil (Nabil Shaban).

Crozier (Patrick Ryecart) has been conducting experiments in brain transference, his ultimate aim being to transfer the brain of the Mentor leader, Kiv (Christopher Ryan), into a new body, it having outgrown its own. He has also been using a cell discriminator device to pacify the belligerent King Yrcanos (Brian Blessed), a Krontep warrior, who is currently lying on a bed in the laboratory.

The Doctor and Peri make their way back to the laboratory. The Doctor starts to disconnect the circuitry but is discovered by Sil, who decides to use the cell discriminator on him. The process has already been started when Yrcanos suddenly revives and starts smashing up the laboratory. Eventually the warrior escapes into the tunnels.

The Doctor's mind has apparently been affected by the process he has undergone, and he becomes callous and self-interested. He offers to help Crozier repair the lab and assists Sil with some interplanetary currency speculation before betraying Peri to the Mentors. His bewildered companion is chained to the Rock of Sorrows on the jagged coastline outside the city and the Doctor tries to get her to confess to being a spy from Thoros-Alpha.

The Doctor objects. He cannot clearly remember the events, but is sure that the evidence being presented has been falsified. The Valeyard states that it is impossible to tamper with the Matrix.

While escorting Peri back into the base for further questioning, the Doctor is ambushed by Yrcanos and flees. Peri then accompanies Yrcanos – who wishes her to become his bride – as he resolves to locate an Alphan resistance movement which he assumes is present on the planet. The Lukoser turns out to be Yrcanos's loyal equerry, Dorf, who has fallen victim to Crozier's experiments.

Crozier has meanwhile found a temporary body in which to house Kiv's brain. It is that of a Mentor fisherman found floating dead in the sea. The transfer is achieved successfully after several nerve-wracking false alarms – Kiv had ordered that both Crozier and Sil be killed if the operation failed.

Yrcanos finds the Alphan resistance group and Peri manages to win over their leader, Tuza (Gordon Warnecke). They all head for Alphans' weapons dump but are ambushed by the Mentors' guards and knocked unconscious.

As neither the Doctor nor the Alphans are suitable candidates for the transference of Kiv's brain, Crozier must find another host. He wonders if Peri would be suitable. The Doctor, now acting more like his true self, goes to the Induction centre – the area where new Thoros-Alphan prisoners are taken for conditioning with brain implants – to see if he can find anyone else. He frees Tuza, rescues Yrcanos and Dorf from a cell, and then heads off to save Peri, who is being prepared to become the ultimate recipient of Lord Kiv's intelligence. Dorf is killed by guards and, in a rage, Yrcanos destroys the control centre. The Alphan slaves mill about in confusion as their brain implants are no longer operative.

Before he can rescue Peri, the Doctor is taken out of time by the Time Lords and transported to their space station to begin his trial. The transference operation is completed successfully by Crozier, and Kiv awakes in the body of Peri, whose own mind ceases to exist. Yrcanos, along with Tuza, has been temporarily frozen in time by the Time Lords, but he is released at this point and forces his way into the laboratory. Unable to stand the sight of his intended bride possessed by Kiv's consciousness, he fires a phaser indiscriminately about the room, destroying everything within – the result which the Time Lords had intended to achieve, to eliminate the threat which they considered the transference equipment to pose to the natural course of evolution.

The Doctor is aghast at what he has seen and angrily disputes the Inquisitor's claim that the High Council had no choice but to intervene. He asserts that there is more to the Trial than has so far been revealed, and that he intends to discover what it is.

WHO FAX

● Novelised as *Doctor Who – Mindwarp* by Philip Martin in 1989.
● Episodes released as part of *The Trial of a Time Lord* boxed set on BBC Home Video in 1993.
● Working titles: *The Planet of Sil*, *Mindwarp*.
● Location recording took place at Telscombe Cliffs, East Sussex.

- This segment of *The Trial of a Time Lord* provided the first example in *Doctor Who* of the new HARRY digital image manipulation process. It was used to colour Thoros-Beta's sky and seas and to provide the image of Thoros-Alpha in the sky.
- This was the final appearance of Nicola Bryant as Peri.
- Nabil Shaban returned to play the part of Sil, while comedy actor Christopher Ryan played Lord Kiv.
- It was originally proposed that much of the Mentors' dialogue would be spoken in their own alien language and translated by way of on-screen subtitles, but this idea was dropped as posing too many problems.

QUOTES

- 'My original idea was that there was someone playing around on a planet, actually using another race to do all their slave labour for them. There was the élite, which was the Mentors, Sil's race. Although the planet did not have a lot of resources, they could manipulate the universal stock market to profit. That's how they lived, by investing. But they were also meddling, and selling arms to anybody. They'd invest in various underdeveloped worlds – sell to both sides, see who was going to win, and make a contract with the winners. It was a form of colonisation. They were also manipulating their biology to provide a means of extending life. Crozier was a genetic genius.' Writer Philip Martin interviewed by Neil Penswick for *Doctor Who Magazine* Issue 150.
- 'After the hoo-ha over *Vengeance on Varos*, perhaps after all the comedy bits had been cut out, I think I compensated by saying to myself that I'd put in plenty of comedy this time. I thought "Even if they cut it there'll be some left." In fact, Eric Saward edited it more heavily than I ever imagined, diluting my whole conception. New characters appeared which weren't even mine.' Writer Philip Martin interviewed by Neil Penswick for *Doctor Who Magazine* Issue 150.
- 'It suffered from problems in rehearsal. Because there was a certain high level of comedy it was almost stylised, which you could see in the way Crozier, Yrcanos and Sil operated. Central to all this should have been a cohesive force, which was the Doctor, but in rehearsal Colin Baker saw how the other actors were playing it and he started to do it as well. This affected the whole story, the whole balance was

wrong, and it just appeared to be a bit of a send-up.' Writer Philip Martin interviewed by Neil Penswick for *Doctor Who Magazine* Issue 150.

● Sil's costume was the same as in *Vengeance on Varos*, but a new mask was created by effects designer Peter Wragg. 'The main part was made from a softer material than before – a prosthetics foam into which we'd put a green base colour. That fitted like a hood over Nabil Shaban's head, leaving a circle with his face exposed. We then had to provide separate pieces of foam which could be applied by Make-up to Nabil's face, covering his cheeks and his chin, so that any facial movement or change of expression would be reflected in the mask.' Peter Wragg interviewed by Patrick Mulkern for *Doctor Who Magazine* Issue 123.

● 'Sil's race on Thoros-Beta, the Mentors, are all different. Some can walk, some can stumble along, some have to be carried like Sil. It seems that the more their brains develop, the more the capability to move around is restricted. The less a Thoros-Betan can move around, the more intelligent it is.' Philip Martin interviewed by Paul Cornell for *Doctor Who Magazine* Issue 125.

● 'Sil's horrible in a way, but children love him because he's like them, he's full of bluster and bombast, even though underneath he's very uncertain. He's like a child who's pretending to be an adult, really. When I came to write him second time, I was rather apprehensive that he might be a one-story character, but with Nabil's contribution, when I came back from the studio I could hear the whole gallery laughing along with his performance.' Philip Martin interviewed by Paul Cornell for *Doctor Who Magazine* Issue 125.

Parts Nine–Twelve (7C)

PRODUCTION DETAILS

Studio: 30.07.86–01.08.86 in TC3, 12.08.86–14.08.86 (studio unknown)

After a short recess to allow the Doctor to come to terms with Peri's death, the Valeyard rests his case for the prosecution. It is now the Doctor's turn to present a case for the defence. He announces that by showing the court an adventure from his own future, he hopes to demonstrate that he mends his ways.

The Doctor is now travelling with a young girl named Melanie – a keep-fit fanatic who has him exercising and drinking carrot juice – and their latest adventure begins when the TARDIS picks up a distress call from someone aboard an intergalactic liner, the *Hyperion III*.

The *Hyperion III* ferries between Mogar and Earth in the year 2986, and amongst its present cargo are precious metals from Mogar and a mysterious light-shielded hydroponic section containing several giant vegetable pods. A passenger, Grenville (Tony Scoggo), is recognised by one of his fellow travellers, Kimber (Arthur Hewlett), as being a man named Hallet. He dismisses this as a case of mistaken identity, but his actions are suspicious and he later disguises himself as a crew member in order to gain access to the cargo hold.

Arriving on the *Hyperion III*, the Doctor and Mel are arrested as intruders. They meet the ship's Commodore, 'Tonker' Travers (Michael Craig), who is an old acquaintance of the Doctor's. Travers is sceptical of the Doctor's explanation for his arrival here and claims to know nothing of any mayday. However, he tells the ship's security officer, Rudge (Denys Hawthorne), to allow the two travellers the freedom of the passenger quarters – if the Doctor is up to no good, he will incriminate himself in time.

The Doctor and Mel join the rest of the passengers, who include a group of botanists led by thremmatologist Professor Sarah Lasky (Honor Blackman). It is they who are responsible for the hydroponic section in the cargo hold, and also for a guarded isolation room which is off-limits to everyone else.

Grenville disappears and one of his shoes is found by the ship's incinerator. The implication is that he has been murdered. The Doctor suggests that Mel investigate the hydroponic section on her own.

The Doctor again tells the court that the Matrix is wrong, asserting that this section of evidence was different when he reviewed it earlier. He has a strong feeling that he is being manipulated and that the evidence is being tampered with.

Mel is shown around the cargo hold by the ship's communications officer, Edwardes (Simon Slater) – who, to her horror, is electrocuted when he touches a metal grille surrounding the hydroponic section. The electrical discharge also causes creatures within the pods to start moving and ultimately to break out. A guard who arrives to investigate Edwardes' death, having been alerted by Mel, is killed by the creatures.

The Valeyard sneeringly registers this as another death to the Doctor's credit.

Also on board the liner are three Mogarians, natives of Mogar who have to wear special breathing apparatus to survive in the same atmosphere as humans, oxygen being poisonous to them. They berate the Commodore for steering the vessel too close to a black hole, and also complain about Earth's mining of Mogar for metal. One of the Mogarians later turns out to be Grenville/Hallet in disguise. An undercover agent and an old friend of the Doctor's, it was he who beamed the distress signal to the TARDIS. Before he can reveal his reasons for doing so, however, he is poisoned by persons unknown.

Lasky and her assistants try to cover up the fact that the pods in the hydroponic section are now empty. The Doctor and Mel, however, are highly suspicious of the thremmatologist and trick their way into the guarded isolation room. There they find Ruth Baxter (Barbara Ward), another of the Professor's assistants, who is slowly turning into a mutant form of plant life.

Mel manages to record on tape some alien voices which she has overheard plotting the destruction of animalkind. The tape is subsequently stolen, however, and she suspects that the culprit could have been the liner's stewardess, Janet (Yolande Palfrey). At the Doctor's suggestion, she goes to search Janet's cabin. The Doctor then makes for the liner's communications room and smashes the equipment with an axe.

The Doctor again protests that this is not what really happened.

While Mel is in Janet's room, it is entered and wrecked by one of the alien plant-creatures, or Vervoids. Another of the creatures overhears Bruchner (David Allister), a member of Lasky's team, plotting to destroy them, having realised the threat that they pose to the human race. The Vervoids determine that he should be the next to die.

After burning the team's notes, Bruchner obtains a gun and heads for the flight deck. He manages to set the ship on a suicide course for the Black Hole of Tartarus before succumbing to a cloud of poisonous marsh gas emitted by a Vervoid in the air conditioning duct. The presence of the gas prevents the liner's human crew from entering the flight deck to alter course, but Rudge summons the two Mogarians, Atza (Sam Howard) and Ortezo (Leon Davis), who can do so without suffering any ill effects.

It transpires that Rudge and the Mogarians have been planning all along to hijack the liner. Now that they have seized control of it, they refuse to hand it back to the Commodore. The Mogarians are angry about the human exploitation of their home planet, while Rudge is in it simply for the money – this is to be his last tour of duty. The Mogarians' plan goes awry, however, when an unseen figure enters the flight deck and throws acid on their face masks, allowing the liner's air to penetrate and suffocate them. With his allies dead, Rudge is easily overpowered.

The Vervoids (Peppi Borza, Bob Appleby, Gess Whitfield, Paul Hillier, Bill Perrie, Jerry Manley) begin a reign of terror on the ship, systematically wiping out the human crew and passengers.

Another of Lasky's assistants, Doland (Malcolm Tierney), is revealed to be behind the murder of Hallet and the Mogarians. He plans to bring the Vervoids to Earth for use as cheap slave labour. However, he too is killed by the creatures. The Doctor realises that the liner's occupants are in a terminal situation: it is a case of kill or be killed. The Commodore asks for his help.

The Doctor points out to the court that this proves his assistance was requested. He was not interfering.

The Doctor realises that rather than try to kill the Vervoids, it would be better to encourage them to grow. There is in the cargo hold a metal called vionesium, which has properties similar to those of magnesium and emits a bright light when exposed to air. The Doctor tells the Commodore to switch off all the lights on the ship. This causes the Vervoids to return to their lair, where the Doctor and Mel use vionesium bombs to expose them to intense light. The creatures' growth accelerates out of control and they turn brown and crumble to dust as their energy reserves are used up.

As the Doctor completes his defence, the Valeyard states that the charge against him must again change. The Inquisitor agrees that Article 7 of Gallifreyan Law can be invoked. The Doctor now stands accused of genocide.

WHO FAX
● Novelised as *Doctor Who – Terror of the Vervoids* by Pip and Jane Baker in 1988.
● Episodes released as part of *The Trial of a Time Lord* boxed set on BBC Home Video in 1993.

- The working title of this segment of *The Trial of a Time Lord* was *The Ultimate Foe* – a title more usually associated, incorrectly, with episodes 13 and 14. The title *Terror of the Vervoids*, by which it is now more commonly known, was a later invention, not used at the time of production.
- Locations: none.
- Eric Saward is not credited as script editor for these episodes as, by the time they were drafted, he had resigned from that post.
- This was the first story to feature Bonnie Langford as Melanie. Her surname of 'Bush' is not given on screen in this season.
- The model of the *Hyperion III* was designed by Kevin Molloy, who wanted to capture the feel of an art-deco ocean liner. It was three feet long and vacuum-formed in thermal plastic.

QUOTES

- 'We'd been abroad, and on our return we met John Nathan-Turner in a lift at the BBC. He said "Where on Earth have you been? We need a story." So we wrote the Vervoid story. We were never part of the decision to make the Trial a format for the season – there was some discussion I believe, but we weren't there. We were told only that the Doctor was on trial in the previous two adventures, and our brief was that we had to provide the Doctor's defence in a story set all within the studio.' Co-writer Pip Baker interviewed by Richard Marson for *Doctor Who Magazine* Issue 137.
- 'We had a meeting in John's office, and both John and Eric Saward wanted a whodunit in space.' Co-writer Jane Baker interviewed by Richard Marson for *Doctor Who Magazine* Issue 137.
- 'We came to an arrangement where we would write an episode a week and run it down to Television Centre on the Sunday. They would read it on the Monday and phone us back to say "Proceed." After we'd done two we went in and spent a day with Eric Saward going through and discussing how it fitted in with the rest of the concept. We still didn't know what the outcome of the trial would be – we were never told. The last two episodes were being kept very much a secret. We were being asked to put things in for which we were given sort of half explanations – the suggestion that the Matrix had been tampered with, for instance. We never really understood why. Anyway, we delivered the scripts and there was this great silence, so we phoned the office and the next thing we heard was that

Eric had left the BBC.' Pip Baker interviewed by Richard Marson for *Doctor Who Magazine* Issue 137.

● 'I was delighted with the *Trial* scripts, and with the freedom I was given. I expected there to be a house style, and I remember saying to John Nathan-Turner, "What does this spaceship look like then?" and "Who's deciding this?" He said, "Well – you!" I thought, "Oh my God!" I'd never really been a sci-fi buff, though I'd watched the show occasionally, so it was really nice to come in so fresh.' Director Chris Clough interviewed by Richard Marson for *Doctor Who Magazine* Issue 135.

● 'It was like an Agatha Christie set on a banana boat! We wanted to give it some style, which is why the designer picked up on the Agatha Christie theme, and we also wanted the cabins to be quite small, because all the space would be reserved for the cargo. Like the QE2, it had an airy lounge and a nice open space for the cargo hold, with small cabins. The thing I always remembered about past *Doctor Who*s was having vast open sets, and I couldn't stand that.' Director Chris Clough interviewed by Richard Marson for *Doctor Who Magazine* Issue 135.

● Six Vervoid costumes were made, as a collaboration between the Costume Department and the Visual Effects Department. The masks were the creation of the effects designer, Kevin Molloy. 'The script said that they had to be humanoid vegetables, bipedal, and very vicious. I had to give the design a lot of thought, so that it would be more than just a carrot with teeth, and I researched into pictures of carnivorous plants.' Kevin Molloy interviewed by Patrick Mulkern for *Doctor Who Magazine* Issue 123.

● 'I hated my first episode as Mel – and I had to watch it at the press call. I was sitting at the back and I loathed it. My first couple of scenes were me bobbing around with a skipping rope, and I thought, "Oh no, they're all going to think I'm going to be doing aerobics all the time." But that kind of started it off – they wanted energy and they wanted kind of a strong character. They wanted a character who wasn't dissimilar to me in some respects. I knew people would be saying, "Oh, she's just being her" – until the storyline was established and I could participate in that.' Bonnie Langford interviewed by Richard Marson for *Doctor Who Magazine* Issue 131.

Parts Thirteen–Fourteen (7C)

PRODUCTION DETAILS

OB: 23.06.86, 24.06.86, 30.06.86–04.07.86

Studio: 16.07.86, 17.07.86 in TC1

The Inquisitor calls the Keeper of the Matrix (James Bree) into the Court and he denies that the Matrix can be tampered with as the Doctor has alleged. He states that entry into the Matrix can be achieved only with the Key of Rassilon, which he alone holds. The Doctor accuses the Valeyard of tampering.

Two coffin-like containers arrive at the trial ship. Inside the pods are Glitz and Mel, who enter the courtroom. Glitz states that he has been sent here to assist, and when the Inquisitor asks by whom, the reply comes from the Matrix screen. An image of the Master appears, proof that the Matrix can indeed be breached – the Master has a copy of the Key of Rassilon.

The Master wants Glitz to testify, so the Doctor asks him about the secrets. Glitz reveals that the Sleepers from Andromeda had been stealing secrets from the Matrix while based on Earth. The Master confirms this and goes on to explain that the High Council of Time Lords used a magnetron to throw Earth across space, causing the fireball which devastated it. They then arranged for the planet to be renamed Ravolox, so as to divert suspicion from themselves. Fearing that the Doctor would discover the truth, the Council made a deal with the Valeyard to the effect that he would receive the Doctor's remaining regenerations upon the Doctor's execution. The Master also reveals that the Valeyard is an amalgamation of the Doctor's darker side, somewhere between his twelfth and final incarnation.

The Valeyard flees into the Matrix through the Seventh Door, which is located just outside the courtroom. The Doctor follows, taking Glitz with him, and finds himself in a fantasy world created by the Valeyard. After many deceptions, he confronts his future self, who had disguised himself as a Dickensian clerk named Popplewick.

The Doctor realises that the Valeyard intends to wipe out all the Time Lords present at the trial by using a device – variously described as a megabyte modem, a maser and a particle disseminator – which he has secreted in the Matrix and which is linked to the screen in the courtroom. The Master, meanwhile, intends to use the ensuing chaos on Gallifrey to take over as the supreme ruler of his own people. He has enlisted the services of Glitz, but his plans are halted when he becomes trapped inside his TARDIS in the Matrix.

The Doctor induces an anti-phase signal in the telemetry unit, causing the particle disseminator to backfire. Mel, who had followed him into the Matrix, has already gone back to warn the Time Lords in the court, and they escape unscathed when the machine blasts energy through the Matrix screen. The Valeyard is apparently killed in the back-blast.

The danger over, the Doctor returns to the courtroom, where the Inquisitor informs him that all charges against him have now been dropped. She is also able to tell him that, contrary to what was seen in the trial evidence, Peri was not killed on Thoros-Beta but is now Yrcanos's Queen.

As the Doctor prepares to leave, the Inquisitor invites him to run once again for President of Gallifrey. He declines, asking only that the new Council treat the entrapped Glitz with clemency. He then departs with Mel in the TARDIS.

As the Inquisitor leaves the court she asks the Keeper of the Matrix to arrange all necessary repairs. When the Keeper turns, however, he is revealed to be the Valeyard.

WHO FAX

- Novelised as *Doctor Who – The Ultimate Foe* by Pip and Jane Baker in 1988.
- Episodes released as part of *The Trial of a Time Lord* boxed set on BBC Home Video in 1993.
- Working title: *Time Inc*. The title *The Ultimate Foe*, by which this segment is now more commonly known, was the working title of parts nine to twelve.
- Locations: Gladstone Pottery Museum, Stoke on Trent, Staffs; Camber Sands, East Sussex.
- Some stock barrel-organ music was used for the scenes featuring Popplewick's Fantasy Factory offices. This was 'Can You Handle This?', composed by Ken Jones and Keith Grant from an LP called *Hymns, Carols, Mechanical Instruments*.
- A five-second flashback of Peri and Yrcanos from part eight of *The Trial of a Time Lord* was used at the end of the final episode to reinforce the concept that Peri had not died but had gone on to marry the King.

- Eric Saward is credited as script editor on part thirteen, which he extensively rewrote from Robert Holmes's draft after Holmes died, but not on part fourteen.
- The cat badges worn by Colin Baker during the season were designed and hand-painted from Colin's own cats, Eric and Weeble, by Maggie Howard of Maggie's Moggies.
- Parts nine to fourteen were voted the favourite segment of *The Trial of a Time Lord* by the *Doctor Who* Appreciation Society in their season poll, and part thirteen the favourite individual episode.

QUOTES

- 'Jane had a rather strange conversation with John just after Eric had left. He said, "There's a taxi on its way to you with a script in it. Read it tonight and come in in the morning." And he wouldn't say any more. So the taxi came, and we discovered it was script thirteen. We went in the following morning and the first ten minutes was just the usual coffee and gossip. But there was another person there as a witness to ensure that John didn't tell us anything that was in script fourteen, because of copyright difficulties. Obviously he wanted us to provide a replacement, but he couldn't tell us how the series was supposed to end! There were thirteen episodes leading up to a conclusion that wasn't there. We said we'd think about it, and then John said he wanted it within the week!' Co-writer Pip Baker interviewed by Richard Marson for *Doctor Who Magazine* Issue 137.

- 'There was trouble with the scripts on the last two episodes. Bob Holmes died, Eric Saward left and withdrew his script, and we went into shooting the last script, I think, the week after Pip and Jane delivered it. So, not a lot of time. But it was good in that I'd worked with Pip and Jane in preparing the Vervoid story, so we knew each other. Also, by then we'd chosen the location, so they wrote the last script to kind of fit the location. We'd found this pottery, because in Eric's script there was a long discussion about going round in circles. We'd looked at power stations, cooling towers and so on, and the pottery was the most practical. In the event, it needn't have been there at all.' Director Chris Clough interviewed by Richard Marson for *Doctor Who Magazine* Issue 135.

- 'The original character of Mr Popplewick was meant to be thin and weasly, rather like Scrooge and typically Dickensian. We went through zillions of characters in our minds, and everything was a bit boring. So I thought, "Well, obviously that avenue is a dud, otherwise we'd have solved it by now, so start from totally the opposite end of the thing and go for a large, fat man." In the new script, the Valeyard turned out to be Popplewick all along, but that wasn't the first intention at all.' Director Chris Clough interviewed by Richard Marson for *Doctor Who Magazine* Issue 135.

● 'We delivered the script on a Tuesday. John and Chris read it and then we had a meeting in an observation room for half an hour. I think the script ran to about 38 minutes. We then took some out and Chris said "Let me go into rehearsal and see what we can cut there." You see they were shooting episodes thirteen and fourteen before the Vervoid story. At rehearsal it was still too long. After the producer's run, we told John to leave us alone to sit down and cut it, and we knew there was going to be heartbreak, because we had to cut four minutes and that meant losing some lovely comedy scenes. Some of the actors pretended not to speak to us in rehearsal – they were genuinely a bit hurt.' Co-writer Jane Baker interviewed by Richard Marson for *Doctor Who Magazine* Issue 137.

● 'The fact that the final episode of *The Trial of a Time Lord* was 30 minutes long was a mistake, but it was so complicated we couldn't think of a way of cutting it down. We looked and looked and looked and just could not think of a way of getting five minutes out of it. John Nathan-Turner had to go to Jonathan Powell, who liked the show and said "Okay".' Director Chris Clough interviewed by Richard Marson for *Doctor Who Magazine* Issue 135.

COMMENT

DJH: Considering that the viewing audience had had to wait eighteen months for The Trial of a Time Lord, *it is fair to suppose that they were expecting something really good. Unfortunately what they got was mediocre.*

The first segment promises a lot, but this promise eventually comes to nothing as none of the mysteries it poses are satisfactorily resolved in later episodes. The triumph of this section of the story is Sabalom Glitz. Perfectly cast and played by Tony Selby, this character stood out head and shoulders above the rest.

Parts five to eight are a mess. A lot was expected of Philip Martin after his promising debut story, Vengeance on Varos, *but this sequel has a plot which is simply too shallow to support four episodes. As a result there is a great deal of running up and down corridors, getting captured, escaping, being recaptured, and other general padding. The majority of the cast are uninspired, Gordon Warnecke as Tuza being the weakest link. Brian Blessed plays Yrcanos so totally over the top that any subtlety there may have been in the script is completely lost.*

The Vervoid segment is by far the best. The plot is straightforward, the monsters are eerie and menacing, and the whole thing leads to a satisfactory climax. The cast are great: particularly Michael Craig as the Commodore and Yolande Palfrey as Janet, although Honor Blackman as Lasky seems to be just going through the motions rather than really getting her teeth into the role. Even Bonnie Langford's debut as Mel is okay. At least she shows some individuality and determination, and a singlemindedness to investigate regardless of the Doctor's wishes. This is refreshing after the wasted opportunity that was Peri.

Of course, in any mystery, the resolution is all-important, and in this case it is completely botched. The story ends leaving the viewer wondering what all the fuss was about. One of the casualties of the final two episodes is Mel's character, which is markedly different from how it was established on screen in parts nine to twelve.

While a fourteen-part story was a brave and ambitious project to undertake, and while the production team should be praised for attempting something previously untried on this scale, The Trial of a Time Lord *ultimately failed due to a collision of circumstances largely outside the control of those in charge. Yet another wasted opportunity. (7/10)*

MS: *The idea of having the Doctor on trial for his life throughout the whole of the 23rd season was an interesting parody of the real-life events which were affecting the production of the series. But to have such a linking theme over fourteen episodes is almost bound to result in the story becoming a complicated mixture of on-going plot strands and individual storylines. Casual viewers had no chance of following the plot if they tuned into the season halfway through, and even many fans who watched the whole event were uncertain as to the logic of its conclusion.*

The season begins well, with the extremely impressive and complex model shots of the TARDIS being dragged towards the space station, but the first segment within The Trial of a Time Lord *is less of a story in its own right than the establishment of a mystery that remains unresolved until the beginning of part thirteen.*

The second segment has the bonus of a returning enemy from the previous season, but Sil's character is not used to its full potential this time. In terms of plot, this segment is a rather standard run-about, populated with over-the-top characters like Yrcanos.

The next four episodes see an improvement. The tale of the Vervoids on the Hyperion III *space liner has its roots in whodunit-style thrillers like* Murder on the Orient Express*; and, unlike the other segments of the season, these four episodes could have stood up as a story in their own right.*

The acting of the supporting cast in the last two segments of the story is generally far superior to the rather over-the-top performances of most of those in the first two. Colin Baker's commendable portrayal of the Doctor is the one unchanging constant which manages to keep the story from becoming totally incomprehensible.

By the time they reach the final two parts of The Trial of a Time Lord, *most viewers have forgotten about the mysteries set out in the first four parts, and the rest of the story's climax is a muddle of surreal images which make little sense. In fact, as the Doctor leaves with Mel, a companion from his own future, he creates a time paradox. So many of the answers and explanations are crammed into the final two episodes that the pace becomes frantic. Perhaps the final mystery posed by* The Trial of a Time Lord *is, what was it really all about? (6/10)*

SJW: *A fourteen-part Doctor Who story is not necessarily doomed to fail. The 1965/66 adventure* The Daleks' Master Plan *was only two episodes shorter, and that was superb. In that case, however, the plot was relatively uncomplicated and did not require the viewer to remember details from the early episodes in order to enjoy the later ones. Those with only a casual interest could pick things up as it went along. The same can certainly not be said of* The Trial of a Time Lord, *which is convoluted in the extreme.*

The most successful segment is the third one, featuring the Vervoids. This is partly because the tedious courtroom scenes are kept to a minimum, allowing the story to flow rather better than during the other segments, but mainly because the script itself is entertaining and quite easy to follow, complemented by Chris Clough's well-paced and stylish direction. *The cliffhanger endings of episodes nine and ten are particularly noteworthy, being easily the most dramatic of the season. The 'whodunit' element could perhaps be considered rather unsatisfactory, leaving a few loose ends and unanswered questions, but on the other hand this is entirely in keeping with the Agatha Christie motif, Christie's own stories often being full of holes and highly implausible in their resolution.*

The other three segments are difficult to assess in isolation, as they don't really tell self-contained stories. The concluding one is notable, however, for containing some superb imagery in the scenes set in the Valeyard's fantasy domain within the Matrix. This segment is again very well directed by Chris Clough and, after the relative disappointment of his opening episodes for the story, it's nice to be able to say that Robert Holmes's final credited script, that for part thirteen, is a good one.

A brave attempt, but in the final analysis it just doesn't come off. (4/10)

SEASON TWENTY-FOUR

Time and the Rani (7D)

EP	DATE	TIME	DURN	VIEWERS	CHART POS
1	07.09.87	19.35	24'44"	5.1	71

[Details are for the episode as a whole]

PRODUCTION DETAILS

Studio: The TARDIS scenes for the pre-credits sequence were recorded on 20.04.87 in TC8

The TARDIS is attacked by a powerful force whilst in flight and the sixth Doctor (Sylvester McCoy) and Mel (Bonnie Langford) are both knocked unconscious. The ship then materialises on the planet Lakertya, observed by one of the natives, Ikona (Mark Greenstreet). The main doors open and the Rani (Kate O'Mara) enters – it was she who was responsible for the attack. She tells an unseen companion to leave the girl but to bring the Doctor. As she leaves, a lumbering, hair-covered creature (Richard Gauntlett) enters. The creature moves to the Doctor's side and turns his prone body over. The Doctor's face blurs and changes as he regenerates into a new form.

WHO FAX

- This sequence was shown before the main *Doctor Who* titles at the start of the 24th season.
- The effects of the TARDIS in space were computer generated by the CAL Video company, who had also created a new title sequence for the seventh Doctor.
- As Colin Baker had turned down the invitation to return to the series to reprise the role of the sixth Doctor in a regeneration story, Sylvester McCoy donned a curly blonde wig to play him for the few seconds before the regeneration.

AFTERWORD

Suddenly it was all over. The sixth Doctor was no more. No final swan-song story for this Doctor, just a few tears to mark his passing. In the end, all that was left was a legacy of eight stories and the promise of what might have been.

Stories: Appendix

The sixth Doctor has also appeared in other productions which, while not forming a part of the established *Doctor Who* canon, are detailed here.

In A Fix With Sontarans

DATE	TIME	DURN
23.02.85	18.05*	8'46"

*Time is the start time of *Jim'll Fix It*, not of the *Doctor Who* segment.

PRODUCTION DETAILS

Studio: 20.02.85 (studio unknown)

The Doctor is making hurried adjustments to the TARDIS console when the ship's matter transporter activates and Tegan appears. The Doctor apologises to his former companion for her sudden transportation here and asks for her help as there are two Sontarans on board. She agrees, and assists him in cutting off all main sources of power on the TARDIS. The Sontarans have with them a vitrox bomb, which requires a considerable amount of power to activate it. The Doctor predicts that when they find there is no power, the creatures will return to the console room.

Tegan reactivates the matter transporter and a young boy named Gareth Jenkins appears, dressed in a similar manner to the sixth Doctor. Tegan is concerned that Gareth should be returned to Earth, but the newcomer offers to stay and help in repelling the Sontarans. Tegan fetches a box for Gareth to stand on, so that he can reach the TARDIS controls, and he then assists the Doctor in making further adjustments to the console, priming its energiser unit.

The interior door to the console room explodes as two Sontarans enter. The leader introduces himself as Group Marshal Nathan of the tenth Sontaran Battle Brigade. When Gareth is introduced to them, they recognise his name and are pleased to have captured such an important prisoner. They explain that in the year 2001, a Sontaran attack on Earth will be defeated by a defence force led by a Gareth Jenkins. They plan to kill the boy now to ensure the future success of their invasion. The Doctor, however, knocks their gun away and shouts to Gareth to activate the energiser. Gareth does so, and the Sontarans dissolve in a jet of smoke.

The danger seems to have passed, and the Doctor asks Gareth how he had the knowledge to operate the TARDIS. Gareth replies that he has seen the Doctor do it on the telly. Just then an image appears on the scanner. Tegan describes it as monstrous, and the Doctor agrees that it is revolting. It is Jimmy Savile.

WHO FAX
- *In A Fix With Sontarans* was a one-part mini-story shown within the BBC1 light-entertainment programme *Jim'll Fix It* – a series in which Jimmy Savile OBE makes viewers' dreams come true.
- Eight-year-old Gareth Jenkins had written in asking if he could see Colin Baker and go inside the TARDIS.
- The story was written by Eric Saward, and directed by *Jim'll Fix It*'s director Marcus Mortimer.
- The name of the Sontaran Group Marshal was changed from Stern to Nathan by actor Clinton Greyn during recording. His subordi-

nate, Turner, was not named on screen.

● Alongside Colin Baker as the Doctor, Janet Fielding reprised her role as Tegan, complete with the air-hostess uniform which she had worn in her earliest *Doctor Who* stories. Clinton Greyn and Tim Raynham played the Sontarans, as they had done also in *The Two Doctors*.

● The sketch was originally to have featured Nicola Bryant playing Peri, but she was out of the country on holiday so the script was changed to incorporate Tegan instead.

COMMENT

In A Fix With Sontarans *is a very complex and far-reaching story, in which the abilities of the TARDIS are tested to the full. The episode is really held together by Gareth Jenkins, who plays himself. He is so important to the plot that the build-up to his appearance is carefully crafted, and his apparent woodenness in the face of first the Doctor and then the Sontarans is merely a mask for his real intentions. It is obvious that he could have held the story together on his own. The inclusion of another Doctor in the guise of Colin Baker and the gratuitous use of Tegan are totally superfluous. Overall, this is one of the better sixth Doctor stories!*

Yes, okay, we're joking. In A Fix With Sontarans *is actually one of the rare examples of* Doctor Who *being featured on another BBC TV programme with the Doctor played in character and by the regular actor.*

Slipback

EP	DATE	TIME	DURN
1	25.07.85	10.08	10'33"
2	25.07.85	11.44	10'22"
3	01.08.85	09.50	10'19"
4	01.08.85	11.26	10'14"
5	08.08.85	09.44	10'09"
6	08.08.85	11.36	11'36"

PRODUCTION DETAILS

Studio: 10.06.85 in studio B11 at BBC Broadcasting House

CREDITS

The Doctor	Colin Baker
Peri	Nicola Bryant
Bates/Snatch	Nick Revell
Computer Voices	Jane Carr
Seedle	Ron Pember
Maintenance Service Drone 934/	
Steward/Time Lord/Maston	Alan Thompson
Shellingbourne Grant	Jon Glover
Captain Slarn	Valentine Dyall
Studio Managers	Colin Duff, Wilfred Acosta, Sarah Rosewarne
Production Secretary	Kate Abercrombie
Sound Effects	Dick Mills
Incidental Music	Jonathan Gibbs
Theme Music	Ron Grainer
Arrangement of Theme Music	Peter Howell
Writer	Eric Saward
Director/Producer	Paul Spencer
'Pirate Radio 4' Producer	Jonathan James-Moore

On board the space-craft Vipod Mor, two crewmen are killed by a creature inside the ventilation ducting.

On board the TARDIS, meanwhile, the sleeping Doctor hears a whispering voice in his dreams. The ship then unexpectedly material-ises next to the Vipod Mor. Investigating, the Doctor and Peri discover that the Vipod Mor's computer has developed a split personality and intends to travel back in time to re-start the Universe, shaping it into a more structured and ordered place.

A further danger is presented by the fact that the Vipod Mor's captain is cultivating a deadly virus with which he intends to wipe out the crew – this being a fit of pique caused by the fact that he has not had an opportunity to meet Peri, whom he quite liked when he saw her on the ship's monitors.

The Doctor tries to thwart the computer's plan but is prevented from doing so by the Time Lords, who tell him that this event has always been and is what will start the Universe in the first place.

WHO FAX
- Novelised as *Doctor Who – Slipback* by Eric Saward in 1986.
- Released on audio-cassette in 1988, together with the audio version of the 1975 TV story *Genesis of the Daleks*, as part of the BBC Radio Collection.
- Working title: *The Doomsday Project*.
- Slipback was transmitted as part of a three-hour Radio 4 programme generically titled *Pirate Radio 4*. Presented by Steve Blacknell, the show featured many items and interviews, with the *Doctor Who* segments broadcast at the rate of two episodes per programme.
- The stock background music in episode three was Philippe Entremont's arrangement of *Satie: Gymnopédie No. 1* from the LP *Bournville Selection*.
- *Slipback* was the last work undertaken by actor Valentine Dyall – the Black Guardian from the TV series – before his death on 24 June 1985.

COMMENT
While Doctor Who *fandom was generally up in arms about the temporary cancellation of the programme following the final episode of* Revelation of the Daleks, *the appearance of a six-part radio story was a welcome means of filling the gap. Unfortunately, Eric Saward's script owes more to Douglas Adams than to* Doctor Who, *with a squeaky American-voiced computer, a captain who spends all his time in a lava-bath cultivating psychosomatic diseases, and a crumbling android who thinks he's a butler. The production is entertaining in its own way, but the comedy element is far stronger than the dramatic.*

The Ultimate Adventure

Producer	Mark Furness
Director	Carole Todd
Writer	Terrance Dicks

Colin Baker Tour Dates:

05/06/89–10/06/89	Newcastle Opera House, Newcastle Upon Tyne
12/06/89–17/06/89	Theatre Royal, Nottingham
19/06/89–24/06/89	Grand Theatre, Leeds
26/06/89–01/07/89	Theatre Royal, Brighton
03/07/89–08/07/89	Edinburgh Playhouse, Edinburgh

10/07/89–15/07/89	Grand Theatre, Wolverhampton
17/07/89–22/07/89	Theatre Royal, Northampton
24/07/89–28/07/89	Marlow Theatre, Canterbury
31/07/89–05/08/89	King's Theatre, Southsea
07/08/89–19/08/89	Congress Theatre, Eastbourne

The Doctor – who is now travelling with Jason (Graeme Smith), a young man from eighteenth-century France – is summoned to Downing Street by the Prime Minster (Judith Hibbert), who asks him to help foil a plot to kidnap a US envoy (Christopher Beaumont). During the course of the adventure which follows, the Doctor and Jason are joined by the nightclub singer Crystal (Rebecca Thornhill) and the small furry alien Zog (Stephanie Colburn) and battle against the mercenary Karl (David Banks), Cybermen, Daleks and an amorous bar-owner, Delilah (Hibbert), before finally rescuing the envoy.

WHO FAX
● *Doctor Who – The Ultimate Adventure* was the fourth *Doctor Who*-related stage play to be produced in Britain. Previously there had been *The Curse of the Daleks* (1965), *Seven Keys to Doomsday* (1974) and *Recall U.N.I.T.* (1984).
● The play started its run with Jon Pertwee playing the Doctor. Colin Baker took over partway through the tour.

COMMENT
When Colin Baker took over the lead role, a number of adjustments were made to the play's scripts to accommodate the differences in character between the third Doctor and the sixth. These ranged from quite significant changes – such as the reworking of the scenes set in Paris 1798 to turn the sword fight from a relatively serious affair into a comic one – to relatively minor alterations of dialogue – such as the amendment of the third Doctor's line 'He's reversed the polarity of the neutron flow' to 'He's reversed the linearity of the proton flow'. Other minor changes were improvised by Baker during virtually every performance.

Overall, the play was enjoyable family entertainment and, while it got off to a slightly shaky start, all the problems had been ironed out by the time Colin Baker took over. Baker's excellent re-creation of the sixth Doctor was invariably a highlight.

4: Rewriting the Myth

Every era of *Doctor Who* brings new elements to the series' developing mythology. Story after story, new facts are invented by the programme's writers and added to what is already known of the Doctor's universe. Some new pieces of this ever-growing jigsaw puzzle interlock neatly with what has gone before, while others fit so poorly that the viewer is forced to start rebuilding the picture from scratch. Many hardcore *Doctor Who* fans expend great amounts of time and energy trying to find an order which gives all the seemingly contradictory facts and storylines some kind of logical continuity.

Plot continuity has always been a bugbear of long-running television programmes. It could be argued that good continuity is essential in a popular soap opera for the sake of believability, but is it important in a fantasy-orientated series such as *Doctor Who*? Colin Baker certainly considered that it was, as he told the fanzine *The Colin Baker Interview* in 1987:

'I think it is important not to ignore it totally. I did fall out with the script editor, Eric Saward, on a couple of occasions. For instance, on *The Trial of a Time Lord*, I remember reading the script and saying, "Hang on a minute Eric. As I recall, from watching the episodes before I came into the series, Peter's Doctor was made the Lord President of Gallifrey at the end of *The Five Doctors* because of his actions in nobbling Borusa. Don't you think that if you're going to put the Lord

President on trial, there should be some mention of that fact? Not only the fans but also the general viewers in this case are going to remember it." Eric's reply to that was, "What do you want me to do then?" I said, "Well, can't we write in a little scene where we explain that he is not the Lord President any more?" So he put in two lines which short-circuited the problem.

'Yes, I do believe that continuity is very important. In the end, one has to recognise the fact that, of the five million people who watch *Doctor Who*, it is only a thousand or so who are going to examine it in detail, and the remainder are going to be perfectly happy. But I think I would agree with a lot of the fans, because I am often put in the position of going to conventions and having to make up excuses for all these things. Whenever I spotted anything in the script and it could be altered, I would alter it. I did not have as much input on scripts as Tom Baker did, but then he played the part for seven years. Towards the end, though, I was putting a few extra bits in.'

In fairness, it should be noted that the Doctor's status as President of the Time Lords was one of the points on which writers were specifically briefed during the initial planning meetings for *The Trial of a Time Lord*. It was suggested that an explanation might be included to the effect that there had been a change in Gallifrey's system of government during the Doctor's absence and that consequently he had lost his former position. It seems however that this point must have been lost in the translation of the original ideas into script form.

Continuity was certainly not something which Eric Saward or John Nathan-Turner ignored during this period. On the contrary the sixth Doctor's era is noted for the unusually large extent to which it drew on the series' own established mythology.

Saward, in common with previous script editors, considered that while continuity should not be accorded such an inordinately high priority that it got in the way of telling a good story, care should be taken to keep faith with the series' viewers by avoiding major discrepancies. Consequently he sometimes consulted on such matters with *Doctor Who* fan Ian Levine – whose input, made without payment or credit, he found extremely helpful – as did producer John Nathan-Turner.

Many new facts are learned about the Doctor himself during the eight stories of his sixth incarnation. His first adventure, *The Twin Dilemma*, shows how extreme and unpredictable the after-effects of regeneration can sometimes be, while his last, *The Trial of a Time Lord*, presents a distillation of all his darker aspects in the form of the Valeyard. In *The Two Doctors* he is seen to suffer a psychic trauma when his second incarnation is apparently put to death, and later he communicates with his other persona telepathically across space.

Viewers are also introduced to a number of old acquaintances from earlier incidents not seen in the TV series. In *The Twin Dilemma* there is Azmael, a retired Time Lord with whom the Doctor once spent a pleasant drunken evening beside a fountain on the planet Joconda; in *The Two Doctors* it is revealed that he first met Joinson Dastari while attending an inaugural function as a representative of the Time Lords, before he fell from favour with them; in *Timelash* the TARDIS materialises on Karfel, where the Doctor is honoured for having saved the population from a disaster during a visit in his third incarnation with Jo Grant and another companion; and in the Vervoid segment of *The Trial of a Time Lord* he arrives on the space-liner *Hyperion III* too late to save the life of his old friend Hallet, an undercover law enforcement agent, but still in time to come to the aid of Commodore 'Tonker' Travers, a man for whom he apparently caused some trouble during a previous encounter.

In *The Two Doctors*, the second Doctor and Jamie are seen to be undertaking a mission for the Time Lords – something which surprised many fans as, during his own era, this Doctor had not even admitted his origins until the end of his last adventure, *The War Games*. This is an example of a change occurring as a result of a misunderstanding on the part of the writer. Robert Holmes had always been under the impression that it was the second Doctor who had routinely undertaken missions for his own people, as the price of his continued freedom, when in actual fact it was the *third* Doctor who had done so. Some interesting theories have been advanced by fans to account for the apparent inconsistency which arose from this. One ingenious explanation is that after the momentous events of the 1973 story *The Three Doctors*, it was not only the third Doctor who was rewarded by the Time Lords by being given a new dematerialisation circuit for his TARDIS, but also the first and second Doctors, by each being allowed a completely new lease of life. This would certainly account for some of the developments seen in *The Two Doctors*, and also for some of those in the earlier anniversary story *The Five Doctors*, but it is only one of many possible explanations.

The Doctor's trusty TARDIS features prominently in a number of the stories of this period. In *Attack of the Cybermen* the ship temporarily discards its familiar police box form after the Doctor repairs its chameleon circuits, appearing first as a decorated cupboard, then as a pipe organ and later as an ornate gateway; in *Vengeance on Varos* it becomes stranded in a galactic void owing to a fault in the transitional elements, requiring the trans/power system to be relined with zeiton 7; in *The Two Doctors* viewers learn that a TARDIS's briode-nebuliser has to be primed with the Rassilon Imprimatur – a print of symbiotic nuclei within the physiology of every Time Lord – before it can be used; in the same story, the sixth Doctor is heard to express considerable envy on discovering that his second incarnation is now able to operate his TARDIS with a Stattenheim remote control unit, provided by the Time Lords; and in *Timelash* the ship is used as a deflector shield to neutralise a Bandril missile.

Along with the introduction of a number of new returning characters – the evil arms dealer Sil and his fellow Mentors, the exiled Time Lord chemist the Rani and the intergalactic mercenary Sabalom Glitz – the sixth Doctor's era saw the return and development of a number of well-established adversaries from previous seasons.

Attack of the Cybermen could almost be considered a sequel to the sixties classic *The Tomb of the Cybermen* as it sees the Doctor being forcibly returned to that story's setting, the tomb complex on the planet Telos. Here he has a new battle with the creatures' ultimate leader, the Cyber Controller, who has apparently recovered from the damage inflicted upon him at the end of his debut story. This time, viewers also meet Telos's original inhabitants, the Cryons – creatures who can exist only in extreme cold – with whom Lytton, the mercenary first encountered working for the Daleks in the fifth Doctor story *Resurrection of the Daleks*, has now allied himself. The Cybermen's plan turns out to involve the use of a time ship, captured from another race, in order to crash Halley's Comet into the Earth and thereby prevent the destruction in 1986 of their original home planet Mondas, as seen in the first Cyberman story *The Tenth Planet*. In the end, however, their scheme is defeated and the Controller finally destroyed.

It has become traditional over the years for subtle – and sometimes not-so-subtle – changes to be made in the Cybermen's appearance for each new adventure. *Attack of the Cybermen* is one exception to the rule, however, as this time the creatures' costumes are almost exactly the same as in their previous outing, *The Five Doctors*. The only variations are provided by a black-camouflaged Cyber Scout in the sequences set in the London sewers – the site of the Cybermen's base on Earth, as they were in the 1968 adventure *The Invasion* – and by the Cyber Controller, who looks somewhat bloated in comparison with his underlings and whose helmet is notable for having a domed top and a lack of any side handles, echoing some of the distinctive features of the original helmet as seen in *The Tomb of the Cybermen*. Director Matthew Robinson had also intended that the Cybermen seen on the surface of Telos should wear transparent, globe-shaped space helmets over their heads, but this idea was dropped at a late stage as it was found that the globes had a tendency to steam up and impede the actors' movements.

The Doctor's arch-enemy the Master returned to plague him once more in *The Mark of the Rani* – with no explanation given for his miraculous escape from the apparently fatal predicament in which he was last seen at the end of the Season 21 story *Planet of Fire*. His powers of hypnotism – somewhat neglected during the fifth Doctor's era – are very much in evidence here, as is his familiar Tissue Compression Eliminator weapon, but his characteristically devious scheme is directed towards what seems – for him – a remarkably unambitious end. His main aim is simply to disrupt the course of Earth's history by thwarting the start of the Industrial Revolution – although in the process he also plans, as usual, to humiliate and kill the Doctor!

The Trial of a Time Lord has the Master setting his sights rather higher as, by revealing to the court the High Council's corrupt deal with the Valeyard, he contrives to bring about their downfall, creating insurrection on Gallifrey and leaving a power vacuum which he intends to fill. He has once again miscalculated, however, and ends up trapped inside his own TARDIS, lodged within the Matrix.

The Sontarans also reappear during the sixth Doctor's era, having their fourth on-screen skirmish with the Time Lord. Little new information is learned about them on this occasion, though, apart from the fact that they are vulnerable to attack with a chemical called coronic acid. They are still as bellicose as ever, still attempting to gain the secret of time travel – something which they were seen to have achieved in rudimentary form in Season 11's *The Time Warrior* and which they tried to take by force in Season 15's *The Invasion of Time* – and still locked in their seemingly endless intergalactic war with the shape-shifting Rutans, described on this occasion as 'the Rutan Host'.

No era of *Doctor Who* would be truly complete without at least one story featuring the series' most famous monsters, the dreaded Daleks. *Revelation of the Daleks* is the first story to present viewers with two different Dalek factions: one – with the traditional grey livery – loyal to the Supreme Dalek on their home planet Skaro, the other – with a new, highly effective white and gold colour scheme – created by Davros on the planet Necros to do his bidding. Continuity with previous Dalek stories is excellent, the splitting of the Daleks into two opposing blocs being a highly logical development after their earlier clashes with Davros, their progenitor.

The idea of Davros deliberately creating new mutants to serve as recruits for his Dalek army is also a fitting reference back to the creatures' origins on the radiation-soaked Skaro, and provides the opportunity for a particularly memorable image – that of the transparent, partly formed Dalek in the incubation room on Necros. The concept of a transparent Dalek first appeared in David Whitaker's book *Doctor Who in an Exciting Adventure with the Daleks* – the novelisation of the Daleks' debut story from 1963/64 – but could not have been realised in the TV series at that time, so it is nice to see it reaching the screen here.

Another important development in *Revelation of the Daleks* is the scene where one of Davros's Daleks appears to hover some distance off the ground when exterminating the characters Natasha and Grigory, finally providing the answer to the age-old question as to how the Daleks can conquer a galaxy when they can't climb stairs!

Davros's own evolution is taken a stage further in this story. He is represented for the most part as a disembodied head within a life-support unit, which is actually just a decoy to fool potential assassins – although whether it is a clone or a projection or a mechanical automaton of some sort is never made entirely clear. When the real Davros finally appears, however, it is obvious that he has developed some previously unsuspected powers: he immobilises the assassin Orcini with a stream of blue lightning projected from his forefinger and – like the Dalek in the incubation room – demonstrates an ability to hover effortlessly in mid-air. A rather more prosaic development occurs toward the end of the story when he has his remaining hand blown off by a burst of gunfire from Orcini's squire, Bostock!

Ever since they were devised in 1969 by writers Terrance Dicks and

Malcolm Hulke, the Time Lords have been an increasingly important part of *Doctor Who*. Their contribution to the series' mythology is developed significantly during the sixth Doctor's era, and most notably in *The Trial of a Time Lord*. This is the third time the Doctor has been placed on trial by his own people; in *The War Games* he stood accused of interfering in the affairs of other planets, and in *The Deadly Assassin* he was erroneously charged with the President's assassination.

The trial takes place on a giant space station, into which the Doctor's TARDIS is drawn by the mental energy of the assembled Time Lords, and the evidence is presented on a huge screen linked to the Matrix – the computer which acts as the repository of all Time Lord knowledge, as established in *The Deadly Assassin* and expanded upon in a number of later adventures. In charge of the court is the Inquisitor, and presenting the case for the prosecution is the Valeyard.

At the beginning of the story, the Doctor learns that during his absence from Gallifrey he has been deposed as President due to his neglect of his duties – the reference which Colin Baker had asked to have inserted, as mentioned at the start of this chapter. At first, he is told that the proceedings are merely an inquiry into his behaviour, ordered by the High Council. The charges are that he is guilty of conduct unbecoming a Time Lord, and that he has broken the First Law of Time – which appears to relate here to interference in the affairs of other planets, although at earlier points in the series' history it was the law which prevented a Time Lord from crossing his own time stream. The Valeyard considers that the sentence imposed upon the Doctor at his last trial – presumably a reference to the one in *The War Games* – was too lenient, and before long he has had the inquiry changed into a formal trial, with the Doctor's present and future lives at stake if he is found guilty. Later, the charge is changed again, under Article 7 of Gallifreyan law, to one of genocide, the Doctor's own evidence having shown him destroying the Vervoid race in a future adventure. Clearly the Gallifreyan judicial process works rather differently from any here on Earth!

During the course of the trial, it becomes apparent that the Matrix is by no means as inviolable as its Keeper – a figure not featured or referred to in any previous story – asserts. The Master has gained access to it using a copy of the Key of Rassilon and, at his urging, Glitz tells the court that thieves from Andromeda had previously been stealing hi-tech secrets from it for some time before their actions were finally discovered. The Doctor's trial is in fact part of an elaborate cover-up by the High Council to prevent anyone from finding out about the drastic measures they took to prevent their secrets from getting out; measures which involved moving Earth – the base for the Andromedans' operations – light years across space, devastating it with a fireball. As seen in the opening segment of the story, Earth is now known as Ravolox and inhabited by primitive peoples such as the Tribe of the Free. This continues the trend of previous Time Lord stories in suggesting that their race's hold on power – which the Doctor states has been absolute for ten million years – has had a highly corrupting influence.

Further features of the Matrix are observed in the closing stages of the story as the Doctor, Glitz and Mel enter it through the Seventh Door – a portal, situated just outside the courtroom, which is opened by placing the Key of Rassilon against a sensor pad – and as all three become caught up, along with the Master, in a fantasy domain created by the Valeyard – scenes highly reminiscent of those in *The Deadly Assassin*, also written by Robert Holmes, in which the Doctor battled another adversary within the Matrix.

Considering its relative brevity, the sixth Doctor's era saw some significant changes taking place in and some important additions being made to the *Doctor Who* universe: a legacy which would remain with the series and which would be further built upon in later years.

PART THREE – FACT

5: Production Development

The sixth Doctor's era broke with recent precedent right from the outset, the newcomer's introductory story being placed not at the beginning of a season but at the end of one. This was a consequence of John Nathan-Turner's desire to establish the new Doctor before the series went off-air for the summer. It could therefore be considered rather surprising that the production team then chose to make him mentally unstable in the aftermath of his regeneration, leaving viewers uncertain as to what he would be like in later stories. They took this decision partly with a view to keeping all their options open but also in a conscious effort to try something new, making the sixth Doctor highly impetuous and unreliable, as Eric Saward explained to *Doctor Who Magazine* in 1984:

'Because the Doctor has always been slightly seedy after regenerating . . . and because we wanted to make the sixth Doctor different we decided to make the regeneration so extreme that it would resemble madness. The swings of mood were amazing – if he had been walking around on the streets, he would have been a strong contender for a psychiatric hospital! So the whole behavioural aspect of the Doctor in *The Twin Dilemma* was quite deliberate – I wanted to explore what happened after the regeneration.'

Saward acknowledges that this idea could not be sustained for long:

'It's an obstacle to developing a story. Personal traits in the way a character approaches a problem are interesting, and a writer can use them, but when a character is utterly unreliable, one doesn't know how he's going to act or which way he's going to go, it creates endless problems.'

In view of this, the sixth Doctor became noticeably more stable in his first full season, Season 22, allowing the emphasis to be shifted towards the stories themselves. One thing which remained unchanged, however, was his garish, multicoloured costume, the initial inspiration for which had come from John Nathan-Turner.

'John very much wanted to achieve a kind of development from one Doctor to another,' recalled the costume's designer, Pat Godfrey, in *The Frame*. 'He wanted to get the feel of the previous Doctors' costumes by going back to a more Victorian shape, but he also wanted to make the new one look very bizarre, rather fairground and clown-like. He even suggested that I could give the character spotted trousers, but that was a direction we chose not to follow. John wanted a garish costume – his own words were "a totally tasteless costume" – which is actually very difficult to achieve as one has to be tastefully tasteless.

'The other constraints I was given were that the shirt had to have a question mark on each collar and that there couldn't be any blue anywhere in the costume as it would have caused problems with the electronic effects.'

This brief continued John Nathan-Turner's policy of giving his Doctors highly stylised, uniform-like costumes, rather than simply eccentric collections of more conventional clothing as had been worn by the Time Lord's earlier incarnations. The very distinctive nature of the sixth Doctor's costume had an obvious impact on the style of his stories, in that it precluded any possibility of him making an unobtrusive entrance into a situation and inevitably meant that he became the centre of attention. It also had another, less obvious repercussion, as Pat Godfrey explains:

'This really arose from a technicality of working in colour television. When colour was first introduced we were trained in how to design for it. We were shown a scale of 0 to 100, where 0 was black and 100 was white. We were told that the maximum range that video cameras could cope with at that time was only about 30 – in other words, the darkest and brightest colours in the picture could be no more than 30 points apart on the scale. So because the Doctor's costume was very bright, I had to move everything else up the scale accordingly. If the companion's costume had been in very subtle hues it would have been washed out by the Doctor's, so hers had to be bright as well.'

This knock-on effect extended not only to the series' costumes but also to other aspects of the production, most notably the sets. The end result was that the overall look of the sixth Doctor's stories tended to be very gaudy and unsubtle – a development which John Nathan-Turner later acknowledged to have been to the series' detriment, although he was unaware of it at the time.

Season 22 also saw important changes being made in the style and pacing of the series' scripts. These came about as a direct consequence of the decision – reportedly taken by Alan Hart, the then Controller of BBC1 – to double the length of each episode, with a concomitant halving of the number of episodes per season. The new episode length was originally to have been 50 minutes but was eventually fixed at 45 minutes when John Nathan-Turner pointed out that, with fewer title sequences required, a 50-minute episode would actually have demanded *more* than twice the usual programme content, increasing the strain on the series' budget and resources.

The extended episode length was welcomed by Nathan-Turner. 'I feel that the show lends itself more easily to that formula,' he told the fanzine *Zygon*. 'I know that's a kind of outrageous thing to say after 21 years of the old format, but it provides an opportunity for us as programme makers to examine the relationship between the Doctor and his companion . . . and to find out more about the guest characters, to flesh them out more.'

Notwithstanding this potential advantage, both Nathan-Turner and Eric Saward realised that the transition from the old format to the new would require careful handling. In an interview for *Doctor Who Magazine*, Saward later explained the challenges it had presented:

'It involved, from my point of view, an attempt to talk to our writers about a format of which I had no experience, although obviously I'd written 50-minute things myself for other programmes. While rethinking the format, we were very careful to keep the essence of the show, which is a fantasy/SF adventure story. We couldn't just cobble together two 25-minute episodes, because a compilation of two fast-running parts is very off-putting – it jars. We had time to stop and think a bit more, although we did have to keep on hammering away with the action.'

Saward considered that the transition had been achieved relatively successfully and was disappointed when the powers that be decided to revert to the traditional 25-minute format for Season 23, feeling that another season of 45-minute episodes would perhaps have been better. This was a view with which John Nathan-Turner concurred, as he told *Doctor Who Magazine* in the same September 1985 interview:

'Yes, I think it did work. Inevitably when there's a change in something which has been a tradition for such a long time, there's a kind of apprehension from the front office that it won't work. Now we're rethinking again. We've got material which has been written for 45-minute slots and will have to be split up again. Those scripts we do finish up using will have to be restructured. There's more to it than just splitting it down the middle. It would have been lovely to have done one more season in that slot to get it exactly right, but we were both surprised and delighted that we achieved accuracy so quickly.'

Another significant change in storytelling style arose from the fact that, unlike his predecessor, the sixth Doctor had just a single companion. This was a change which Eric Saward actively supported, as he revealed to *Doctor Who Magazine*:

'From my point of view, both as script editor and as writer, you can do much more with just one companion. The Doctor and the companion can have a much stronger, better-defined relationship and they can relate to each other in a more positive way. When you've got more than one companion you're farming out lines which could be said by one person. Also, if you've got so many people in a confined space like the TARDIS, it's difficult to give them a lot of positive action. That became very apparent with three companions. It's also a problem to deal with so many sub-plots. Thus the return to the old idea.'

What Saward found rather less appealing was the nature of Peri's character, which he considers to have been weak and 'feminine' in all the worst ways. Neither was he any happier with Peri's successor, computer programmer Mel Bush, whom he recalls to have been conceived purely to fulfil Nathan-Turner's desire to have a companion with red hair – possibly with a view to his intended casting of the part.

The original character outlines for Peri and Mel were both relatively detailed. The former was prepared by Nathan-Turner along with Saward and writer Peter Grimwade, while the latter was entirely Nathan-Turner's work. In his book *Doctor Who – The Companions*, the producer gave his own account of the factors which had shaped Mel's development:

'One of the changes we decided to make [for Season 23] was a change of emphasis in humour. I have always maintained that *Doctor Who* should have a helping of wit rather than slapstick. In order to make this helping more than ample I decided to devise a companion whose basic character gave the writers more opportunity for fun and humour; a character who, by her very nature, placed the Doctor in humorous situations.'

Thus Mel was conceived as a get-up-and-go health-and-fitness fanatic with a mane of red hair who would rush impetuously into dangerous situations and keep the Doctor on his toes in more ways than one, often chiding him about his tendency towards portliness.

Nathan-Turner did however admit, in his introduction to *Doctor Who – The Companions*, that he was wary of making the Doctor's companion too strong a character:

'One of the problems I discovered with companions of my own devising was that the more rounded the character, the more it required development. And development of character takes air-time and this reduces the amount of dramatisation air-time and before you know where you are, a science-fiction adventure series is taking on a soap-opera flavour. So, slowly but surely, writers and script editors *and* producers decide to play down the character development of the companion (in any case after 23 years we know comparatively little about the Doctor) and concentrate on the drama of the story.'

When he came to cast the part of Mel in December 1985, almost six months after he had first devised the character (his original outline being dated 5 July 1985), Nathan-Turner made a very surprising choice. He later described to *Doctor Who Magazine* how this had come about:

'I was having a meeting with the agent Barry Burnett, and he said, "Is there any other casting I can help you with; what about the new companion?" and I said, "You have a client who is perfect for it from the way I've described it, but I don't know if she'd be interested, or whether it's really a good idea or not." He said, "Who's that?" and I said, "Bonnie".'

The selection of popular variety artist Bonnie Langford to play Mel was not well received by Eric Saward. In an interview for *DWB* in 1992, he commented: 'Bonnie Langford, I'm convinced, was Nathan-Turner's most cynical piece of casting.' Ian Levine, speaking in the same interview, added: 'I'm not alone in believing he hired her not simply because in his opinion she'd be good for *Doctor Who*, but because he saw her as a big draw for Teynham Productions' pantomimes.' Teynham Productions was an organisation run by Nathan-Turner and others which mounted regular Christmas pantomimes during this period.

The casting of Bonnie Langford was also unpopular with many fans, who saw it as an extension of the recent policy of featuring 'guest stars', frequently best known for their comedy work, in prominent *Doctor Who* roles. Examples included comedienne Beryl Reid as captain of a space freighter in *Earthshock*, Rodney Bewes of *The Likely Lads* as an android trooper in *Resurrection of the Daleks* and Kate O'Mara, most famous for her roles in the soap operas *The Brothers* (opposite Colin Baker) and *Triangle*, as the Rani in *The Mark of the Rani*.

As some critics saw it, this influx of 'celebrity' actors damaged *Doctor Who*'s credibility, bringing inappropriate 'light entertainment' connotations to serious roles and making it more difficult for viewers to suspend their disbelief – a vital factor in the impact of any science fiction or fantasy series. The *Doctor Who* audience, it was argued, would be unable to dispel from their minds the popular image of Bonnie Langford as a precocious song-and-dance performer who had come to prominence as a winner of the *Opportunity Knocks* talent contest and as a child star in roles such as that of the obnoxious Violet Elizabeth Bott in London Weekend Television's *Just William* series.

John Nathan-Turner, however, was unswayed by such criticisms, pointing out that Langford's popularity with youngsters could attract many new viewers to *Doctor Who*. 'Bonnie is a terrific little actress,' he told *Doctor Who Magazine*, 'and anybody who has seen her in the West End in *Peter Pan*, which is something a darn sight more recent than Violet Elizabeth, will realise that. I think of myself as ambitious in casting terms, and I know that Bonnie has the potential to make the part totally unirritating, as opposed to Violet Elizabeth.' Nathan-Turner also rejected the more general criticisms of the 'guest star' policy, arguing that it attracted valuable extra publicity for the series.

Another objection to which the production team often had to respond at this time concerned the increasing level of violence in *Doctor Who*, and particularly in the six stories which made up Season 22. This season was, without question, exceptionally bleak and oppressive in emphasis, dealing with such heavy themes as video nasties, genetic experimentation and cannibalism; and, added to this, the plots themselves became rather more gory and horrific in content, featuring disturbing scenes of torture, dismemberment and suffering.

'I've always felt,' says Eric Saward, 'that if you're going to show violence, you should also show the horrific effects of it. If you hit somebody, it hurts; it hurts your hand for one thing, and it certainly hurts the person you hit. If you hit them in the face, they're going to get a black eye or a bloody nose. Similarly, if you shoot at somebody's hand, they're going to lose fingers, as Davros did in *Revelation of the Daleks*. That's a terrible thing to happen, but if you present an action-adventure story in which there's no apparent consequence to the violence then I think you're cheating the audience.

'I'll never understand Mary Whitehouse's point of view. She seems to want a bland, safe little world in which everything is quiet and ordered and the traditional class structure is completely in place. That's simply confirming a stereotype and is an evil portrayal of society. In the same way, if you offer an audience blandness, it's a corrosive thing. I would argue with anybody on this point. To pretend that there's no consequence to violent conflict is to cheat and to deceive.'

This graphic portrayal of violent incidents certainly brought a greater degree of realism to *Doctor Who*. It is also fair to mention that Season 22 was planned on the basis that the episodes would be going out at around 6.20 p.m., and not in the 5.20 p.m. slot to which they were eventually allocated. These factors were of little comfort, however, to the many viewers who remained concerned at the sheer number of violent incidents presented, and at the depiction of gratuitously unpleasant images such as that of the character Shockeye killing and biting into a rat in *The Two Doctors*. The inclusion of such scenes was generally felt to be quite at odds with the series' traditional 'family viewing' appeal – as was the introduction of a blatantly sexual overtone in the form of Peri's titillating outfits and the recurring subplot of aliens lusting after her body.

Some commentators even went so far as to suggest that Season 22 marked a temporary departure from the strong moral standpoint which had previously been one of *Doctor Who*'s most distinctive and popular features. No longer, it was said, was there any clear delineation between good and evil in the stories. The actions of supposedly noble or heroic characters – such as Lytton in *Attack of the Cybermen*, the Governor in *Vengeance on Varos* and Orcini in *Revelation of the Daleks* – were criticised as being almost as questionable as those of the villains themselves, and even the Doctor's tactics did not entirely escape reproach. Although *The Trial of a Time Lord* saw the production team making a considerable reduction in the level of violence – a response to a specific instruction from Michael Grade, the Controller of BBC1 – many still consider this arguable lapse in the series' basic morality to have been a major failing of the Colin Baker era.

Eric Saward sees these criticisms as naïve:

'There have never been moral absolutes. The Doctor has been responsible for many deaths throughout the series' history. The portrayal of characters such as Lytton and Orcini perhaps reflected a more accurate image of life than had been attempted before. Remember that soldiers honoured as heroes have often killed many people, an activity that would be seen as totally unacceptable in peace time.'

Another criticism often made of the Colin Baker era was that it placed an excessive reliance on *Doctor Who*'s own history and mythology to provide the inspiration for new plots. Examples are numerous; and in this regard, *The Trial of a Time Lord* did nothing to improve matters. While fans could pick up all the continuity points, other less-committed viewers were probably completely alienated – a supposition supported by the season's comparatively low ratings.

Speaking at a convention in November 1985, during the period when scripts were being commissioned for *The Trial of a Time Lord*, John Nathan-Turner gave a dismissive response to criticisms that the series had been drawing too heavily on its own past:

'I don't think it's been drawing too heavily. I think the mix has been about right. Something which has a 22-year history should not dismiss its heritage. At the same time it shouldn't pander to it. I don't think we've overdone it. There are facts and figures one can produce to show that the popularity of the Daleks and the Cybermen is above that of all the other old enemies, and it would be totally foolhardy to dismiss them. They constitute the majority of our returning villains.'

Eric Saward, however, feels that the series did indeed become over-reliant on its own mythology at this point, and had indicated to *DWB* in 1988 that he was never in favour of such an approach:

'I think that it was John's idea to feature a past element in every story [of Season 20] but it was something I wasn't very interested in. I mean, we had had the Cybermen in the previous season and that had worked; but personally I wanted us to move on. Looking back, it was a fault both John and I fell into. The season and the celebration failed because of wanting to relive history. I must say that this was done, certainly on John's part, to please the fans rather than the general public.'

Saward went on to say in the same interview that as far as the scripts went, '*Doctor Who* should have the highest rejection rate in the department . . . because they are very difficult things to write well. The writers tried their best and were paid for their efforts but the scripts should nevertheless not have been made.' However, as Saward explained, Nathan-Turner did not like rejecting material.

Accepting that John Nathan-Turner would very often request stories featuring popular monsters such as the Daleks, the Cybermen and the Sontarans, it might perhaps be asked why the writers could not then have made original and inventive use of them, just as their predecessors had done during other eras of the series' history. Eric Saward puts this down to the fact that the concepts were in many cases very dated:

'Attitudes have changed a great deal in the last twenty years: schoolchildren no longer accept as gospel what is said by their teachers; adults no longer become staid and over the hill at 45; and no one now believes that the police are like Dixon of Dock Green. It's the same with good, imaginative writers: they prefer to invent their own projects – it inspires them – rather than try to breathe life into a tired old concept like, say, the Daleks. When they are asked to use such concepts, their work often reflects the tiredness of the original idea.'

There is no doubt that during the mid-eighties *Doctor Who* drew on its own mythos to a far greater extent than at any other point in its history. *The Trial of a Time Lord* came in for some particularly heavy fan criticism for this, and indeed for its general incoherence. Philip Martin, one of the writers of the fourteen-part epic, had a number of reservations about it, as he later told *Doctor Who Magazine*:

'It suffered from being simultaneously commissioned. Bob Holmes died after his second draft, there were problems with the final storyline – there were six or seven writers altogether – and we never knew where we were going. Then the script editor left, and when we reached the final episode it was all so confusing I couldn't follow it. And I had been there at the beginning! The story as it eventually reached the screen seemed to have little left of our original idea.'

Eric Saward admits that almost all the scripts commissioned during the Colin Baker era were heavily rewritten by him – a fact which he attributes to the difficulties experienced by incoming writers in coping with *Doctor Who*'s especially challenging format:

'My attitude towards script editing was that what the writer wrote ought to be, wherever possible, what was produced. But *Doctor Who* is one of those old-fashioned shows which is very difficult to write. It requires strong characterisation, strong stories, action, humour, adventure, thrills; the whole gamut. Other shows like *Casualty*, for example, simply aren't that demanding. I'm not knocking *Casualty*, but it's got a stock setting, stock characters and stock situations. The writers just have to weld on their own idea: a road accident, a schizophrenic on the run with a meat axe, or whatever. Half the work is done for them, because they are using the established elements. In *Doctor Who*, the only ongoing characters are the Doctor and the companion. The rest, the writers have to invent for themselves.

'The problem is that modern television writing makes writers very lazy. Up-and-coming writers are used on soaps like *EastEnders*, which have stock characters, and on shows like *Casualty*, which require, to my mind, a limited amount of characterisation and plotting. My experience – and I tried many, many different writers – was that a lot of them just couldn't characterise to the standard that was wanted. Their imagination wasn't developed sufficiently. I mean, imagination is not a gift one is given at birth; it's something which can be developed. The more one works at it, the stronger it becomes. And a lot of writers never have that opportunity. The reason so much rewriting went on by me and by my predecessors was that it was very hard to find people who could do it well.

'Another problem was getting writers to work within the constraints of what could be achieved on our budget. The first hour of my discussion with any writer would always be about the technical limitations: what could be done, what couldn't be done, the number of sets we could have, the number of talking parts. I mean, we would always try to do whatever the writer wanted, but I would have to say things like, "Never give a creature tentacles, because we can't manage that." There were certain things we just couldn't do, because we didn't have the money or the time. The writers had to be realistic about what could be achieved. I assume that Terrance Dicks, Douglas Adams, Christopher Bidmead and all the other script editors down the decades must have said very similar things to their writers, because it's pointless sending a writer away to write something and then finding out that it can't be done.'

Speaking to *DWB* in 1988, Saward recounted some of the behind-the-scenes problems encountered on *The Trial of a Time Lord*:

'Bob Holmes wrote the first four episodes which, given the pressures, were okay on paper. But Jonathan Powell didn't like them. We got this memo saying, "Didn't like this, or that, thought this was too silly . . ." and all the rest of it. So alterations were made which he accepted and which went into the final programme.'

The original idea had been that Holmes would also write the final two episodes of the story. These would have ended the season with the Doctor and the Master locked in mortal combat and with a question mark hanging over the outcome. Saward says that this was agreed with Nathan-Turner and that the writing of the scripts was taken forward accordingly.

A further development then occurred, however, when Saward decided to resign his post as script editor. He had, as the sixth Doctor's era progressed, become increasingly unhappy working alongside Nathan-Turner, rarely seeing eye to eye with him over production decisions, and he decided at this point that it was time he left the series. Despite this, when Holmes fell ill after completing only a draft of the story's penultimate episode, Saward accepted Nathan-Turner's invitation to finish the work on this script and to write part fourteen himself, according to the agreed outline. As Saward recalls, when Nathan-Turner eventually saw the script for the final episode, he reneged on what had been agreed and refused to accept the cliff-hanger ending to the season. Saward consequently withdrew permission for the use of this script – a decision he declined to reconsider, although Nathan-Turner wrote to him in conciliatory terms in an attempt to persuade him to do so. Nathan-Turner then had to commission from Pip and Jane Baker a last-minute replacement.

Following these incidents, Saward gave *Starburst* magazine an interview in which he aired his criticisms of Nathan-Turner:

'I was getting very fed up with the way *Doctor Who* was being run, largely by John Nathan-Turner – his attitude and lack of insight into what makes a television series like *Doctor Who* work.'

He went on to say that his former colleague had, amongst other things, brought pantomime aspects to *Doctor Who*; neglected important tasks in favour of trivial ones, such as making arrangements for and attending fan conventions in the USA and approving merchandise for BBC Enterprises; been reluctant to work with experienced people in case they undermined his authority; taken insufficient interest in the series' scripts; and made poor casting decisions.

As Saward had a day-to-day involvement with the series' production, his comments must clearly be accorded considerable weight; and equally critical opinions of Nathan-Turner's qualities as a producer have been publicly expressed by a number of others involved in *Doctor Who* during the mid-eighties, including writer and director Peter Grimwade, actor Anthony Ainley (who played the Master) and Ian Levine. It should be noted, however, that Nathan-Turner also has many friends and supporters amongst those who worked on the series at this time. These include stars Colin Baker, Nicola Bryant and Bonnie Langford, writers Pip and Jane Baker, and directors such as Fiona Cumming and Nicholas Mallett, all of whom have given quite the opposite impression of the contribution made by the producer, praising him for his strong support of their work, for his enormous energy and for his fierce commitment to the series. This is not of course to suggest that anyone has been less than truthful in their comments on Nathan-Turner; it is simply a reflection of the fact that there seems to be a very wide divergence of opinion amongst those who worked with him, making him arguably the most controversial figure ever to have been associated with the series.

Despite this divergence of opinion, some fans came to believe that the multitude of problems with which *Doctor Who* was beset during this period were almost entirely the fault of John Nathan-Turner. Whilst it is certainly true to say that all matters pertaining to the production of *Doctor Who* on a day-to-day basis were ultimately the producer's responsibility, it can also be said that some of the difficulties the series faced – the frequent, damaging changes of transmission days, times and episode lengths; the postponement of Season 23; Michael Grade's public attacks on the programme and its production team; and ultimately Colin Baker's ousting from the programme after *The Trial of a Time Lord* – were matters largely if not entirely beyond the producer's control. While opinions may legitimately differ as to the artistic merits of the sixth Doctor's stories, the vociferous criticisms sometimes directed at Nathan-Turner with regard to scheduling and other decisions taken by BBC management would appear to be unfounded.

If *The Trial of a Time Lord* can be seen as a case of art imitating life – Michael Grade and his colleagues having made it abundantly clear that the series itself was still on trial – then it could be argued that there are certain respects in which, conversely, life imitated art during the Colin Baker era. It was as if the unpredictable, mercurial, explosive character of the sixth Doctor was actually being reflected in the dramatic real-life incidents surrounding the series!

Whatever else might be said, this was undeniably the most troubled and eventful period of production in *Doctor Who*'s long history.

6: From Script to Screen – *Revelation of the Daleks*

To try to analyse comprehensively the development of a *Doctor Who* adventure is not an easy matter. A television production is the result of many months' work by a large number of people, and what is ultimately seen on screen may have been affected and influenced in greater or lesser degrees by all of them.

Unless one is afforded a fly's-eye view of every production meeting and every aspect of the creative process, then any attempt to try to chronicle the production is limited by the memories and personalities of those people to whom one speaks.

Bearing all this in mind, what follows is an in-depth look at the making of just one of the sixth Doctor's stories. It reveals the process of creating a *Doctor Who* story at this point in the series' history and some of the behind-the-scenes discussions and thought which go into a production, a factor common to every story.

The production chosen for this case study is *Revelation of the Daleks*, the final story of the twenty-second season, first transmitted in 1985. For helping us to compile our information, we are grateful to several people, in particular the writer Eric Saward, the director Graeme Harper, the designer Alan Spalding and the visual effects designer John Brace, each of whom took the time to speak to us in great detail about their respective contributions, and to costume designer Pat Godfrey, who gave an earlier interview to *The Frame*.

The Scripts

Every *Doctor Who* adventure which appears on screen starts life as an idea. This idea may be in the mind of a writer, it may come from the producer or the script editor, or, as is more often the case, it may develop out of a discussion between two or more of these people.

Once the initial contact has been made, a story outline or synopsis will generally be commissioned from the author. Assuming that all is well when that is delivered, one or more of the actual scripts themselves will then be commissioned. Depending on the status of the writer, these stages may be compacted or expanded accordingly.

In the case of *Revelation of the Daleks*, the initial idea came from John Nathan-Turner, who decided that he wanted a Dalek story with which to close the season. He also wanted Eric Saward to write it, as his previous Dalek tale, *Resurrection of the Daleks*, had been very well received.

'I actually went off contract for six weeks to write *Revelation of the Daleks*,' recalls Eric Saward. 'I went away to Rhodes for three weeks round about June/July 1984, had a nice holiday, enjoyed myself, and wrote the scripts.

'I wanted to do something about a planet which specialised in dealing with the dead. I worked out a rough storyline – and it was *very* rough – and went through it with John, and he said "Okay".'

The initial inspiration for the story came from an Evelyn Waugh novel. 'When I was on holiday I re-read *The Loved One*, which is Waugh's skit on how the Americans view the dead. I had first read it many years before, and I remembered that there is a character in it called Joyboy, who is a make-up artist for the dead. He is a very sad character. He is in his thirties, still living with his mother, and is pursued in the novel by an even more lonely and sad woman. I took the idea of Mr Joyboy and made him Mr Jobel, and the poor infatuated woman became Tasambeker. I really should have killed her in the first episode and put her out of her misery!'

Holidaying in Rhodes while writing the scripts provided Eric with the ideas for many of the character names that he used. 'The local goddess of fertility on Rhodes is called Tsambeker, with a silent "T", and I just took it phonetically as Tasambeker. Stengos ran the local ferry. Cara was a type of potato that we had fresh from the ground out there – I just changed the spelling to Kara. Orcini was the Grand Master of the Knights of St John who used to be on Rhodes. He defended Rhodes against Suleiman the Magnificent, the Turkish Sultan, and managed to hold out against 100,000 troops for about six months with only 600 Knights and 2,000 auxiliaries. Suleiman was so impressed by their bravery that, when he eventually won, he freed the Knights that had survived. I took the myths rather than the reality and created my warrior Orcini who is always looking for the mythical "great kill". Of course there is no such thing as a "great kill" or a "perfect kill", but in his mind there is because it's noble, it's honourable. Reaching that ideal is what spurs him on to hunt Davros.'

As Eric recalls, there was no pressure from Terry Nation, the Daleks' creator and copyright holder, to include Davros in the story. Rather, this was an idea which John Nathan-Turner suggested and with which he was very happy to go along:

'Davros was included because I thought someone had to be behind the planet's operations. Davros had decided that he was going to be the self-appointed Great Healer, and I wanted him initially to appear honourable. Kara was meant to be the unpleasant one. But it didn't quite work out in either case.

'The thing about the Daleks is that when you come to write them, they're very boring. They're boring to listen to for any length of time – that stilted monotone. Davros is a much more interesting character. He speaks relatively normally so he can sustain conversations which the Daleks can't, and he is therefore convenient to use at the centre of the plot. In which case the Daleks themselves take just a supporting role.

'I believe that nowadays the Daleks can't be taken seriously. They're far too old-fashioned to be seen as a deadly and ultimate evil. That's the reality. They're no longer this great, frightening creation that Nation thought they were.

'The plot developed further when I wondered what Davros could be doing running this place. The most heinous thing anyone can do when running a cemetery is to sell the bodies. That seemed obvious, if not particularly original, so I used it.

'The other thing I wanted to do was to take the development of the

Daleks one stage further. Their history seemed to me to have been very chequered in terms of what they could and couldn't do. Considering that they're supposed to be so powerful, their early beginnings were very feeble and crude; needing to draw electricity from the floor and so on. I thought that perhaps it was about time for them to be able to reproduce themselves, so that they could go anywhere and be anything that they wanted.'

Perhaps the strangest character in *Revelation of the Daleks* is the DJ. 'The idea for him came about one evening when I'd been out for a meal and was driving back home in my car. I turned on the radio and there was an incredibly boring DJ on the air. Now, prior to this I'd thought that if one was going to have a super-cryogenic planet then there would be problems. I've always wondered about the cryogenic idea, because if people could come back after 200 years, imagine what state they would be in! All their technology, their thinking, everything would be redundant. The world would have moved on so far and they would have become so out of touch that they would instantly die of nervous breakdowns! I'd reasoned that there would have to be some way of keeping the frozen people up to date, but hadn't yet decided how. Then, when I heard this lunatic DJ, who was trying to be incredibly serious but at the same time hip, I knew I had to have him! That's how the character was born.

'The DJ is completely at odds with the place. He sits there and plays music and passes on notes from the folks and so on, but he is so cynical about it all. I made him really rather grotesque, and he had to be grotesque.'

Revelation of the Daleks was commissioned to fit the new 45-minute episode format which *Doctor Who* was assigned for its 22nd season. As Eric explains, this required a slightly different approach from that used in writing the traditional 25-minute episodes: 'A 25-minute episode tends to be rather frenetic, because it's zooming up to the cliff-hanger. The 45-minute ones were paced a little slower. There was never any intention to create an artificial cliff-hanger halfway through. I'm told that *Revelation of the Daleks* was cut up into four parts for sale to America, but I had nothing to do with that.'

Eric recalls that when his scripts for the two episodes were completed and delivered they were found to be too long and required shortening, but that little other adjustment was called for. 'If the script is there and it's working reasonably well, most of the director's time is spent on the other aspects of the show – casting, designing and so on – and so I didn't have that much to do with the actual process of making it.

'I first saw it performed at the producer's run, and I was in the studio for almost all the recording. The first time I saw it all together was in John's office when Graeme delivered the rough cut. I thought he'd made a good job of it, and it had come together well.'

Pre-production

Once the scripts have been drafted, the first person to be contracted to work on a *Doctor Who* is generally the director. In the case of *Revelation of the Daleks*, which had been conceived as the grand finale of the season, John Nathan-Turner was looking for someone who could not only convey the story effectively but also bring a sense of spectacle to it. The man he chose was Graeme Harper, whose work on the fifth Doctor's farewell story, *The Caves of Androzani*, had greatly impressed him.

'When we'd finished *The Caves of Androzani*,' recalls Graeme, 'John asked if I would come back and do one in the following season, to which I replied "Yes". At that time he wasn't sure which story it would be, or where or when we would be filming, but I knew that if I wanted to do another, then the chances were that I would be able to.' It was in fact around June 1984 that Graeme was approached by John to direct *Revelation of the Daleks*. 'At first I wasn't sure how this would fit in with my other commitments, but about three months later, when I knew exactly what I was going to be doing, my agent went back to John and told him the dates on which I would be free. Fortunately they tied in with John's schedules.'

Once Graeme was confirmed in November 1984 as the director, the next task was to bring on board the key creative personnel. Most BBC departments at this time operated some form of rota system whereby staff were allocated to shows for a whole year in advance. Occasionally the director, in consultation with the producer, would specifically request a particular designer, in which case it would then be up to the appropriate department head to say whether or not that designer happened to be free, as would occasionally be the case, or alternatively whether or not he or she could be freed up from a pre-arranged assignment.

To handle the visual effects for *Revelation of the Daleks*, Graeme asked for and got John Brace. 'John had worked on several *Doctor Who* episodes throughout his career, and we knew each other anyway, so it was lucky that he was available.'

John was equally pleased to be returning to *Doctor Who*. 'Working in the Effects Department, a designer got the opportunity to be involved in many different types of programmes, but to be allocated to *Doctor Who* allowed particular scope for creativity. There were spaceships and monsters, there were explosions, it was a fantasy world. So to have a *Doctor Who* was good news, and everyone wanted to do them.'

The first thing the director does when joining a production is to read the scripts.

'I didn't understand one bit of them at first,' laughs Graeme. 'They were quite complex and I remember going through them suggesting where we might be able to clarify the plot. Even with this, the story was very complicated.

'As an overall fantasy, however, it was well written. I remember it being very wordy, featuring some almost Shakespearean characters. This was one of its strengths, and it worked.

'I saw the story as a pastiche on the 1973 Richard Fleischer film *Soylent Green*, in which the problems of overcrowding and starvation on a future Earth are both solved by making food (the soylent green of the title) from the people.'

In reading the scripts, the director gets many casting ideas, and these are next discussed with the producer.

'The first conversations a director would have after considering the script would be about casting: the areas and the kinds of characters involved, and whether or not there were going to be any guest stars,' says Graeme. 'While those discussions were going on for *Revelation of the Daleks*, I was also talking with the designer about the look and feel of the production and about how we could realise it.

'Soon into those discussions would come the Costume and Make-up Departments – but not *too* soon unless there was something very special required. Visual Effects would also be involved quite early on, and all the while John Nathan-Turner would be listening in and occasionally asking how much all this was going to cost!'

The production team had approximately six weeks – which included a break for Christmas – between starting work on the story and going away on location. This timescale meant that many things had to be worked out quickly, always with an eye on the budget.

'I remember discussing the concept for the planet,' recalls designer Alan Spalding. 'It was supposed to be a death planet. It contained a modern cryogenic plant, but at the same time maintained a tradition of death similar to that found in ancient Egyptian society. Designing the modern aspects was fine because I could make them futuristic and different, but the ancient elements we found difficult to resolve because Graeme argued that there wouldn't be Earth-type graves and all the associated iconography. I therefore had to aim for impressive and different visuals with a very low budget.'

The costume designer, Pat Godfrey, also remembers that money was tight. 'I think the costume budget for this story was, in all, about £5,000. This had been worked out at the beginning of the season, before the scripts had been completed, and as it was a Dalek story they'd thought that they wouldn't need too many extra costumes. Unfortunately, there turned out to be a lot of characters in the cast, so the money was spread very thinly.'

The scripts also presented some unusually demanding effects requirements, ranging from exploding glass Daleks through to simple prop bombs, guns and knives, all of which had to be realised by the Visual Effects Department. To try to get around the budgetary restrictions, John Brace took a somewhat radical step: 'We needed all sorts of Daleks – grey Daleks and white Daleks, Daleks that blew up and crystal-clear Daleks in an embryonic stage – and also a large polystyrene sculpture of the Doctor. I went to BBC Enterprises and explained that there was no way that the production could afford to have all these constructed but I knew they had in the past taken visual effects props and other interesting items for exhibition and they may have had some old Daleks that we could modify. As discussions evolved with the production associate June Collins and Julie Jones of BBC Enterprises, we decided that we could make new Daleks and Enterprises would buy them back from the programme when production was completed.

'Enterprises were fine with the idea, but my own Department's reaction surprised me. They didn't think that I should be able to do this. "What are you doing making deals with Enterprises?" they asked. "You're just an effects designer. We manage the Department! If you have problems with your budgets come and see us." However I *had* been and seen them and they had looked and said, basically, that I was stuffed! They had said that this was television, not films. That this was the real world, and that I had to work within my budget.'

Graeme Harper's previous *Doctor Who* story, *The Caves of Androzani*, had consisted of four 25-minute episodes. Although the amount of material required to be shot for the two 45-minute episodes of *Revelation of the Daleks* was the same, the new format placed much greater demands on the director and his team. 'There was a lot to do in the studio,' recalls Graeme. 'They'd changed to a 45-minute format, but it felt as though we didn't have the time in the studio. Whereas in the 25-minute format it was just about possible to scrape through with an occasional overrun, on *Revelation of the Daleks* I think we worked until eleven o'clock every night. We just couldn't fit it all in.'

On Location

One way of maximising studio time is to film as much material as possible on location. Like many *Doctor Who*s at this point in the series' history, *Revelation of the Daleks* made quite extensive use of location filming.

Location filming is normally carried out prior to any studio recording and takes place at whatever venue the production team have decided is best suited to the requirements of the story.

It can take many weeks of effort to find a suitable location. The director and the producer will first discuss the most important criteria and then, in conjunction with the production manager and members of the design team, start to think about places where all these can be met. As travelling time must come out of the time allotted for filming, it is usually important that the chosen location should boast all the required features within easy reach of one another, and that it should be fairly close to the production base of Television Centre in west London.

Where *Revelation of the Daleks* was concerned, the team felt that the mortuary complex of Tranquil Repose was the central image of the story and should be the prime location. Alan Spalding remembers that it was quite tricky to find. 'We wanted a building which was very futuristic-looking. Because of the Egyptian death motif, we had in mind something which suggested hi-tech pyramids. We wanted the ancient culture to be reflected in a modern design. We eventually found somewhere by going through lots of books and looking for unusual buildings and architecture. It was the IBM office complex at North Harbour, Cosham, near Portsmouth. This fitted the bill perfectly. It had all the right qualities.'

IBM allowed the crew eight hours' filming on their premises and, instead of taking a fee, asked the BBC to make a donation to a local school.

'It was a perfect location,' affirms John Brace. 'It had little tunnel entrances so that we could establish that the place extended underground, and it was all black glass on top. In our production, the building was supposed to look incredibly nice on top, although underneath it was throbbing with evil.'

The main location having been chosen, all the other requirements were found nearby. The place where the TARDIS lands was represented by a large hill and woodland area of the Queen Elizabeth's Park nature reserve in Petersfield, near Southampton. The scenes when the Doctor and Peri, and later Orcini and his squire Bostock, approach Tranquil Repose, were shot at a disused aerodrome in the Poole area.

The script's description of the planet Necros was quite difficult to realise, as Alan explains: 'The story was supposed to be set on a bare, stark planet, but we weren't allowed to go too far away to shoot it. It was quite a difficult brief. We couldn't go to the Yorkshire Moors or Fylingdales or anywhere like that as we weren't originally supposed to have any overnight stays.'

Prior to going on location, a director usually needs to have worked out a detailed schedule for the filming. 'There are some productions on which it's not critical to have worked out all the camera angles and so on beforehand,' says Graeme, 'but on something as complex as *Doctor Who*, everything has to be well planned.

'The director is constrained by the requirements of all the various departments – Design, Effects, Make-up, Costume – as to the order in which certain things have to be done, because of construction and setting-up times. Even the availability of certain actors and actresses can sometimes dictate whether their scenes have to be filmed first or last. The whole process must be planned very carefully. You have to know what you're going to do. You have to know all the shots, the angles and how they will develop. This is essential because you haven't got time to try to work it all out when you are already there. It really has to be done in advance.'

With this in mind, the director and his team will normally go on a recce – an advance visit to all the chosen locations – to start working out how the camera will be positioned in relation to the artistes and to any special props or sets required, and also to try to anticipate any problems which might arise.

When on location, the standard method of working is to rehearse each scene immediately before it is filmed, this process being repeated as many times as is necessary until the director is happy with what has been shot. 'I would talk through any major dialogue scenes the night before with the artistes,' says Graeme, 'and any changes would be agreed with the writer. Otherwise, it would all have been blocked out and planned beforehand, so I would know what I was hoping to achieve on any particular day.'

The major problem with going on location as opposed to working in a studio is the unpredictability of the weather. In a studio it can be made to rain or snow on cue; gale-force winds can be created, and so can hot, balmy sunshine. Out in the wilds of the English countryside, however, the unit are at the mercy of the British weather and can encounter considerable difficulties. This was certainly the case on *Revelation of the Daleks*, as Graeme Harper recalls:

'Bearing in mind that we were due to be filming in January, I'm sure we must have wondered what would happen if it snowed. I had never really worried about it though. Snow can actually give you a longer working day, because it makes things brighter.

'Anyway, we went away on location for four or five days, and the first couple of days went by with no problems at all: everything we had planned to film was done, and all was on schedule. And then the snow came overnight. We were due to film at Queen Elizabeth's Park the next day, and had to try to get there through a foot of snow! In the end we had to alter the schedule, and as a result we lost one of our major effects sequences.

'At the Park there was a valley where we were going to stage a battle between the Daleks and the two "Don Quixote" characters, Bostock and Orcini. There was going to be a massive gun battle and, as the major feature of this, we were going to prove that the Daleks could fly. This had never been done before, and we had all wondered how they got about so easily over all manner of terrain. During the battle a Dalek was going to fly up, twenty feet in the sky, and then explode. That was going to be a major effects piece but, once the snow arrived, we couldn't get the equipment up there. It had all been planned and worked out, but the spring-device that was going to launch this Dalek into the air couldn't be set up. I was disappointed to lose that.'

Eric Saward, however, cannot recall this scene at all. 'It might have had something to do with the one in part two where Orcini destroys a Dalek on location, as what was seen on screen was not what was scripted.'

The original script for this scene has two Daleks suddenly appearing on a ridge behind Orcini and Bostock. The mercenaries open fire with bastic-headed bullets, capable of penetrating solid rock, but the Daleks are unscathed. Ducking behind a rock, Orcini manages to blow off the eyepiece of one of the Daleks, which then topples down the bank, allowing him and his squire to slip away.

'I had tried to carry through the idea that Daleks are very difficult to destroy,' explains Eric. 'I had written that Orcini just damaged the Dalek, but this was changed on location so that it exploded.'

Although it caused the abandonment of the planned battle scene, the snow did have certain fortuitous consequences, as Graeme notes: 'We had always planned to do the opening sequences of the story at the end of the shoot, and the change in the weather meant that we could have the Doctor and Peri landing in a snowy landscape next to a frozen pond. It really brought over the feeling of icy desolation that we were trying to achieve.'

Mention of the pond reminds Alan Spalding that it had not been easy to find. 'We had decided to use the South Downs area because we wanted the bleakness and the lack of vegetation that you find there. Then we had to try to find a pond, and at first we couldn't because ponds just don't happen in chalk. Mike Cameron, the production manager, hunted and hunted, but it seemed that there just wasn't one to be found on the South Downs.

'In the end we found one on a farmer's property. The farmer had built it for his cattle to drink from. There was a little island in the middle and a boat which we used to get out to it. Graeme decided that the boat would be a good place to position the camera for the shot where the alien hand emerges from the water.'

Using a frozen pond in the middle of winter posed particular problems for John Brace and his team. 'There was thick ice all over this pond and we had to break it up in order to get into the water to set up the effects.

'In view of the fact that we needed to get underwater to achieve the effect of a hand emerging, I asked for my Department's diving section to come out. The diving section was in fact Jim Francis and Dave

Barton, two other visual effects designers, and it was difficult to get my management to accept that you could have three designers on one location. I kept explaining to them that it wasn't three designers, it was one designer and two divers.'

The location sequences for *Revelation of the Daleks* were filmed from 7 to 10 January 1985. As a final note, this was the last *Doctor Who* location shoot ever to be done on film. The use of outside broadcast (OB) video cameras had since 1974 become increasingly prevalent, and from Season 23 onwards all of *Doctor Who*'s location work would be done in this way.

In Studio

The first studio work to be undertaken for *Revelation of the Daleks* was one day of filming by the Visual Effects Department to create all the model scenes required for the story.

In keeping with the usual pattern at this point in the series' history, the main studio recordings then took place at Television Centre in two separate blocks, the first of two days' duration on 17 and 18 January 1985 in studio TC1 and the second of three days' duration between 30 January and 1 February in TC8. Cast rehearsals were held at the BBC's Acton rehearsal rooms from 3 to 16 January for the first block and from 19 to 29 January for the second.

All the scenes involving the futuristic sets were recorded in the first block and all those involving the underground areas were done in the second, this split being dictated by the logistics of the story. Normally, a certain proportion of the studio space would have to be left empty to meet the BBC's strict safety regulations, but for *Revelation of the Daleks* Alan Spalding got special dispensation to fill the studio completely so as to fit everything in.

Recording of *Doctor Who* in the eighties was invariably done out of story sequence. The exact recording order would be worked out by the director based on which sets were going to be available in each studio. All the scenes which used one particular set would generally be recorded together, then the crew would move on to the next set and record all the scenes taking place there, and so on. In this way, an actor could sometimes find himself performing his death scene before he had even recorded his entrance!

There were two alternative approaches which directors could take to studio work. One, known as the rehearse/record method, involved each scene being rehearsed on camera immediately before it was recorded, just as on location. The other entailed all the rehearsals being completed during the day and then all the recording being done during the evening. The method used was generally a matter of choice for the individual director, depending on the facilities available, and for *Revelation of the Daleks* it was the latter which Graeme Harper chose.

Each day's studio recording would have to end at 10 p.m. sharp, the only exception being where the director had – as on this occasion – obtained permission to go into overtime (an expense which had to be agreed). The studio house lights would be switched on at the appointed time, even if the cast were in the middle of a scene, and the cameramen and other technical personnel would leave for the night. The scene-shifters would then come in to take down (strike) any sets which were not required for the following day's work, and to erect any new ones which were.

To indicate some of the considerations involved in making a *Doctor Who* story during the Colin Baker era, we now present a complete scene-by-scene summary of *Revelation of the Daleks*, taking in comments as appropriate from Eric Saward, Graeme Harper, Alan Spalding, John Brace and (from an interview conducted for *The Frame*) costume designer Pat Godfrey. Make-up designer Dorka Nieradzik was unwilling to contribute to this book, but her recollections are also reported, based on an interview by Brenda Apsley which appeared in the 1986 *Doctor Who Annual*.

Part One

A planet in space. The TARDIS arrives on a mist-blown snowy hillside.

JB: 'We used three smoke machines here. The tricky thing about this shot was that we had left the TARDIS's blue lamp behind and we had to knock something up on location.'

AS: 'I didn't want to see any trees but we had to in the end. I wanted it totally blank, but it wasn't to be.'

GH: 'I liked it actually, because it got away from the "Dorset sand pit" look.'

Peri (Nicola Bryant) emerges and wanders down to a large pond. She throws into the water the remains of a nut-roast roll on which she has been nibbling. The Doctor (Colin Baker) follows her down. They are both wearing blue – the official mourning colour on Necros – as the Doctor intends to honour local customs. The Time Lord has come here to honour the late Professor Arthur Stengos, one of the finest agronomists in the galaxy. As the two travellers turn away from the lake, an alien hand emerges from the icy water and snatches Peri's roll.

JB: 'The hand belonged to Ken Barker, the stuntman who played the mutant creature.'

Alerted by the splash, the Doctor and Peri turn back in time to see the water erupt in a small explosion.

JB: 'We had to have a woofer [a compressed-air device used for simulating explosions by propelling dust and debris with a blast of air] rigged under the water. We had to rig all that up in one day, although we had already put in an underwater scaffold.'

The Doctor and Peri head away, not seeing a ragged figure (Ken Barker) emerge and start to follow them.
In a mortuary complex elsewhere on Necros, Takis (Trevor Cooper) is putting the finishing touches to the burial mask of the President's late wife, currently lying in state in the main hall. Jobel (Clive Swift), the chief embalmer, congratulates him. Meanwhile other workers are putting the finishing touches to the arrangements of small blue flowers – herba baculum vitæ, or staff of life – and peacock feathers which line the hall.

AS: 'A lot of actors won't work with peacock feathers because they're supposed to be bad luck, but we didn't have any problems here. We had a thousand of the little blue flowers specially made.'

Tasambeker (Jenny Tomasin), a dumpy, unattractive attendant, fawns over Jobel and tells him that the presidential shuttle is on the way. When Jobel has gone, Takis and his friend Lilt (Colin Spaull) tell Tasambeker that she is wasting her time – Jobel isn't interested in her.

GH: 'When I read the script, certain people came straight to my mind. I knew that Takis and Lilt were going to be Laurel and Hardy. If you watch them, even though they're sinister guys, they have this sort of double act going. Trevor Cooper, who plays Takis, does all these kind of Laurel and Hardy things and mannerisms.

'When it came to Jobel, I just knew that it had to be Clive Swift playing the part. I knew that if I could get him, then he would bring a lot to the character.'

Dorka Nieradzik decided to give Jobel an obviously Marcel-waved auburn toupée which deliberately did not match his own grey hair. The intention was to make him appear quite vain, as if he thought that by putting on the toupée he would appear younger, and that everyone would be fooled into thinking it was his own hair – which of course they were not.

GH: 'I knew that Tasambeker had to be Ruby from *Upstairs, Downstairs*, played here, as there, by Jenny Tomasin.'

AS: 'There isn't actually any set there in the main hall. It's just done with foreground props and a big arch – which was originally made for *Little and Large*. There's virtually nothing on the sides, just space. The idea was to convey a sort of Egyptian high-tech decor.'

As Jobel and the assistants leave to prepare themselves, two outsiders, Natasha (Bridget Lynch-Blosse) and Grigory (Stephen Flynn), cross the hall and, following a map, enter one of the corridors.

The Doctor and Peri are attacked by the creature that has been following them. It is an horrific mutant, its skin peeling from its body, with broken, yellowing teeth and saliva running from its mouth. Peri beats the beast with a stick until it frees the Doctor.

JB: 'We provided a rubber stick for Nicola to use. It was made to look like a lump of wood from the forest.'

GH: 'When *Doctor Who* went over to the longer, 45-minute episodes, I believe the intention was to reach out to a bigger, more family and more adult audience. With the agreement of John Nathan-Turner, we went as far as we dared with the horror, bearing in mind the timeslot and the audience. The intention here was to be a little more frightening.'

AS: 'The make up was by Dorka Nieradzik and was excellent. Prosthetics were her speciality.'

GH: 'Dorka was fairly unknown to me before this story. I'd worked with her when she was an assistant, but I'd never really known what she could do: the talent that was about to burst forth. She really is someone very special in make-up.'

Dorka provided the mutant with some false teeth made by specialist dental technicians to look as if they were in the process of melting away. She left some hair on his head to give him a pitiful look, and also to make him less frightening and more humanoid, thereby conveying the idea that Davros had been experimenting on him and that his mutation was the result of the experiment.

The fight is being watched on monitor screens by a hippy-like character. This is the DJ (Alexei Sayle), an employee of Tranquil Repose, who is narrating events to the other, less active residents.

GH: 'The DJ was a very difficult character to cast. We could have gone for a real disc jockey, someone like Jimmy Savile or Alan Freeman, a "name" whom everyone would know and love, and just placed him in the story. But would we have got a performance or would we have had to rely on that familiar persona? Alternatively, we could have gone for a character actor, but that would have meant losing the value of some good publicity.

'We went through a whole host of names and eventually started thinking about going for alternative comedy or something. Alexei had just made *The Young Ones* and *Whoops Apocalypse* and had been very good in them, so we knew that he was a talented actor as well as being a comic, not to mention being larger than life, zany and interesting as a character. So we approached him with the idea and he liked it.'

AS: 'We were going to make the DJ very sixties-orientated and a collector of sixties ephemera. As we were doing this in the mid-eighties it seemed like the past, but it didn't quite work because we couldn't get the right objects. The trouble with a lot of sixties items is that, even now, they look quite futuristic. The idea that he collected things from the past didn't quite gel because they looked like things from the future! We should maybe have chosen art deco or something that was more obvious. The items were very hard to find as well, which surprised me.'

ES: 'Alexei Sayle turned out to be very good casting. When I saw him at the producer's run he was very flat and I thought, "Oh God, what have we done here." But that is how Alexei works. He is a very shy man and very awkward – until, that is, it comes to the performance, and then the energy comes and suddenly he's away. I thought he did it very well.'

Elsewhere in the complex there is a life-support unit containing the disembodied head of Davros (Terry Molloy), who is attended on by a white Dalek. Davros has been watching the DJ on a monitor but now orders him silenced, and the sound is cut off. Davros then sees on the monitor that the Doctor has arrived, and comments that his lure has worked.

JB: 'Davros was supposed to be just a head, with life support systems surrounding him. Because later there would be explosions going on around it, and Terry Molloy was inside, we had to make it practical. We used techniques to confuse the eye so that it wasn't obvious that the rest of Terry's body was in there. I think the most difficult thing was trying to make his head spin round. Colin Gory was my assistant, who had been working on this problem in the workshop while I was away filming. He decided to put Terry on a swivel chair such that he had to squeeze himself into position from underneath with the full head make-up on, and the rest of the tank was then put on top of him.'

Natasha and Grigory make their way through the complex. On level seven they kill a guard. Davros alerts Takis that there are bodysnatchers at large.

GH: 'This was Bridget's first job on television, although she had done some theatre. I met her at an actors' workshop. I knew Stephen from a fringe theatre production that I had directed. I wanted to give him a break.'

The Doctor and Peri talk to the mutant. Before he dies, he tells them that he has been conditioned and is a product of the Great Healer's experimentation.

As Natasha and Grigory penetrate further into the complex, the DJ reads some dedications and Tasambeker orders Takis and Lilt to find the intruders. Davros orders Tasambeker brought to him.

The DJ, now dressed as a fifties leather-clad rocker, is still reading dedications. He picks up on his screen the picture of the Doctor and Peri coming towards the complex.

Davros overhears Takis and Lilt discussing what might be in the catacombs. A Dalek then announces that Kara is ready to speak with him, and an image of the woman appears on his monitor.

Kara (Eleanor Bron) is an industrialist who is helping to finance Davros's operations on Necros. Davros pleads for more money and Kara agrees to see what she can do. When the communications link is broken, she is obviously ill at ease. She asks her secretary Vogel (Hugh Walters) if Orcini has arrived, and is told that he has.

GH: 'Eleanor Bron was another immediate casting choice on reading the script. I phoned her up and she said yes. Eleanor had some very strong ideas as to how the part should be played, and she was brilliant.'

AS: 'It was quite deliberate that all the parts of the city that weren't to do with death were white, while the catacombs and corridors of Tranquil Repose were either black or had black elements in them.'

Natasha and Grigory have located the cryogenic storage unit for which they were searching. They open it to find it occupied by a mannequin. The body they sought – that of Natasha's father, Stengos – is missing.

AS: 'That unit opened up and was fully operational, but all the rest were just vacuum-formed repeats.'

The two 'grave robbers' are interrupted by guards, who fire on them as they flee.

JB: 'An armoury called Baptys provided all the working guns. The BBC often uses them.'

The Doctor and Peri arrive at a wall which blocks their path. The Doctor points out to Peri that the occupants of Tranquil Repose are not dead – they are simply resting in suspended animation. He then helps her over the wall.

GH: 'This was filmed at the Goodwood horse racing ground. When they went over the wall, Nicola accidentally kicked Colin between the legs, so his expression of concern over his broken watch is genuine.'

Natasha and Grigory find themselves at a door leading down into the underground areas of the city. They head down into the tunnels to look for a service lift to take them back to the surface. Suddenly Natasha hears a Dalek approaching and they press themselves into an alcove.

GH: 'I had made a decision that, although we didn't have loads of money, I really wanted to have great lighting effects, which I got from Don Babbage. The idea was to light it from the floor and make it reminiscent of the style of *Alien*, with the interesting shadows and dark, dingy passageways.'

AS: 'The under-city corridors were based on Highgate cemetery. The idea was that this was an ancient cemetery which had been buried under the new city, but that elements of the new technology were still represented there. That corridor was so tight and cramped. It was actually a circular set so that we could go round and round and make it look as though there were many long corridors.'

The Dalek, leading some guards with a covered body on a trolley, passes by. Natasha and Grigory continue on and stumble into a red-lit room in which a heartbeat sound can be heard.

GH: 'That room was lit with red gels and also floor-lit, which is time consuming to do because of all the potential shadows.'

Davros is following the progress of Natasha and Grigory on his monitor.
Natasha and Grigory discover a rack of human brains bubbling in liquid and, in the far corner of the room, a transparent Dalek containing the remains of a human head – it is that of Arthur Stengos (Alec

Linstead). Stengos pleads with Natasha to kill him, becoming more and more Dalek-like with every sentence. She finally raises her laser pistol and destroys her father and the Dalek. As Natasha and Grigory flee from the room, they find Takis, Lilt and some guards lying in wait for them, and are taken prisoner.

GH: 'The shot where Stengos opens his eye was meant to be much more frightening than that. I don't know what went wrong but it was meant to be really frightening. I think he opens his eye a fraction too soon.'

JB: 'To do a glass/acrylic Dalek was going to be very expensive and time-consuming, so I took it to a specialist firm, Denny's, down at Shepherd's Bush. They did a lot of the BBC's plastics work. The main reason I sent that outside was because we had so much other stuff to construct that there was just no time to fit it all in. They supplied us with the three sections – top, middle and bottom – all made out of clear acrylic plastic. Other considerations were that it had to be lit, an actor had to be in it, and we had to be able to see him. We raised it on a platform to get the lights under it.

'I was glad that it wasn't seen very often, because as well as being very fragile, it collected dust like a magnet. By the time we had finished recording it looked very tacky and damaged. Dorka had a lot of trouble fitting in all the prosthetics and make-up, with the tubes and everything.

'We also had to consider that this Dalek was required to explode. Whatever else we did, we weren't going to be blowing up the perspex one, because the material splinters and is sharp and dangerous. We had to construct another Dalek out of lightweight vacuum-formed plastic just for the shot where it blows up.'

Kara receives Orcini and Bostock into her office. Orcini (William Gaunt) is a Knight of the Grand Order of Oberon, a hired assassin, and Bostock (John Ogwen) is his squire. Kara is hiring them to kill Davros.

GH: 'I chose William Gaunt to play Orcini because I'd worked with him a couple of times and knew what he could do. I saw the character as a sort of Don Quixote figure, and I find Gaunt a very elegant and classical actor. I'd worked with John Ogwen on *District Nurse* in Wales, but he hadn't worked very much in England. I felt it was time we saw more of his talent.'

PG: 'I wanted to give Bostock and Orcini camouflage jackets, but it was decided that they should be more Che Guevara-type characters, so we hired their costumes from a costumier and just added some small details to them.'

Dorka Nieradzik decided that, as Orcini was a mercenary who had found fame for his bravery and skill, she would make him up with some scars on his face, as the legacy of a former battle. She also gave him long hair tied back in a leather thong, the aim being to achieve a 'Buffalo Bill' look.

The Doctor and Peri walk through the outer boundaries of Tranquil Repose. The Doctor explains that he was suspicious when he heard the reports of Stengos's death and of his internment in Tranquil Repose, and this is why he has come here.

JB: 'This was done at an enormous disused airport which I had to relate to some model shots later. There were strange, monolithic lumps of concrete dotted around, and Alan put statues and painted scenery along one side of the runway. It all gave the impression of huge monuments dotted around the approaches to the mortuary pyramid.'

AS: 'Of the statuary and scenery that we brought with us, the BBC scenic artist handled the painted ones and a guy called Derek Howarth worked on the sculpted ones.'

Jobel gives his workers a pep-talk prior to the President's arrival.

PG: 'The mortuary workers' uniforms were all dentist's tunics, which were specified in the brief. We had to send them all out to be dyed professionally to make sure that the colour was consistent. As these costumes would have been fairly boring on their own, I came up with the idea of a cap with coloured stripes on it which would continue down on to the face. I had recently read an article about face painting in an issue of *Vogue*, so I worked with Dorka Nieradzik to produce the right effect.'

Kara gives Orcini a box-like electronic device, telling him that it is a transmitter which he should use to send her a signal when he and his squire have reached the under-city. Unknown to Orcini, the device is in fact a bomb with which Kara hopes to destroy Davros and his Daleks.

Tasambeker arrives to see the Great Healer. Davros tells her that he is pleased with her work and that he wants her transferred to his personal staff.

The Doctor and Peri finally arrive at the entrance to Tranquil Repose.

AS: 'The entrance to Tranquil Repose was filmed on location with a glass painting of pyramids over the top. There was a decorative pond outside the IBM building and the statues were recycled from the ones we had used at the airfield.'

A Dalek passes by behind the two travellers as they enter the complex. Peri catches sight of it, but does not know what it is. She and the Doctor go to investigate, but it has vanished.

JB: 'There wasn't anyone actually inside that Dalek – we pulled it along on a wire.'

Takis and Lilt torture Natasha and Grigory to try to gain information about any co-conspirators. They force the alcoholic Grigory to drink from a flask which he has hanging on a strap around his neck.

In an area which he describes as the Garden of Fond Memories, the Doctor has found a giant gravestone carved with a huge image of his face. As he stands lost in thought, believing that he must be destined to die on Necros in his current incarnation, the gravestone topples forward and falls on top of him.

(End of part one.)

JB: 'The gravestone was carved by Derek Howarth from our specifications. He's a clever sculptor who works with hot wires rather than knives. I would have liked the prop to have been very much thicker, but that would have doubled the price.

'When it finally fell, blood was supposed to come out of the statue's eye.'

GH: 'We did do that but it was cut, I think because it was too grim for the end of an episode. There is a continuity reference to it a little later.'

Peri rushes over to the fallen monument but is intercepted by Jobel, who smarmily tries to ingratiate himself with her. The Doctor is in fact unscathed and pushes his way out from under the lightweight imitation stones. His clothes are marked down one side with fake blood. He determines to find out who had the statue erected.

Grigory is now drunk and Lilt can get no sense out of him.

Inside Tranquil Repose, the Doctor and Peri are met by Tasambeker, who gives them a sales pitch about the facilities it has to offer.

Takis uses a communications screen to find out the ETA of President Vargos's ship. The computer voice (Penelope Lee) tells him that a second ship is also en-route for Necros.

AS: 'The screen was done using inlay rather than overlay, because it was not a blue screen. We just replaced a part of the picture with another image.'

Tasambeker shows the Doctor and Peri a promotional video of the DJ explaining the service he offers of relaying loved ones' messages to the Tranquil Repose residents.

GH: 'The DJ's video was a pre-recorded sequence played in through the small monitor screen on the desk there. It was actually the very first thing we did in studio.'

Bostock and Orcini are nearing Tranquil Repose when they see a white Dalek. Orcini lets rip with his machine gun and the Dalek is destroyed in a violent explosion. Orcini comments with pleasure that the bullets are fitted with bastic heads.

AS: 'This was when we choked everyone as a pall of black smoke from the Dalek blew over the camera crew.'

JB: 'The explosion was rigged up by Jim Francis. As there were other things going on that day, we created the Dalek shell in the workshop and brought it out with us so that we could achieve the effect as easily as possible. However, we had a problem with the wind changing direction all the time, and the smoke from the explosion blew straight at us afterwards. Ideally one would plan the shots so that it blew the other way.

'We had to pre-cut and break the shell of the Dalek. Jim manufactured a number of explosive charges to be set off in sequence: maybe one to lift the thing off the ground, one for light and one for smoke. Sometimes we needed a "pretty" explosion rather than a powerful one. Often, too, when the script said "and it blows up" we had to overstate it, because all you see of an explosion is a subliminal image. The actual effect is always better if it is bigger and more impressive than it would be in real life.'

Davros speaks to Kara via her communications screen and reports that a Dalek patrol has been attacked. He tells her that he is sending some Daleks to 'protect' her against insurrection. Kara thanks him through gritted teeth. Afterwards, Vogel tells Kara he suspects that Davros has realised what they are up to. Kara looks forward to Davros's death so that she will control the provision of food for the whole galaxy.

The Doctor decides to pay a visit on the Great Healer while Peri goes with Jobel to see the DJ. When his companion has gone, the Doctor is captured by two white Daleks and led off.

Fighting off Jobel's amorous advances, Peri slips into the DJ's room.

AS: 'The DJ's studio and Kara's office were slightly expedient, and I wasn't too happy with them. They were actually the same set, just changed around a bit. There wasn't enough money to build another set so we had to make do.'

The DJ is impressed that Peri is actually from America on Earth. He explains that he has based his style of presentation on some recordings brought back from Earth by his great-grandfather.

GH: 'Some of that music playing in the background is genuine. You can't get permission to use most American music as it would cost a fortune, but there are good cover versions and sound-alikes that you can use.'

JB: 'The DJ's headphones were specially constructed by Andy Lazell.'

Davros congratulates Tasambeker on a job well done. He quizzes her about her feelings for Jobel, encouraging her to watch him on the security cameras and then see if she doesn't hate him enough to kill him.

The Doctor has been placed in a cell with Natasha and Grigory. As he tries to free himself from his manacles, they tell him what they have seen. He gets one foot free.

In Kara's office a signal is received from Orcini – he has entered the catacombs under Tranquil Repose. Two Daleks enter the office, and, after exterminating Vogel, order Kara to accompany them back to Davros.

GH: 'That is a standard post-production extermination effect. When things have been established over a period of time, you don't just come along and change them for the sake of it.'

Takis and Lilt talk covertly to Jobel about moving against the Great Healer. Jobel is interested but wary.

GH: 'Although Jobel is a slightly camp character, he's real. All the characters are real to me. He's nicely underplayed and, although he's somewhat outrageous, he's real.'

Davros has been watching the discussion on his monitor and is infuriated by Jobel's duplicity. He offers Tasambeker the chance to become a Dalek and says that to show her total obedience she must kill Jobel.

JB: 'For that shot of the Dalek eyestalk in the foreground, we couldn't get the Dalek close enough to the lens because the camera was in the way. So we took an eyestalk off a Dalek and moved it in by hand.'

Orcini decides to release the prisoners and use them as scapegoats to divert attention from his own operations.

Tasambeker tries to warn Jobel that he will die unless he leaves. He will not listen, and cruelly snubs her again. In fury, she plunges a filled hypodermic into his chest and kills him.

GH: 'The hypodermic was filled with liquid and we originally had a shot of it emptying once it had been stuck into Jobel. Again, that was cut as it was too horrific.'

JB: 'The needle was wired with a spring so that it collapsed into the syringe. Jobel was then fitted with a body plate with a needle already attached to it. With careful camera angles and editing, the whole thing came across as effective and real.'

Tasambeker is exterminated by two white Daleks.

Peri uses the DJ's viewing screen to find the Doctor. The DJ shows her how to speak to him. The Doctor responds by telling her that she is in danger. He instructs her to get back to the TARDIS and to warn the President's ship not to land.

Davros has heard this warning and sends his Daleks to bring Peri to him and to kill the DJ.

The DJ bars Peri's exit, saying that it is too dangerous for her to go. He suggests that she uses his own radio transmitter to warn the President's ship.

The Doctor leaves Natasha and Grigory to destroy the incubation room. When Natasha attempts to fire her gun, however, she discovers that its power pack is exhausted. Davros orders that a specimen be activated, and another transparent Dalek materialises in the room. Grigory changes the controls on the incubator tanks in an attempt to stop the process.

Bostock and Orcini arrive at Davros's base and, killing the guard, burst in. Caught in the crossfire from their machine guns, Davros is killed. Orcini feels it was too easy, however, and he is right. The head in the life support unit was artificial; the real Davros suddenly appears on the steps behind them.

GH: 'The only reason I can think of for my use of close-ups when Davros appears on the stairs is that Terry Molloy might not have been in his base at the time. I suspect, because of time, we just had him standing there, and I took the shots accordingly.'

Bostock throws a knife at Davros but it thuds into the back of his chair, just missing his neck.

JB: 'We didn't throw the knife, we just had it stuck in there. The cutting from the hand throwing the knife to the knife in the back of the chair gives the impression of it hitting its target.'

Davros's white Daleks enter the chamber and fire at Bostock and Orcini. Orcini's false leg is hit and blown away, and Bostock is winged by an exterminator blast. Davros, in his chair, hovers above Orcini, transfixing him with a bolt of blue lightning from his hand.

JB: 'Gaunt was standing there with one leg strapped up behind him, hopping about, and we rigged a little charge to disconnect his fake leg for the shot where it gets blown off.

'Davros's chair was difficult to recreate. The original didn't exist, so we had to re-build it all without much reference material. It was quite expensive.'

GH: 'The shot of Davros hovering above Orcini was a very complicated one to achieve. We had Davros set up on a block against a black background, and that image was then superimposed on the shot of the room with Orcini down on the floor. The crackling blue light came from a Van der Graff generator which was also in the studio, and the spark of electricity was added to the main image in post-production, as were the red glow under Davros's chair and the blue glow over the lightning bolt.'

PG: 'Davros's costume was from stock, so we just patched it up and made it reusable.'

The transparent shell has now converted into a fully formed white Dalek, and it rises up to hover menacingly over Natasha and Grigory. It exterminates them, but then explodes due to Grigory's tampering with the equipment.

JB: 'We got hold of a chap, Stuart Evans, who produced Dalek models commercially, and borrowed one of his kits, so that we could get it up high enough. The problem was that, with the limitations of studio space, we could never have got the depth of field to have had a full-sized Dalek floating up in the air. It wasn't physically possible, because the Dalek needed to be close to the camera. We initially thought that if we went for a model, and put that in front of the camera, it would look as though it was a giant Dalek.'

GH: 'We ended up doing the shot of the model Dalek in an effects studio and then adding it to the main picture in post production. It was simply the best and easiest way of getting the effect I wanted.'

JB: 'The model wasn't actually blown up. The explosion was achieved in post-production by using a video effect.'

The President's spaceship has apparently been turned away by Peri's transmitted warning. The DJ has now rigged up in his studio a large gun which he describes to Peri as firing a highly directional ultrasonic beam of rock and roll. He hopes that this will repel the Daleks.

Kara arrives in Davros's laboratory. Davros accuses her of trying to kill him, but Kara denies this. Davros gives back to Orcini the communicator device which he earlier confiscated and instructs him to operate it. Before the Knight can complete the sequence, Kara admits that the device is in fact a bomb. Orcini knifes Kara in response to her treachery, and she falls dead on the floor.

JB: 'The knife worked in a similar way to the hypodermic in the earlier scene; the blade slipped back into the handle.'

The DJ manages to destroy two Daleks with his gun, but is exterminated by a third. The Doctor, listening over the speaker system in the caverns, hears what has happened. Turning a corner, he himself then runs into two Daleks, who escort him away.

Takis and Lilt monitor the landing on Necros of the second space-ship which was earlier detected approaching.

JB: 'We had a special model filming day to do all these scenes. We built a platform and dressed it with bits and pieces to represent the landing pad, and then the spaceship was built. It descended on an air ram, which was hidden by the tower with the flashing lights.'

The Doctor is taken to Davros, who tells him that he survived their last encounter by using an escape pod. While Davros gloats over his achievements, Orcini and the Doctor have a furtive exchange of gestures, agreeing an unspoken plan. The Doctor then draws Davros's attention, allowing Orcini to retrieve Kara's bomb. When asked about the fate of the Tranquil Repose residents, Davros explains that those whom he considered worthy have been converted into Daleks, while the others have been sent to Kara's processing plant to be turned into a protein-rich foodstuff for sale to the starving masses of this part of the galaxy. When he has created sufficient new Daleks, he plans to invade the neighbouring planets to which the food has been supplied.

JB: 'When we came to get Davros's mask done, we found that the sculptor who had done it the previous time had left, so Dorka took on that responsibility and arranged for it to be re-made.'

Takis and Lilt meet the new arrivals – grey Daleks. Ignoring the two men's attempts to bargain, the Daleks demand to be taken to Davros.

JB: 'Two of these Daleks were originals and two we had built. We got the fibreglass workshop to make up some of the basic components, then the carpenters turned these into final structural pieces and added casters and seats and all that kind of thing. When a designer's got only two or three assistants and so much work to do, then it's useful to be able to get the carpenters to screw and bolt these things together.'

Peri arrives in Davros's laboratory, escorted by a white Dalek. Davros prepares to activate his new Dalek army, but Bostock has revived and manages to shoot his hand off before he can do so. Bostock is then exterminated by a Dalek.

JB: 'We went through a couple of exploding hands getting that shot. The hand was made from brown foam and we gave him green blood.'

The grey Daleks battle with Davros's white Daleks, eventually defeating them. They sweep into the laboratory and order Davros to return with them to Skaro to stand trial for crimes against their race. The white Daleks will be reconditioned to obey the will of the Supreme Dalek. Davros draw their attention to the Doctor, but they retort that his appearance does not match their records. They intend to hold him until his identity can be verified.
When Davros has been led away, the Doctor uses Orcini's gun to blind the grey Dalek left on guard. Peri then attaches to it a grenade taken from Bostock's pocket, blowing it up.

JB: 'We always had to be careful not to reveal too much of the insides of a Dalek! All the paper debris which flew into the air after the explosion was deliberate. This was an idea I got from Jim Francis. When you blow something up, it always seems to come down too soon, immediately after it's happened; explosions happen too quickly, and you just get balls of smoke. But if you add these bits of paper, they float down slightly later and it looks a lot more effective.'

Orcini intends to use the bomb to destroy the complex before Davros and the Daleks can escape, and he tells the others to get out while they can.

The Doctor tells Takis and Lilt that Davros has created a demand for synthetic protein and they must continue to supply it. They can use the protein-rich 'staff of life' plant as a new raw material – there's certainly enough of it about.

As everyone races for the exit, the Dalek ship takes off. Orcini detonates the bomb, just too late to stop the ship. Davros has escaped again.

JB: 'The model, constructed by Bill Pearson from my brief, reflected all the elements from the location and from the glass shots: the pyramids, the pool, the statues, the sky. Freon was used for the smoke coming out of the bottom of the ship as it lifts off. There's an awful lot of work goes into a model like this and then we blow it up! Explosions are especially tricky to do on a small scale.'

As the base rocks with explosions, the workers mill about in the smoke and confusion.

GH: 'The picture shake was all done in post production. It was Quantel shaking the picture electronically rather than us shaking the cameras physically.'

When the excitement has died down, Takis and Lilt prepare themselves for the task ahead – rebuilding the processing plant.

The Doctor decides to take Peri for a holiday, but the picture freeze-frames just as he is about to state the intended destination.

(End of part two.)

GH: 'The very last word – Blackpool – was cut because the series had been just put on hold and a decision was taken not to trail the following season.'

Post-production

While the filming and recording of a *Doctor Who* adventure accounts for the raw material of what is eventually seen on screen, the diary of a production does not end there. A period of many months can pass between the time a writer first submits his script and the time the story is eventually transmitted, and the proportion of that period which is spent in the studio – about one day per 25-minute episode – is very low indeed compared with that spent on work carried out both before and after the recording sessions.

The early part of this chapter covered the pre-production work on *Revelation of the Daleks*; now Graeme Harper describes the general post-production process: the work which takes place once all the filming and recording has been completed.

'I would sit down with all the recorded material copied on to VHS tapes encoded with a timestamp [a clock with which each frame can be uniquely identified]. From these I would be able to work out all the "ins" and the "outs" – in other words, the exact frames on which I wanted to cut into and out of each scene – and the order in which I wanted all the shots to come. In the process I also selected which of the different takes I wanted to use.

'I can't remember whether or not we did an "off-line" edit on *Revelation of the Daleks*. I seem to think that we didn't. An "off-line" edit is where the director supervises a rough cutting together of the show to see how it all fits. Gaps may be left for any post-production work which is still under way, and certain sequences may later be lengthened or shortened by any special video effects which are to be added.

'I think that in this case we went straight to an "on-line" edit – constructing the show from my notes, cutting it according to how I wanted it to be, and to what would hopefully be the correct length.

'It would generally take about two days of work to end up with a basic edit. That would then be shown to John Nathan-Turner, we would go through it with him in the edit suite, and he would suggest changes depending on how he had visualised the show as looking. Any necessary changes would take another day to make.

'We would have to lift off any shots which required electronic video effects and put them on a tape to go over to the Video Effects Workshop. There we would add in John Brace's model work, the Dalek exterminator effects and so on. These treated shots would then be put on to a tape and dropped back into the master tape containing the rest of the programme.

'In the week's gap which had occurred between the end of the location filming and the start of the studio rehearsals for *Revelation of the Daleks*, I had worked with the film editor (Ray Wingrove) to cut together all the film sequences: the fight with the mutant and so on. Once these sequences had been agreed with John, we did a basic film dub [added the sound] and transferred them all to video. These were also ready then to be dropped into the master tape as and where appropriate.

'Dick Mills at the Radiophonic Workshop would have got a copy of the original "on-line" edit – the one without all the effects added – together with notes showing where and what all the effects were going to be. This was so that he could start putting a basic track of special sounds together. I would go to the Workshop and sit down with him and the composer, Roger Limb, to go through where all the sounds were needed and what I was looking for in the way of music. Eventually Dick would get a copy of the master tape and he would then be able to add more sounds to complement the effects sequences.

'Dick and Roger would go away and do all their work for two weeks, and when they had finished I would go and listen to everything that they had done, before we got to the dubbing session. In that way we could adjust anything that wasn't working. The next time I would hear their work would be at the dub, when we could again make minor changes if necessary.

'I tend not to give detailed instructions to a composer. I think my direction to Roger was simply to make the music big and orchestral. I know the music is electronic but I wanted something huge and orchestral. Roger managed to give me that and came up with a stunning, electronically produced, orchestral sound. Dick Mills also composed some "death music" for part two.'

Roger Limb, interviewed for *Doctor Who Magazine*, had the following recollections of working on *Revelation of the Daleks*:

'You sit down first with your director, and your relationship with him is crucial for the whole operation. You don't just decide where the music is going to be and what it is going to do in an emotional sense. You also consider the actual sounds themselves. Graeme Harper was very good like that; he really gave me a lot of help in that way. He bullied me a lot, but he knew what he wanted and made me go for it. He made me look for things that I might not have automatically thought of. He was a good director from my point of view. He didn't know anything about music, but he knew exactly what he wanted the music to do. When I played some music, he knew it was something he *didn't* want. The important thing is to find out what the director *does* want.'

Once all the music and special sounds have been dubbed on to the master tape at the sypher dub session, that is then the end of the director's job. All that remains is for the completed programme to be scheduled and transmitted.

Transmission

The two episodes of *Revelation of the Daleks* were eventually transmitted at 5.25 p.m. on Saturday 23 March 1985 and Saturday 30 March 1985 respectively, bringing to a close the 22nd season of *Doctor Who*. The closing episode achieved a notable success in attracting 7.7 million viewers, the second highest rating of the season, bettered only by the first episode of the opening story, *Attack of the Cybermen*, which had attracted 8.9 million. The average viewing figure for the story was 7.55 million viewers per episode, slightly above the season average of 7.12 million. Although very respectable, this was still rather lower than what the series had been achieving in the recent past. The season as a whole also fared rather less well than most previous ones in the weekly television chart – perhaps the best guide to a programme's success or failure – its average position being a disappointing 61st.

One reason for the lower-than-normal ratings was that HTV/ Goldcrest's new film series *Robin of Sherwood* was transmitted by ITV in direct competition with most of the episodes. Word-of-mouth publicity for this new fantasy-orientated show was very good and, given the choice between this and the known quantity of *Doctor Who*, many casual viewers opted for the greenwood forests rather than the desolation of Necros.

Revelation of the Daleks was repeated in 1993 as the sixth Doctor's entry in a series of BBC2 repeats to celebrate *Doctor Who*'s thirtieth anniversary. The repeat was of the overseas four-part version, rather than of the original two-part transmission, and it ran on consecutive Friday evenings from 19 March to 9 April inclusive in a 7.15 p.m. slot following repeats of *Stingray* and *The Man From U.N.C.L.E.*

Credits

Producer	John Nathan-Turner
Writer/Script Editor	Eric Saward
Director	Graeme Harper
Production Associate	Angela Smith (replaced Sue Anstruther at late stage)
Production Manager	Michael Cameron
Production Assistant	Elizabeth Sherry
AFM	Jo O'Leary (replaced David Tilley at late stage)
Designer	Alan Spalding
Design Assistant	Adele Marolf
Costume Designer	Pat Godfrey
Make-Up Designer	Dorka Nieradzik (replaced Elizabeth Rowle at late stage)
Visual Effects Designer	John Brace
Video Effects	Dave Chapman
Prop Buyer	John Watts
Lighting Director	Don Babbage (replaced Henry Barber at late stage)
Technical Co-ordinator	Alan Arbuthnott
Sound Supervisor	Andy Stacey
Grams	Howard Jones
Camera Supervisor	Alec Wheal
Vision Mixer	Dinah Long
Videotape Editor	Steve Newnham
Floor Assistant	Anna Price
Crew	11
Title Music	Ron Grainer
Incidental Music	Roger Limb
Special Sound	Dick Mills
Film Cameraman	John Walker
Film Sound	Steve Gatland
Film Editor	Ray Wingrove

7: Cancellation Crisis

Rumours that *Doctor Who*'s 23rd season had been cancelled by the BBC first began to circulate amongst the series' fans over the weekend of 23 and 24 February 1985, but it was not until the following Tuesday, 26 February, that the first public confirmation came in the form of a report by journalist Patrick Hill in the London evening newspaper, the *Standard*:

> *Dr Who* is being dropped by the hard-up BBC for the first time in 22 years.
>
> It has decided that *Dr Who*'s adventures are too expensive to produce.
>
> BBC1 Controller Michael Grade has ordered the series, which stars Colin Baker, to be suspended for at least 18 months.
>
> *Dr Who* fans have launched a campaign to try to persuade Mr Grade to change his mind.
>
> The series has been seen on TV at least every nine months over the past 22 years and regularly attracts nearly eight million viewers.
>
> A BBC spokesman said: 'We intend to make a lot of new drama this year and cannot afford to do that and produce *Dr Who*.
>
> 'The Doctor is being rested, but will be back next year.'
>
> The last episode will go out on March 30.

Within hours of Mr Grade's decision, some of the programme's 110 million fans worldwide in 54 countries where it is shown, had begun their campaign.

An army of fans began mustering letters of complaint about the series being rested.

One fan said: 'If public opinion can change the BBC's mind over *Dallas*, then we hope we can do the same.'

London record producer Mr Ian Levine, a lifetime fan and member of the British *Dr Who* fan club, said: '*Dr Who* is now more than just a TV programme. For 22 years it has been a way of life. We are calling on all fans to write to Michael Grade to urge him to change his mind.'

A spokesman for the British branch of the *Dr Who* Appreciation Society, which has over 3,500 members, said: 'This news has been a great shock to us. We will be meeting to discuss exactly what we can do to help save one of the country's favourite programmes.'

A spokesman for the *Dr Who* fan club added: 'We want all our members to write to Mr Grade.

'At present 30,000 letters have already been sent. We have got to save this programme and we are calling on members of the public to help us.'

This short article marked the start of an incredible whirlwind of press coverage and fan activity the like of which *Doctor Who* had never seen before. The first national report came just a few hours later courtesy of the BBC itself on the children's news magazine programme *Newsround*, and this was quickly followed by brief items on BBC1's main evening news bulletins at 6 p.m. and at 9 p.m., both featuring a short clip from the most recently transmitted episode, part one of *The Two Doctors*. New developments then occurred daily.

On Wednesday 27 February, the rest of the media eagerly pounced on the story, seeing in it a chance to indulge in their perennial pursuit of knocking the BBC, which had been at the centre of another major furore less than a month earlier when Michael Grade had dropped the popular soap opera *Dallas* and then been forced to reinstate it due to public pressure. David Saunders, the Co-ordinator of the *Doctor Who* Appreciation Society (DWAS), was inundated by phone calls from newspaper journalists, from TV and radio stations – both national and local – and from fans in the UK and in the USA, all desperate for information. Society representatives were even booked to appear on the BBC's *Breakfast Time* programme and on ITV's rival *Good Morning Britain*, although in the event both appearances fell through – the BBC's because Michael Grade, who was to have responded to the fans' criticisms, was on a skiing holiday in France and reportedly could not be contacted.

On Thursday 28 February, the fruits of all the journalists' endeavours became apparent as the story broke in the national press. Every daily newspaper – not only the tabloids but also the so-called quality broadsheets – devoted space to it, and some – the *Daily Telegraph*, the *Guardian*, the *Daily Express* and the *Sun* – judged it of sufficient interest to merit front-page coverage.

The *Sun*'s report, under the banner headline *Dr Who is Axed in a BBC Plot*, was particularly memorable, and was the only one to take a slightly new angle on the story. Wrote reporter Charles Catchpole:

> *Doctor Who* was axed by the BBC last night, and furious fans claimed it was a plot to back up demands for a higher licence fee.
>
> TV bosses say they cannot afford to make any new shows about the famous time-traveller for 18 months.
>
> But even the BBC's own men see the axing of the show – a hit for 22 years – as a cynical bid to whip up support for an increase in the fee.
>
> One official said: 'This is absolute madness. *Doctor Who* is getting around nine million viewers.
>
> 'There's a strong feeling that the high-ups are using it as part of their propaganda campaign.'
>
> Actor Colin Baker, who plays the Doctor, said: 'I was staggered. We were all geared up to start work on the next series.'
>
> And sexy Nicola Bryant – his assistant Peri – was said to be 'very surprised and clearly upset.'
>
> Colin said: 'I am contracted to the series, but the decision will mean the BBC probably having to pay off a lot of other people. It doesn't seem good financial sense.'
>
> Patrick Troughton, 54, who was Dr Who in the Sixties, said: 'I think it is just power politics at work. I'm sure the viewers will make their feelings known.'
>
> BBC1 supremo Michael Grade claimed: 'We intend to make a lot of new drama, and we cannot afford to do that and *Doctor Who*.'

But Beeb insiders say each episode of the sci-fi serial costs only £180,000 – against an average £220,000 for drama.

They claim dumping the Doctor will *lose* the Corporation money from sales to 54 other countries. It has a world-wide audience of 110 million viewers.

With just five new episodes left to be shown, fans were launching a massive campaign to save the Doctor last night.

Jeremy Bentham, co-founder of the *Dr Who* Appreciation Society, said: 'The public won't let it die.'

In America, the show's 40,000-strong fan club pledged themselves to raise one and a half million dollars to keep the programme on the air.

This leader article was followed up by a short editorial comment piece inside the paper which, although written in the *Sun*'s usual lurid style, must surely have struck a chord with many of the series' disappointed viewers. Headed *Who Dunnit?*, it read:

There can rarely have been a more popular children's TV show than *Doctor Who*.

Yet this programme is now selected by the BBC to be shelved for 18 months.

The poor dears say that they cannot afford to make another series. *Dr Who* probably costs less than an average TV drama.

So what cheap rubbish is going to be put on in its place?

The life story of Director-General Alasdair Milne? Or just the station signal?

We can tell the BBC how it can start saving real money.

By sacking the over-paid fat heads who came up with this nasty little stunt!

It became apparent as the day wore on that the BBC was trying to play down the story. This was clearly a case of swimming against the tide, however, as interest from other sources continued largely unabated, one of the most notable cases being an interview with Ian Levine, one of the leading fan campaigners, on ITN's *News at One*.

Friday 1 March saw further items appearing in the national press, most of them concentrating on fans' reactions to the postponement and on the pledged financial support from those in the States. The *Sun* and the *Daily Star* both took the opportunity to launch 'Save *Doctor Who*' campaigns, the latter giving over no fewer than five pages to its coverage of the series. Reports also started to appear about the possibility of a record being produced, along the lines of the Band Aid famine relief single, to publicise the series' predicament.

The BBC had by this time had an opportunity to formulate a considered response to the situation, having been caught completely off guard by the initial outcry. This belated damage-limitation exercise began on the afternoon of 1 March when Bill Cotton, Managing Director of BBC Television, took the highly unusual step of telephoning DWAS Co-ordinator David Saunders to inform him that the BBC was issuing a press statement to clarify its position over *Doctor Who*'s future, confirming that the series would be returning in 1986 and in its original format of one 25-minute episode per week. Further evidence that the BBC was finally getting its act together came when a planned appearance by Ian Levine on BBC1's early evening chat show *Wogan* was called off at the last minute, denying the fan campaign a valuable publicity opportunity.

The press release which the BBC issued that day was a cleverly worded piece of media manipulation which made it appear that the Corporation had in some way capitulated to public pressure when in actual fact its position remained completely unchanged. Headed 'More *Doctor Who* in 1986 – Another Miraculous Escape for Fiction Favourite', the release read as follows:

> As every follower of *Doctor Who* knows ... You can't kill a Time Lord. Today Bill Cotton, Managing Director of BBC Television, phoned David Saunders, Co-ordinator of the *Doctor Who* Appreciation Society, to explain the BBC plans.
>
> He said: '*Doctor Who* will be on the air in 1986, as it is in 1985, and as it has been for each of the past 22 years.
>
> 'Instead of running in January 1986 we shall wait until the start of the Autumn schedule, and then *Doctor Who* will be a strong item in the mix.
>
> 'We are also going to go back to the old tradition and have 25-minute programmes rather than the 45-minute version running at the moment. We think that is what the public wants. So does the producer, and his team.
>
> 'The 45-minute series has been a good experiment, but we need

to get back to basics, and to established ways. It also means that with a 25-minute length we can run the series for a greater number of weeks.'

Mr Cotton added: 'We appreciate the passionate support of the fan club in this country, and of fans around the world. We ask them to be a little patient while we get the Doctor back onto familiar rails. I am confident that *Doctor Who* has a great future on BBC1.'

The tabloids, perhaps sensing that they had got as much mileage out of the story as they usefully could, seized on this as a chance to claim that their 'Save *Doctor Who*' campaigns had been a success. The *Daily Star* of Saturday 2 March repeated sections of the press release verbatim, and went on to add:

A Band Aid style record has been planned to raise cash for the Save *Dr Who* cause. Fans hope Elton John and Holly Johnson – both *Who* fans – will take part along with the Village People.

It is the second time in 10 days that Mr Cotton has had to calm angry viewers.

He earlier admitted that the BBC had boobed dropping *Dallas* in mid-series and announced that it would be back next month.

The *Doctor Who* news came on the same day it was revealed that the BBC had paid £500,000 – for an American series it hadn't even seen.

Kane and Abel, based on Jeffrey Archer's best-seller, is being made by Embassy Films which was headed by Mr Grade until 1983.

Mr Grade has a credit on the series as executive producer – but he has no financial involvement in it.

The elusive Mr Grade also entered the fray on 2 March, the *Daily Mail*'s Corinna Honan having actually flown out to the French Alps in order to track him down. His rather brusque comments betrayed a sense of irritation at the sensational coverage given to what he appeared to consider a rather trivial matter:

Of course I care about the *Dr Who* fans, but I'm only thinking about British viewers. Do you know how many watched *Dr Who* last week? Six million. Very low indeed. Two or three years ago it was getting 10 to 11 million viewers.

But there's no reason for anyone to make waves. It's not as if I'm cancelling the series. We've got a lot of work to do on it but the show *will* be back. That's a promise. And it will be better than ever.

The BBC is *not* broke. It's just a question of priorities. A lot of drama shows are reaching their natural end. The writers don't want to write. The actors don't want to act. We need new material.

The policy has been for short-run series in the last couple of years. We hope these new ones will run for more than a year or two.

When challenged to respond to the enormous public outcry which the postponement had generated, Grade dismissed the series' fans as a special interest group and asserted that the rest of the world would barely notice its absence. 'Taking *Doctor Who* off the air is a piece of professional judgment. It is nothing to do with the licence fee coming up. We take a million of these decisions every day of the week. It's just an extraordinary storm in a teacup. Anyway, we've just had our best week in a long time on BBC1 and 2 – over 51 per cent of the total TV audience from 6 p.m. to closedown every day.'

Sunday 3 March saw the DWAS's executive committee holding a meeting with other prominent fans to discuss their next steps. They decided on two courses of action: first, to send all Society members a photocopied letter explaining the current situation and, secondly, to write to Bill Cotton in response to his phone call to David Saunders, requesting some more meaningful assurances on *Doctor Who*'s future.

Saunders began the following day, Monday 4 March, by taking part in BBC Radio 4's topical *Start the Week* programme, answering presenter Richard Baker's questions about the fan campaign. Then, in the afternoon, he travelled from Broadcasting House to Television Centre to deliver the DWAS's letter personally to Bill Cotton's secretary.

Cotton's reply, sent the very next day, had little to offer in the way of further reassurance but was interesting in that it marked the first real attempt by the BBC to suggest that the postponement decision had been taken for reasons other than purely financial. Received by Saunders on Wednesday 6 March, it read in part:

> Our intentions are clear. We intend to continue to produce *Dr Who* for as long as we believe the British public enjoy it. There is no decision to drop it after the next series.

As far as money from America is concerned, I regard that with a degree of scepticism, but I will certainly look into it. However the problem is not just financial, it is also about scripts and resources.

The day of the week, the time it is transmitted and the exact number will be decided over the next few months. What is important is that it will be a major offering on BBC1.

On Thursday 7 March and Friday 8 March, recording sessions took place for the much-vaunted record release to draw attention to *Doctor Who*'s plight. Entitled 'Doctor in Distress', it was written and produced by Ian Levine and his songwriting partner Fiachra Trench, who together had previously supplied the theme music for the *Doctor Who* spin-off *K-9 and Company*. The reported original intention of using the proceeds to further the campaign for the series' return had been dropped once it was realised that this might command insufficient support. It had since been decided that any money raised should go instead to a charitable cause, the National Society for Cancer Relief. Although the hoped-for participation by major-league pop stars still failed to materialise, a number of artistes were then assembled by organisers Paul Mark Tams, a long-time *Doctor Who* fan, and Jeff Weston, the Managing Director of Record Shack, the label on which the record would be released, and for whom some of the artistes recorded.

Under the group name Who Cares?, four *Doctor Who* regulars – Colin Baker, Nicola Bryant, Anthony Ainley and Nicholas Courtney – performed the song alongside a whole host of other celebrities and entertainers. The full list ran to some 25 names: Earlene Bentley, comedienne Faith Brown, Miquel Brown, Warren Cann of Ultravox, Hazell Dean, Floid of the Hot Gossip dance troupe, Bobby G of Bucks Fizz, Steve Grant, Julie Harris, Justin Hayward and John Lodge of the Moody Blues, Jona Lewie, Phyllis Nelson, Richie Pitts from the cast of the musical *Starlight Express*, John Rocca of Freeez, actress Sally Thomsett, Basia Trzetrzelewska and Danny White of Matt Bianco, David Van Day of Dollar and Music Academy, and the group Time UK, consisting of the Jam's former drummer Rick Buckler with Ronnie Ball, Fletcher Christian, Jimmy Edwards, Ray Simone and Nick Smith.

The record was pressed and distributed as quickly as possible and released a week later, on Friday 15 March, accompanied by a video directed by Reeltime Pictures' Keith Barnfather after pop impresario

Mike Mansfield reportedly pulled out at a late stage. ITV's *The Six O'Clock Show* marked the occasion with a short, very lighthearted item featuring clips from the Aaru cinema film *Doctor Who and the Daleks* and interviews with fans and members of the general public. The press, however, showed only limited interest in the record's release, and it received scathing reports and reviews in some of the weekly music papers. BBC radio stations refused to play it, claiming that it was too poor artistically, although it did receive quite good air-play on some of the independent stations.

The next development in the saga came when a fan's letter of complaint about the postponement met with the following reply from Michael Grade in the 23–29 March edition of *Radio Times*:

> The response of *Doctor Who* enthusiasts is bordering on the hysterical given the exact nature of the BBC's decision. *Doctor Who* has not been cancelled, just delayed for a year. The ratings for the current season have been disappointing and we need time to consider the reasons for this. The current series is an experimental 45-minute length and this has not proved as popular as we had hoped. We were looking to make some financial savings in the coming year and it seems that after 21 years a short rest would do the Doctor no harm at all.
>
> Long-running television series do get tired and it is because we want another 21 years of *Doctor Who* that we have prescribed a good rest.

This pronouncement, which again sought to shift the emphasis away from the financial reasons underlying the postponement and towards supposed deficiencies in the series itself, triggered a slight resurgence of press activity. Reports of Grade's comments appeared in several newspapers, most notably in the *Daily Express* of Thursday 21 March 1985, but to the fans' disappointment these merely followed the BBC line, again asserting that the series' future was safe.

At the beginning of April, further rumours began to circulate within fandom, this time to the effect that Season 23, when it did eventually appear, might be reduced from the then standard length of 26 episodes to only 20 episodes. Ian Levine made an announcement about this at a DWAS convention, DWASocial 5, on Saturday 6 April, but John Nathan-Turner, who was next up on stage, denied that any such decision had been taken.

Throughout the period since the news of the postponement first became public, many thousands of *Doctor Who* fans had written individually to the BBC to make their displeasure felt. Most had received just a standard photocopied letter in response, but DWAS member Gavin French managed to extract a personal reply, dated 17 April 1985, from Head of Series and Serials Jonathan Powell. This offered another slightly different slant on the reasons for the BBC's actions:

> We decided to postpone *Doctor Who* for two reasons. Firstly, we have a financial problem on BBC1 and looking at the programmes we decided that *Doctor Who* would benefit from some breathing space. It seems to me that the show does not work in its new three-quarter-hour episodes, and would be much better returned to its traditional 25-minute format. To change the format requires time and I believe it to be entirely advantageous that the producer of the programme has some time to consider it in depth.
>
> As yet we have not decided how many episodes we shall make when the show returns. We plan to have it on the screen by Autumn 1986 and the number of episodes will be decided according to our editorial wishes balanced against the financial means.

To add to the fans' bewilderment, Saturday 20 April saw Michael Grade giving yet another explanation when questioned on the subject during an interview for the Channel 4 chat show *The Late Clive James*. This time, no mention at all was made of any financial problems: 'The truth about *Doctor Who* is that it was a target for a cut, because the show's not doing very well. It's overly violent. It's losing audiences. Its appeal is not what it was. It's not getting new generations of children. We needed time to take it off the air and get it right.'

It was perhaps fortunate for Grade that these statements went unchallenged, Clive James no doubt being unaware that Season 22 had actually achieved quite respectable average ratings of 7.12 million viewers per episode and correspondingly high audience appreciation figures. Nor would anyone with any knowledge of *Doctor Who* have had much difficulty in rubbishing his claim that time was required in order to revamp the series, some quite radical changes having been made in previous seasons without the need for any such delay.

Wednesday 8 June brought further news in the form of a report in the *Sun* stating that Grade, along with Jonathan Powell and BBC Director of Programmes Brian Wenham, had decided to reduce Season 23 to fourteen episodes and subsequently to cancel the series altogether if its ratings failed to improve. The BBC Press Office denied that any such steps were being contemplated, but the fans remained understandably sceptical.

One of the few highlights of this period came with the commissioning of an original *Doctor Who* radio serial, *Slipback*, to go out on BBC Radio 4, in stereo, as part of a new children's magazine programme, *Pirate Radio 4*. Welcome though it was, this was nevertheless regarded by most commentators as being scant compensation for the lack of any new TV stories.

On Saturday 3 August, the *Sun* returned to the subject of the proposed episode count for Season 23, reporting an extraordinary gaffe made by the staff of BBC Enterprises' Sales Director John Harrison:

A BBC TV boss's blunder has confirmed *Sun* forecasts of *Dr Who* cutbacks.

Beeb chief John Harrison wrote a secret telex message to US distributors, saying next year's series will be trimmed from 26 shows to 14 25-minute episodes.

But someone mixed up the telex numbers – and the message went to the American *Doctor Who* Appreciation Society!

This report was again flatly denied by the BBC Press Office, even though photocopies of the offending telex reportedly began to spread amongst fans both in the US and in the UK.

Having been out of the *Doctor Who* news for a while, Michael Grade returned to controversy in September, using the opportunity of an interview on BBC Radio 2's popular *Jimmy Young Show* to launch another public attack on the series, this time explicitly criticising its production team: 'The people who make it have got rather complacent. The show got rather violent and lost a lot of its imagination, a lot of its wit, and was relying far too much on straightforward on-the-nose violence and had failed really to capture a new audience. There's no question of it being killed off. There is going to be another series next year. The problem with the programme was that it had been losing its appeal. I decided that it was time to take stock, to look at the show, to rethink the scripts, to rethink the shape of the programme, to think how we might revitalise *Doctor Who* so that it's going to last another 20 years.'

On Wednesday 18 December, the BBC made an announcement finally admitting that Season 23 would indeed be only fourteen episodes long. This time, the disclosure failed to generate any press coverage at all, not even the *Sun* bothering to report the official confirmation of its earlier scoop. It seemed that the phase of media concern over the postponement had finally run its course.

As the glare of public attention moved away from *Doctor Who*, it was left to the series' fans to take a more considered look at the hectic events of this extraordinary ten-month period, and to try to assess their long-term implications.

It would later be reported that the original news of the postponement had been leaked to the press by John Nathan-Turner, via Ian Levine.

'The day it was cancelled,' recalled Levine in a 1992 interview for *DWB*, 'John and Gary [Downie, his friend and a *Doctor Who* production assistant] came round to my house and spent the whole evening plotting what to do and how to get the press involved. John got me to phone Charles Catchpole of the *Sun*. He'd told me that there were codenames within the BBC that Catchpole would know, so I phoned him and said that I worked on the sixth floor [of Television Centre] under Michael Grade and that my name was Snowball. I said that there was a plot to get rid of *Doctor Who*. While I was talking, John and Gary were busy scribbling away telling me what to say. I told Charles Catchpole how the show made profits for the BBC, how the series was being used in a plot to defend the licence fee increase – John was even reeling off figures off the top of his head for the number of countries that *Doctor Who* was sold to, and for the millions of pounds [it made], for me to quote at him! John was pulling the strings and using me because he couldn't risk being identified as being involved. He knew this whole code thing and exactly what to say. Then we did the same thing with Geoff Baker of the *Daily Star*.'

Had Nathan-Turner and Levine not taken this step, the chances are that the phenomenal media outcry would never have occurred, and that the series could indeed have been cancelled altogether. Nathan-Turner himself has since denied that cancellation was ever a real possibility, but Colin Baker, in a 1989 interview for the fanzine *Kroton*, said: 'Originally it was the axe; it was coming off! Grade back-tracked very swiftly when he found out the reaction was as strong as it was, and it turned into a suspension, which was the only way he could get it back without losing too much face, I suppose.'

One thing on which all parties are in complete agreement is that the postponement decision, apparently conveyed to John Nathan-Turner by Jonathan Powell at a meeting on Monday 25 February 1985, came as a severe blow to the morale of the series' production team and cast. Speaking at a convention in Manchester on 16 November 1985, Nathan-Turner described their reaction to the news: 'It's a horrid thing to happen, to be told that the season you've prepared is kind of pulled from under your feet. I think my feeling was that of the rest of my team and of all the actors concerned, and indeed of all the directors who had been engaged. It's all very well to get your money at the end of the week, but it's far, far better actually to earn it. So I think we all felt fairly devastated.'

Eric Saward recalls that Nathan-Turner was in fact particularly demoralised by the decision. Saward himself remains uncertain as to the reasons for the postponement. 'I really don't know what the thinking was,' he says. 'I'm sure that Jonathan Powell hated the show. He was always very hostile to us at playbacks. Very indifferent, whether the show was good or bad. It seemed he'd really decided that he didn't like us. I think it was entirely his decision. I don't think Michael Grade cared one way or the other.'

Fans have often sought to suggest that the postponement was an act of pure vindictiveness on the part of either Grade or Powell, inspired by their apparent dislike of *Doctor Who*. This analysis overlooks the fact that the series had been unpopular with BBC executives throughout much of its history without ever before having been dropped from the schedules. Programme planners tend to act not on the basis of their own personal preferences but on that of their professional judgment and expertise, weighing up a whole range of different factors before reaching a conclusion. The weight of evidence now suggests that the postponement came about largely as a consequence of the financial problems to which some of the earlier press coverage alluded – and this is a view to which John Nathan-Turner has lent support. Two developments were particularly significant in this regard.

First, there was an enormous outlay involved in producing 104 episodes per year of the new soap opera *EastEnders*, which made its on-air debut in the week beginning 18 February 1985 – the very same week that the postponement decision was taken. The need to finance and support this show, which would soon become the BBC's most successful in the ratings, placed a very considerable strain on the budget and resources of the Series and Serials Department and resulted in a permanent reduction in the number of other programmes which it was able to make.

Secondly, and even more importantly, there was a substantial financial shortfall in the 1985/86 accounting year due to a decision taken by top-level management to bring forward by several months the launch of the BBC's daytime TV service, so as to get it up and running in advance of ITV's rival effort. This rescheduling meant that several million pounds had suddenly to be clawed back from the previously allocated departmental budgets, with cuts being made right across the board. *Doctor Who* was just one of the programmes to suffer, along with others such as *Mike Read's Pop Quiz, Come Dancing, The Hot Shoe Show* and *Crackerjack*.

It can indeed be considered an astute move on John Nathan-Turner's part to have placed in journalists' minds the idea that there might be a link between Season 23's postponement and the BBC's difficult financial position, as Ian Levine told *DWB*:

'John knew that the story of *Doctor Who* being cancelled alone would not have made the front page, but using the angle that the BBC was axing something popular to draw attention to their efforts to get the licence fee raised was extremely cunning and it worked!'

A skilled publicist, the producer no doubt reasoned that a fierce public backlash was the one thing which could save the series if Grade and Powell were truly intent on killing it off.

The resulting furore is certainly reported to have caused considerable consternation amongst the BBC's Board of Governors, who saw themselves being drawn into an unexpected and embarrassing controversy. They regarded the postponement as just the latest in a succession of poor management decisions and apparently took the matter up in forceful terms with Director-General Alasdair Milne. Milne's own view was that Grade, in underestimating the strength of the public's affection for *Doctor Who*, had made a serious error of judgment. On the other hand, however, he admired the way in which his subordinate had coped with the ensuing media circus.

There seemed to be no question of the cancelled season being reinstated, so the production team were left with the difficult task of deciding how to proceed.

The season had been at an advanced stage of preparation when the postponement decision was taken. The scripts for the first story, *The Nightmare Fair* by Graham Williams, had already been distributed to the regular cast and to key members of the production crew, including director Matthew Robinson. This serial, in two 45-minute episodes, would have seen the Doctor and Peri arriving on Blackpool's famous Pleasure Beach (a setting decided upon by John Nathan-Turner after he and Colin Baker made a promotional visit there in 1984 to open a new ride). There they would have discovered that one of the amusement arcades was in fact a deadly trap set by the sinister Celestial Toymaker, a character who had first appeared in an eponymous story in *Doctor Who*'s third season of adventures, way back in 1966.

The second two-parter was to have been *The Ultimate Evil*, written by Wally K. Daly and directed by Fiona Cumming. This would have involved the Doctor and Peri arriving in the peace-loving domain of Tranquela with the intention of taking a holiday, only to get caught up in the devious schemes of an unscrupulous arms dealer, the evil Dwarf Mordant, who hopes to provoke a war between the Tranquelans and their neighbouring race, the Amelierons, by causing them to suffer sporadic fits of extreme violence.

Another two-parter for which draft scripts had already been prepared was Philip Martin's *Mission to Magnus* – previously titled *Planet of Storms*. As Martin later recalled in an interview for *Doctor Who Magazine*, this story, set on the female-dominated planet Magnus, would have featured the return not only of a popular character from Colin Baker's first full season as the Doctor but also of a much more well-established foe:

'I was asked to do a script, again with Sil and maybe involving the Ice Warriors. I'd written a first draft, in which I had the Ice Warriors inside a polar ice-cap, because it suited them being so cold. They were burrowing workshops in the ice-cap, which was beginning to flood the planet, and the people couldn't understand why. This ice environment allowed the Ice Warriors to move freely, because I was always worried about how slow they had been in previous stories.'

The season's longest story, a three-parter, had the working title *Yellow Fever and How to Cure It* (shortened in some later documentation to *Yellow Fever*). Written by Robert Holmes, it was to have been set in Singapore and included return appearances by the Autons, the

Rani and possibly also the Master. In the event, Holmes had completed only a brief outline of the adventure before the season was postponed.

One of the two remaining two-part slots would probably have been filled by a Christopher H. Bidmead story entitled *In the Hollows of Time*. The other would probably have gone either to a story, title unknown, by Bill Pritchard or to one called *The Children of January* by Michael Feeney Callan.

Following the postponement decision, Robert Holmes, Christopher H. Bidmead and Michael Feeney Callan were all asked to continue working on their stories, but in the new 25-minute episode format rather than the old 45-minute one – a request to which all three writers immediately acceded. BBC documentation also indicates that Pip and Jane Baker were commissioned as early as 11 March 1985 – less than three weeks after the postponement decision was taken – to write a story, in four 25-minute episodes, with the working title *Gallifrey*. This is believed to have involved the destruction of the Doctor's home planet. In the end, however, these stories were all abandoned, as were those by Graham Williams, Philip Martin, Wally K. Daly and Bill Pritchard, the cancellation ultimately being seen by the production team to imply that they had to start afresh with some new writers and some new ideas.

In any event, the production team decided that a completely different approach was called for after they learned, in early June 1985, that the postponed season was to be only 14 episodes long. Eric Saward suggested having a season-spanning story in which the Doctor would be seen to be on trial, reflecting the fact that the series itself was still in this situation. This suggestion was readily agreed by John Nathan-Turner and the two men then set about developing a workable format for what ultimately became *The Trial of a Time Lord*.

The basic premise of the story was that the Doctor would be brought back to Gallifrey by the Time Lords to stand trial for his repeated interference in the affairs of other planets. In a conscious allusion to the structure of Charles Dickens' *A Christmas Carol*, the evidence would be presented in three segments – the first concerning an incident in the Doctor's recent past, the second an incident in his present and the third an incident in his future – before the story was eventually concluded in a fourth and final segment. Two pivotal figures in the proceedings of the court would be the prosecuting counsel, the Valeyard and the judge, otherwise known as the Inquisitor, for whom John Nathan-Turner and

Eric Saward developed the following character outline dated 5 July 1985:

THE VALEYARD AND THE INQUISITOR

The Doctor is not very popular on his home planet of Gallifrey. Over the years, his independence of mind has made him many enemies who would like to see him dead.

So when the Doctor is summoned home to stand trial for crimes that could cost him his life, it is decided, by the High Council, that a judge and a prosecuting counsel must be both above suspicion and free of prejudice concerning the Doctor.

After close consultation with the KEEPER OF THE MATRIX, the High Council decide to find suitable candidates from their own future.

To avoid any form of prejudicial selection, the Matrix itself is ordered to draw up a list of qualified candidates. To make the selection even more random, the Matrix gives each candidate a code number, and it is from this list that the High Council choose their INQUISITOR (Judge) and VALEYARD (Prosecuting Counsel). This way only the Matrix knows the identity of the candidates concerned.

THE INQUISITOR is female, middle fifties and very learned. She is also a friendly, agreeable soul with a strong sense of humour. (Although it is tempting to parody contemporary judges, I think it would be more interesting and more fun to play against the accepted stereotype.)

THE VALEYARD, on the other hand, is far less agreeable. He is tall and lean with strong angular features, giving him the manner and appearance of a powerful, predatory bird, whose talons are a sharpness of mind and a verbal dexterity capable of dismembering the strongest and most considered of arguments.

As the trial continues, evidence comes to light suggesting that the Matrix has been tampered with and that the list of jurists it produced was far from unprejudiced.

But who has manipulated the Matrix? And who of the two jurists is involved in the deception?

The Doctor has to find out, while at the same time fighting for his own existence.

The intention was that, somewhere around part twelve of the story, the Valeyard would be revealed to be a corrupt future incarnation of the

Doctor who had manipulated the whole Trial simply in order to destroy his own former persona. Peri was to be killed off at the end of part eight, becoming trapped in a situation from which the Time Lords were unable to extricate her, and a new companion, Mel, would be introduced in part nine. It was also decided at the outset that the Master should put in an appearance as one of the witnesses in the later stages of the proceedings.

The original writers chosen to provide the scripts for the season were Robert Holmes, Philip Martin, award-winning playwright David Halliwell and the late novelist Jack Trevor Story. The idea was that Holmes and Martin would contribute the first two segments of evidence, each in four episodes; that Halliwell and Story would then write two episodes apiece of the third four-part segment, liaising closely to ensure that their ideas dovetailed and could be realised using the same sets; and that Holmes would then provide the final two episodes to form the concluding segment.

On Tuesday 9 July 1985, all four writers travelled to the BBC's Threshold House offices for an initial discussion with John Nathan-Turner and Eric Saward, who explained the format to them and briefed them on their respective contributions.

Despite having made great play in the press of the need for *Doctor Who* to be revamped, Michael Grade had apparently taken no active interest in the formulation of the Trial idea. The only advice he had given John Nathan-Turner, in a meeting reportedly lasting somewhat short of ten minutes, was that the new season should contain less violence and more humour than the previous one. The production team therefore instructed the four writers along these lines, stressing the need to avoid any graphic violence and to make the stories fun and entertaining, albeit with humour arising organically out of the drama rather then grafted on artificially.

While work proceeded relatively smoothly on the segments commissioned from Robert Holmes and Philip Martin, which were given the final working titles *The Mysterious Planet* and *Mindwarp* respectively, the same could not be said of the two-part contributions by Jack Trevor Story and David Halliwell.

Little headway was made on Jack Trevor Story's segment. 'He came up with an idea for his section of the trial,' recalls Eric Saward. 'He said, "I've got an idea of a man sitting in an empty gasometer playing a saxophone." I told him "That sounds wonderful, but I don't think we can use it in *Doctor Who*!" '

David Halliwell's script – working title *Attack from the Mind* – progressed a little further. Halliwell later recalled the plot when interviewed in 1992 by the New Zealand *Doctor Who* fan club fanzine *TSV*: 'It was set on a planet called Penelope which was inhabited by two rival races; the Penelopeans who were extremely beautiful and poetic, and the Freds who were extremely ugly and plodding. At first it seemed as though the Freds were the aggressors but later it appeared that this was not the case.'

Attack from the Mind went through a number of drafts before it was eventually dropped, Eric Saward informing Halliwell in a letter dated 18 October 1985 that it lacked the sort of energy and humour that he and John Nathan-Turner were seeking.

Following this, the production team decided that the four-part gap in the season should now be filled by just a single writer. A submission was commissioned from Christopher H. Bidmead on 29 October 1985 under the working title *The Last Adventure*, although this would later be changed to *Pinacotheca*. In view of the urgency, Bidmead completed his scripts at a rapid pace, sending in first drafts of episodes one, two and three in mid-November, early December and late December respectively, and personally delivering to Eric Saward a second draft of all four episodes on 9 January 1986. On 7 February, however, Saward wrote to Bidmead to tell him that his story segment was being dropped as he appeared to have misunderstood the brief he had been given. The script editor later amplified this by explaining that he had found the scripts dull and lacking in substance from the outset, but that he had been reluctant to pass comment until he had seen the complete story.

With the situation becoming ever more urgent, another writer was then approached to provide the missing four-part segment. This was *Sapphire and Steel* creator P. J. Hammond, whose attempt, commissioned on 10 February 1986, had the working titles *End of Term* and, later, *Paradise Five*.

A fantasy-orientated piece, *Paradise Five* would have seen the Doctor masquerading as a businessman and Mel as a hostess in order to discover the sinister secrets of a planet supposedly designated as a holiday haven for overworked executives, both human and alien. At first sight the Paradise would have seemed idyllic, being run by two seemingly friendly characters called Michael and Gabriel with the assistance of a host of beautiful girls with names such as Stella and Bella and, to perform the menial tasks, a race of creatures known as Cherubs. However, it would ultimately have been exposed as a brash, artificial front for murderous money-making schemes. The Doctor's task would have been further complicated throughout the plot by the fact that the planet was plagued by a race of evil, ghost-like entities called Angels.

According to Hammond, Eric Saward liked this idea but John Nathan-Turner did not, and it was consequently rejected after he had completed just the first episode in draft.

On 6 March 1986, yet another four-parter was commissioned to fill the gap, and this one – working title *The Ultimate Foe* by Pip and Jane Baker – would finally be accepted. In view of the shortage of time, the writers were asked to have the first episode ready in draft form by 17 March, less than a fortnight later, and the other three by 7 April. In discussion with John Nathan-Turner and Eric Saward, they decided to make their plot a 'whodunit in space', paying homage to Agatha Christie.

In the meantime, on 4 February 1986, Robert Holmes had been commissioned as planned to write the final two episodes of the trial, under the working title *Time Inc*. (It is thought that he was also at this point offered the chance to write the missing episodes nine to twelve, but quickly declined.) The intention was that *Time Inc*. would tie up all the outstanding plot threads from the fourteen-part story and provide a dramatic climax to the season. As things transpired, however, Holmes became seriously ill and subsequently died on 24 May 1986, having completed only a rough draft of part thirteen. Eric Saward himself then took over the task of writing part fourteen, and in order to facilitate this he also rewrote completely the latter scenes of Holmes's script, introducing a new character named Mr Popplewick.

This was by no means the end of the season's problems as Saward, who had resigned from the BBC after overseeing the first two segments of the Trial, subsequently had a major disagreement with John Nathan-Turner over the way in which the story was to end. Saward decided to withhold permission for his script for part fourteen to be used, and Nathan-Turner therefore brought in Pip and Jane Baker to write a completely new final episode for the story.

With the eventual transmission of Season 23, it seemed that, at least for the moment, *Doctor Who* had been reprieved.

8: Being the Companion

Doctor Who has always placed a great deal of emphasis not only on the enigmatic Doctor himself but also on those with whom he travels. The companion figures have invariably fulfilled the important dramatic functions of facilitating plot exposition and of providing a point of audience identification, but within these basic parameters have ranged from being well-written and interesting characters in their own right to being little more than pretty girls to keep the dads interested.

As one might expect, the attitude of the Doctor (and, more importantly, of the script writers) to the companion has changed over the years. With the changes which occurred during the seventies and eighties in social attitudes towards sex stereotyping, the role of the companion in *Doctor Who* was under pressure to develop beyond that of the helpless screamer.

When the *Doctor Who* production team were planning the series' 21st season, they were aware that a number of significant changes would have to take place. They knew that Janet Fielding (Tegan) had expressed a desire to bow out along the way, as had Mark Strickson (Turlough). They wanted to lose the Kamelion robot as well, and to introduce a new, female, companion for the Doctor.

In his book *Doctor Who – The Companions*, producer John Nathan-Turner explained that 'the decision to try one solitary companion with the Doctor was an attempt to echo the Pertwee-Jo relationship of the seventies, which had been so successful'. Of course, the Doctor-companion relationship had gone through many variations over the years, but it is certainly true that, with the third and subsequent Doctors, the one-on-one format had seemed to work well, particularly from the point of view of the female companion. It had started with Liz Shaw and then developed through Jo Grant, Sarah Jane Smith, Leela and Romana. In fact it was John Nathan-Turner again who had broken the, by then, traditional format by introducing three companions – Adric, Nyssa and Tegan – to see out the fourth Doctor and introduce the fifth.

In February 1985, Nathan-Turner, Eric Saward and Peter Grimwade, the author of the new companion's introductory story *Planet of Fire*, devised an outline for the character:

Perpugilliam (Peri for short) Brown is a wealthy 18-year-old American student studying Botany. She has long blonde hair which complements her attractive looks. She does not suffer fools gladly and her most charming attribute is an acute sense of humour.

We meet Peri for the first time, while she is on holiday in whichever country we decide to film next season's foreign story.

Peri's mother, Janine, has remarried a man Peri dislikes – Howard. Peri still treasures the memory of her father who died when Peri was 13, particularly as her mother appears to care more for Howard's three children than for Peri herself. It is because of her respect for her father that Peri thinks so highly of the Doctor – to some extent the Doctor replaces the gap in Peri's life. When he died he was of the same age as the Doctor appears now. This never develops further than admiration and close friendship. Peri is the kind of girl who is popular – not just because of her looks, but because her warmth and sense of fun make her appeal to people of all ages.

As Eric Saward recalls, it was John Nathan-Turner's decision to make Peri an American. 'John wanted an American,' he says, 'and his brief was simply that: an American.' In Saward's view, this decision was motivated by a desire on the producer's part to curry favour with the American fans of *Doctor Who*. Nathan-Turner has however denied this. According to him, the decision was taken partly because of the popularity of Tegan – another non-British companion – and partly because he wanted to get away from Earth-UK companions in general, as he felt that their former predominance had lacked credibility.

Having auditioned a large number of actresses for the role, Nathan-Turner eventually chose Nicola Bryant, a young woman just out of drama school. Saward considers that the deciding factor for the producer was Nicola's voluptuousness. Having said this, however, he also accepts that she was the best candidate of all those auditioned. Clearly her attractive appearance and vivacious personality were more than sufficient to outweigh the fact that she lacked the blonde hair specified in the character outline. Another respect in which Nicola failed to meet the initial specifications was that she was not in fact an American – although neither producer nor script editor realised this at the time.

Nicola was born in a small village just outside Guildford in Surrey. 'It was the sort of village where everybody knew everybody else,' she explained in a 1992 interview for *The Frame*, 'and you daren't go out and play up because someone would tell your mother what you'd done. My father's central heating company was there and my mother's family had lived there all their lives. There was no entertainment background at all in my family, except for the fact that my uncle, my father's youngest brother, was very big in amateur dramatics – he actually met his wife while playing in *The Pyjama Game*. I thought he was very funny. I remember as a kid going to see him and thinking "that looks fun", even though I wasn't interested in being an actress at the time. I wanted to be Margot Fonteyn Mk II.

'From as early as I can remember, my very first thoughts were of dancing. I started taking dancing lessons at Bellairs Dance School when I was three, and dancing was all I wanted to do right up until I was eleven when I told my family that I wanted to go to ballet school. Choosing a career at that age is a very difficult thing to do and dancing was a very precarious business, so understandably my parents preferred me to stay at my current school where I could have a better standard of education. This was tough but they thought it was for the best.

'My mother, being such a wonderful woman, realised that I was very upset at their decision. Having noticed in a newspaper that a local amateur dramatics society were auditioning for parts in *Fiddler on the Roof*, she suggested that I go along, even though you had to be sixteen to join and I was much younger. I went for the audition and when they asked what O levels I was doing, I made them all up. I ended up getting the part of the second youngest daughter, and the lady who played my youngest sister was eighteen! They had absolutely no idea I was so young.

'I took all my O levels and A levels and did well, and my father was very pleased. I worked hard, all through the holidays. Boyfriends used to come round and knock on the door and ask if I could come out and I'd say "Oh, not now, I'm doing my Chemistry." I didn't want to go out with boys, I was busy working. I did ten O levels and one O/A level when I was fifteen, then went on to take A levels in Geography, Economics, English and Home Economics.

'Eventually I gave up dancing because the only classes I could now take were modern dance and tap. I didn't like them very much as I was classically trained and wanted to be a classical dancer, and as far as I was concerned anything else was just second best. Either you're going to be Margot Fonteyn or you're not. But I continued to appear in plays put on by the local company. After *Fiddler on the Roof*, I did *The Sound of Music, Snow White* . . . all musicals, simply because I enjoyed them.

'There was an unwritten agreement in our household that once I had done my O and A levels, my parents would support me in whatever I wanted to do. And what I wanted to do was to go to drama school. I wrote to all the accredited schools and got auditions for every one, but they were all sneering about my age. They said "You can't come here at sixteen or seventeen. We want experienced people, people who have been through things in their life." It seemed that they weren't really interested in how good you were, just in how old you were.

'Now, when I went to the auditions I noticed what type of person each school wanted. You're sitting around waiting before it's your turn to audition, and you see the students going past on their way to classes or whatever. You look at the photographs on the wall and can see who has got which part. It's all a case of how observant you are. After I had been turned down, I reapplied to the schools three months later and was accepted by them all. The reason was that, the second time, I acted my interviews. In other words I acted the part of the type of person I now knew each of them was looking for.

'The two most extreme were Central and Webber Douglas. For Central I frizzed my hair, put on black eyeliner and wore jeans in which I'd slashed holes long before it was fashionable to do so. Throughout the audition, I talked in a really common accent. At Webber Douglas, in contrast, I wore a full-length practice skirt, put my hair in a bun, wore

216

no make up, and was a very classical, serious young lady. When they mentioned my age, I turned to them and said, "I'd just like to ask you ...please don't judge someone by the number of birthdays they've had, but by the events that have occurred between them." And that seemed to do the trick.

'I ended up at Webber Douglas. I'm not sure what drama school teaches you, though. I suppose that if you can survive two or three years there then you can probably survive anything that gets thrown at you in the business. However, I came out after getting my diploma thinking that if that was what the acting business was like, then I didn't want to go into it. I found it so aggressive and bitchy, and it was very hard to strike up real friendships with people because everyone was so fiercely competitive. Maybe part of my difficulty was that I came from a very close and loving relationship with my mother, very intimate and supportive, and I was as a result much more sensitive. I pick things up about people and what they're thinking. I have very, very acute hearing. I can walk into a familiar room and tell if the battery needs changing in the clock, because I can hear that the ticking is at a different rhythm from the week before. I actually have to sleep with ear-plugs in because I hear so many sounds. One benefit of this is that I have perfect pitch and can pick up accents easily. The fact that my mother was deaf probably had something to do with it.

'The end-of-term play in my final year at Webber Douglas was the musical *No, No, Nanette*. A director came in from outside the school to audition us and we had about a week in which to prepare. I looked at the book and thought that I was ideally suited to the lead role: sweet, innocent – I *was* Nanette! But as far as singing went, I thought "forget it", because I had had no training. My fiancé at the time – Scott Kennedy, a singer who had played the lead in two or three Broadway musicals and who was at Webber Douglas doing a post-graduate course – encouraged me and said that of course I could do it. He coached me for a week and I just went for it. I auditioned and I read the piece and I sang the song. I didn't really think anything of it because I didn't think they'd give me the part – but they did!

'I was married to Scott at eighteen, incredibly young, in my final year at Webber Douglas, and then walked straight into *Doctor Who*. I told John Nathan-Turner that I was 21. I was trying to be older than I was, and I think it was odd for someone who looked even younger to be settled down and married. When I played Peri, I wore my wedding ring on another finger, but I never lied about being married. If I was ever asked, I wouldn't say yes or no, I'd simply say that there was just one person in my life.

'I was very lucky that I landed the part in *Doctor Who* because it gave me back a sense of family. Colin [Baker] and Peter [Davison] were very nice, and so especially was John. John was very paternal and took great care of me. I had three and a half years to develop a thick skin and to realise that there are lots of nice people in the business. I might come across a couple of right so-and-sos but the majority are all right. I think I was so lucky because otherwise I might have given it all up and tried to do something else: married the boss's son or something.

'When I auditioned for *Doctor Who*, John had no idea that I was not really American. I do have dual nationality through my marriage to Scott (although we're now separated), and also my room-mate at boarding school was from New York so I had picked up her accent. I had been playing an American in *No, No, Nanette* and an agent, Terry Carney, who came in to see it, assumed that I was American. He called me up and asked me to go and audition for *Doctor Who*. He didn't want to take on someone new out of drama school unless they had a job, so this was in his interest as well as mine. I told him that I wasn't strictly American but he told me to be American anyway. So I did and I thought that if they weren't happy with my American-ness, they'd just reject me. There was someone from Denver at the office and I thought that if I convinced him then I was doing all right.

'I went through several auditions until it finally got down to a choice between me and one other actress. They decided that they wanted me, but then of course I had to get my Equity card, because they couldn't let me have the part unless I was a member of the union. I had to get all my friends together and do cabaret work around some clubs to gain enough work experience to qualify for membership.'

One aspect of *Doctor Who* which makes it unlike other BBC dramas is the large amount of publicity which it often generates, particularly when there is a change of Doctor or of companion. In Nicola's case, this resulted in her first work being an interview for BBC's *Breakfast Time* programme on 6 July 1983.

'That was really bizarre. The first money I ever earned was from an interview on breakfast television! Funnily enough, Terry Carney hadn't wanted to draw up a contract with me at first, but when he saw me on TV in front of the cameras, he rang me that morning asking me to come in and sign a contract.'

Throughout this first interview for breakfast TV, Nicola maintained the pretence of being American. She used her 'Peri' American accent; she talked about driving, and the difference between the UK and the USA; she said she was 'an American playing an American part' but added (and demonstrated) that she could speak perfect standard English if she wanted to; she even said that she was 21 years old, and then got into a discussion about early *Doctor Who* stories and what she could remember about them.

At the time the interview was conducted, as the interviewers stressed, she had not actually recorded any *Doctor Who*, nor had she even met any of her co-stars, and all she had to go on with regard to the part she was to play was the original character outline. There was therefore only a limited range of questions which could be put to her. One thing which did come up, however, was the suggestion that she might be typecast as playing only American roles. No doubt this concern was justified at the time, but in retrospect Nicola feels very positive about the high profile she gained as a result of playing Peri.

'When I started in *Doctor Who*,' she told *The Frame*, 'I didn't realise how much emphasis the programme would end up placing on me and on my role in it. It was one of those fortunate – for me – bits of timing that the show went through a period of change just before I joined. There had been five companions – Nyssa, Turlough, Adric, Tegan and Kamelion – all working with one Doctor, and in a very short space of time it was back to just the one. Me. So I didn't have to share my dialogue with several others. My first story [*Planet of Fire*], shot in Lanzarote, represented an obvious injection of money and enthusiasm into the show, and it gained a lot of publicity, most of which featured me.'

In interpreting the part of Peri, Nicola was never in any doubt as to how she should be played.

'I knew exactly who she was from day one,' she explained in an interview for *Doctor Who Magazine*. 'I think you've got to. I don't think it's one of those parts that you can go into thinking "Oh, I'll see how she comes out," otherwise you can get yourself into all sorts of difficult situations. I started to think that there was a lot of me in the part as it was written. That's why I felt sure I could play her. But in the event I couldn't say really that there's more than half of me in Peri.'

One of the problems in playing a young, twentieth-century girl when you *are* a young, twentieth-century girl is this great temptation simply to play yourself. How does Nicola see herself as differing from the character she portrayed?

'If it had been Nicola Bryant travelling in the TARDIS rather than Peri Brown, I would not have been so easily *led* by the Doctor. I would have wanted to establish a different kind of relationship with him and I would have expected lessons on how to fly and operate the TARDIS, amongst other things. I think when I began on the show, Peri and I shared a similar adventurous quality mixed with a certain naïveté but that's where the similarity really ends. Many of Peri's reactions were actually based on that American friend of mine from boarding school. She too was away from home, on her own, and insecure – but so full of adventure.'

Nicola had envisaged Peri herself as being 'a naïve innocent; quite a spunky kid, but not really experienced, having a pretty sheltered upbringing, with a domineering mother and a stepfather who wasn't exactly a bundle of laughs'.

What happened in practice was that particular character traits were either emphasised or lost by successive writers on the show – a lack of continuity which Nicola found very off-putting: 'I would suddenly find that a writer had highlighted one particular aspect, which might be one which I had never seen as a major part of the character anyway.'

'The part of Peri was very bland,' asserts Eric Saward when asked about the way the character was treated, 'and writers will never respond to blandness. We did try to use her, but she was generally involved just in a sub-plot. This tends to happen with companions because, first, it gets them away from the Doctor so you don't have a constant inane dialogue going on and, secondly, it means that they can contribute to the story. Peri was used very much in that way, as Nyssa had been before her. She wasn't really developed because she wasn't very interesting as a character.

'I personally think that the companion should be strong. Of the ones with whom I was involved, I thought Tegan was the best, because she was ballsy and she had an energy. But John Nathan-Turner took a different view, and I always found it a struggle. Whenever the writers or I gave Tegan something strong to do, he'd stop it, saying that Tegan was a stupid, dumb Australian! Well, the actress, Janet Fielding, is neither stupid nor dumb, and the character she was playing was devised as a strong, independent woman. I thought it was pointless wasting her as we ended up doing. We could have developed her, had her acquiring skills under the tutelage of the Doctor, but we weren't allowed to. The same goes for Peri.'

Speaking to *Doctor Who Magazine*, Peter Grimwade confirmed that he had been asked by Saward to make Peri's debut a strong one, but that this strength had been rather lost along the way: 'The first draft I did, I made Peri a bit wimpish and vague and Eric said, "This is dreadful. I want her hard and gutsy," and I went away and really re-thought it.

'I came back with a much harder character. They actually used her opening scene as the audition piece, which was very pleasing. I felt I'd cracked it. Then this and other areas were shortened and re-written to accommodate different aspects of the location, because they'd found bits of Lanzarote that they liked.'

Nicola was never consulted by any of the writers regarding Peri's character, but she has a fondness for the scripts written by Philip Martin (*Vengeance on Varos, The Trial of a Time Lord 5–8*) and Robert Holmes (*The Caves of Androzani, The Trial of a Time Lord 1–4, 13*). 'They had real drama and strength in their episodes,' she explains. She also has no doubts as to which story she liked least. '*Timelash* was my pet hate. Nice ideas, shame about the constant harping back to the sixties victim role Peri played. It contained the same *Beauty and the Beast* idea as was in *The Caves of Androzani* but there Peri wasn't weak; she was sick, naïve and inquisitive but not pathetic.'

Peri certainly starts out well enough in *Planet of Fire*, the first of her eleven on-screen stories, which provides a good establishing framework and sketches in a character with some potential. She thinks nothing of attempting to swim a considerable distance to shore in order to escape from a boat on which she has been stranded – even if she does ultimately get into difficulty and has to be rescued by Turlough – and she stands up to the Master with bravado and bluster. It is obvious that Peri likes the fifth Doctor, and so it is perhaps unfortunate that *The Caves of Androzani*, their first full adventure together, is the last for that particular incarnation of the Time Lord. Here, Peri is initially quietly confident, clearly relaxed and happy in the Doctor's company. As the story progresses, however, she contracts spectrox toxæmia, and gradually descends into fever and delirium as the illness takes its toll – although she still manages to answer back to the unpredictable and unstable Sharaz Jek.

Following this escapade, Peri is faced with an unpredictable and unstable Doctor in *The Twin Dilemma*, and it is probably here that her character really starts to shine through. Her loyalty is very apparent as she stands by the much-changed Doctor – even when, in a fit of temporary insanity, he tries to kill her – and so is her resourcefulness as she takes the lead in exploring on Titan 3 and ultimately as she is left with Hugo Lang to hold the fort while the Doctor disposes of Mestor.

The problems with Peri's character really come to the fore in the 22nd season. It seems that, perhaps partly as a result of the switch to the 45-minute episode format, the majority of the writers had little idea of what to do with her. She is at times reduced to a cypher, simply the person to whom the Doctor explains the plot.

She certainly shows little bravado or resourcefulness in *Attack of the Cybermen*, and in *Vengeance on Varos* she becomes the archetypal damsel in distress when Quillam uses her in his transmogrification experiments. Obvious opportunities for use of the character are missed – for example, it is the Governor who persuades Maldak to free him and Peri from confinement when it could so easily have been Peri herself – and the story is dominated by the Doctor and Sil, who get all the best lines.

Matters improve somewhat in *The Mark of the Rani* as Peri is again allowed some independence. She suggests making a sleeping potion to help the afflicted miners – virtually the only occasion on which her experience as a botany student is put to good use – and agrees, albeit nervously, to escort the Master and the Rani as prisoners back to the Rani's TARDIS. She even manages to resist the Master's attempt to hypnotise her – one up to the writers – although she then lets herself down by falling for a rather obvious ploy on the part of the Rani.

Further good material for Peri comes in the next story, *The Two Doctors*, as she has a chance for a fight scene with the temporarily deranged Jamie on board the space station and later acts as a decoy at the hacienda by posing as a student calling for assistance.

This more effective handling of the character is short-lived, however, as in *Timelash* it is straight back to the damsel in distress routine. Again, opportunities are missed: Peri simply stumbles upon the Falchan Rocks instead of actively seeking them out after receiving a cryptic message about a rendezvous there; and she has to be rescued by Herbert when it would have been perfectly possible for her to have thought of using a flambeau herself to frighten off the inquisitive Morlox. Perhaps the worst aspect of *Timelash*, though, is the illogical plot point that the

Borad falls instantly in love with Peri, and then wants to alter her appearance – the only thing which could have attracted him to her in the first place, since he had never met her. This whole subtext, that a woman is worthwhile only because of what she looks like, really had no place in a television programme of the eighties.

The final story of the season, *Revelation of the Daleks*, sees some attempt being made to establish a better rapport between Peri and the Doctor. Another plus point is that, as in *The Mark of the Rani*, Peri is not totally the helpless bystander – she beats off the mutant attacking the Doctor and later manages to elude the fawning Jobel with both verbal and physical rebuffs. Unfortunately, this refreshing self-assurance was never developed further.

What then happened was that *Doctor Who* took an eighteen-month break from the nation's screens following the decision to cancel the original Season 23. During this longer-than-usual pause in production, Nicola and Colin Baker decided that Peri and the Doctor could not go on as they had been. The whinging American wimp that Peri was becoming was not working, and the two actors decided between themselves that, whatever future scripts be might like, they would do their best to show that travelling in each other's company had changed them both.

The Trial of a Time Lord consequently presents viewers with a slightly mellower Doctor, and with a Peri not quite so at odds with him and with their life together. Peri's final two adventures show her at her best. The first segment of the Trial has her going through some highly emotional situations as she grieves the fate of her planet and then has to face the grim prospect of a life of enforced baby-making at the hands of the Tribe of the Free, while the second gives her perhaps the best characterisation and development she ever had. With the Doctor having apparently lost his mind, it is up to Peri to calm the tempestuous Yrcanos, to talk the strangely bland Tuza around to the fact that they are not his enemies, and to attempt to help her fellow traveller as best she can. For this to be Peri's swan song is fitting, as it illuminates previously unexplored aspects of her character and leaves the viewer wanting more.

The two stories of Season 23 are however overshadowed by the bulk of the previous season, in which Peri was simply a victim to be used in order to generate exciting plot twists as the writers saw fit, or simply as a sounding board to explain proceedings to the viewers. This 'generic companion' aspect of the role is what irritated Nicola Bryant most. 'Having talked to the other girls who had played companions,' she told *Doctor Who Magazine*, 'I realised that we had all had the same problem, that just occasionally we would get a story which didn't really seem to be related to our character, but to the *Doctor Who* "companion of all time".'

Part of the identity of any character, whether on stage, film or television, is established by the costumes they wear. After the departure of Romana in 1980, the *Doctor Who* companions, in common with the Doctors themselves, generally wore 'uniforms' rather than 'clothes'; that is, they tended to wear either exactly the same outfits for every story, or slight variations on a theme. As clothes reflect personality, it is not really surprising that as the clothes became fixed, so did the personalities behind them. Peri was no exception to the rule.

The costumes with which Nicola was presented for Peri were both eye-catching and colourful, but not exactly what she would have chosen herself. The Peri 'look' – generally consisting of figure-hugging shorts and skin-tight leotards – apparently came about because of the clothes Nicola chose to wear to her first photo-call. 'I thought she looked so stunning', relates John Nathan-Turner, 'that I asked our costume designers to echo Nicola's own clothes!'

Nicola, however, recalls that there was slightly more to it than that. 'I was asked to bring several outfits along for the photo call,' she says, 'and "short and very fitting" was the description I was given. I never wore short skirts and clingy-fitting tops myself – all I possessed were a pair of shorts and a leotard. I asked John if this would be okay and he said "Great!" Unfortunately, he liked it so much that we got stuck with it.'

The result was a succession of costumes which left very little to the imagination, and which were usually wholly unsuited to the weather on location.

'We filmed *The Caves of Androzani* in Devon,' Nicola recalled in *Doctor Who Magazine*. 'But it was very cold and I had no way of wrapping up, because my costume was in direct continuity from the previous story. I was wearing the same clothes I had worn in Lanzarote. I remember the cameraman saying "Slap your face, love, you're going blue." I got frostbite, then pneumonia. Then Peter [Davison] fell ill too – it was a pretty rough shoot.

'In *Attack of the Cybermen* I started out in a shocking pink leotard and shorts, then got into a sort of red jump-suit. In *Vengeance on Varos* I had a blue leotard and shorts . . . They went out first and bought the shorts – pink, turquoise and even a pair in yellow – and then tried to find matching leotards. In *The Two Doctors* I wore a psychedelic thing which glistened nicely in the sun, but filming in Seville the temperature reached 102 degrees and it was like a thermal blanket – I felt like a roast chicken! I could have used that in Devon!'

She has a pragmatic attitude towards the costumes, however. 'I think that's one of the unfortunate things that comes with the part. The newspapers always want something extra. There's nothing I could have done to escape it, and I wasn't in a position to do so. Other actresses who came into the show often said, "Why don't you put your foot down and say no?" My reply was, "Look, I'd rather be playing Peri and wear that than not be playing Peri." There's just no point in jumping up and down screaming about it. I hoped that a few people would look beyond all that, at the face and at the acting, and judge me on those things rather than on just the outward appearance.

'I was a lot happier with the more realistic costumes I wore during my last season. It was a relief – especially in Britain's climate. I think the things I wore in that season reflected Peri's character slightly more as I had originally seen her. I still had no choice as to what they were, though.'

So what would Nicola's own choice of costumes have been?

'*Planet of Fire* was fine by me, but afterwards I would have been in jeans, T-shirts, sweat-shirts and sneakers. That's the way I saw Peri. Back to shorts in Seville for *The Two Doctors* and then of course period costume for *The Mark of the Rani*. Peri should have worn basically the kind of clothes that real American students lived in – casual clothes of the eighties. I think to have been in jeans and sensible shoes would have added to that more spunky independent feel that Peri began with.'

Nicola joined the series not long before her original co-star, Peter Davison, left. 'I first met Peter at the studio when I came to watch an episode being recorded. I was amazed at how long the hours were. I remember that when I started the shoot in Lanzarote, the director Fiona Cumming said to me, "Just watch Peter as often as you can," so I did, and in that way I learned an awful lot about acting in a short amount of time.'

Nicola recalls that she was initially rather nervous and unsure about the new Doctor, Colin Baker, 'mainly because Peter had been winding me up, saying everything and nothing. He would say "So, you're working with Colin Baker . . . Well, if you have any problems you just call me. And good luck!"

'After a rather bumpy start, Colin and I turned out to be great mates. As actors we have the same strong feelings about our characters – something which even now when we work on video projects together unites us and makes us a strong team. I think it's also to do with the fact that we trust each other on several levels. Colin was really there for me in a very quiet and special way when my Dad died, and that means a lot.'

Nicola decided to leave *Doctor Who* during the 23rd season simply because she felt that three years working on one show was enough. 'As an actor I had to say "Right, okay, I'm going to get out there and see what else there is." I was happy to do so in that I felt that I wanted to go and do something else, but sad to be leaving such a nice bunch of people behind.'

If she could give some advice now, to herself as she was then, what would it be?

'I would tell myself to have even more fun than I did. I was a little more serious then than I am now and perhaps if I had relaxed a little more, then I could have enjoyed it even more than I did.'

It is ultimately down to the production team whether a companion works or fails, and certain key qualities must be present if she is to inspire the writers to use and develop her. Eric Saward's concept of a really strong character was not to see fruition during his tenure on the show and it subsequently fell to his successor, Andrew Cartmel, to create arguably the true 'eighties' companion in Ace. It clearly helps if the producer and the script editor are in accord as to the treatment of the character, and this appears not to have been the case where Perpugilliam Brown was concerned. However, the fact that she is still recalled with so much affection by so many viewers must surely be a testament to the skills of all those involved in bringing her to life.

9: Selling the Doctor

Media

During the eighties, *Doctor Who* enjoyed a healthy relationship with the media. John Nathan-Turner often played the newspapers at their own game, creating 'news opportunities' at every turn and maximising the impact of those celebrity actors and actresses who agreed to appear in the show with strategically arranged press and photo calls.

During the two seasons (and one story) that Colin Baker played the Doctor, almost every story received some news coverage, whether it be because of who was appearing in it, or because of the location, or the monsters, or the companions, or sometimes all of these together.

Such was *Doctor Who*'s press potential for the BBC that their Press Information pack for the week beginning Saturday 17 March had a photograph of Colin Baker on the front announcing that he was the sixth Doctor.

When Colin's appointment was announced on 20 August 1983, there was a wealth of press coverage, but, strangely, the *Daily Telegraph* and the *Daily Express* made no mention of the fact that not long before this they had both announced a completely different actor, Brian Blessed, as having been chosen to play the part. The *Daily Express* report, in the edition dated 1 August, had stated unequivocally that Blessed was to play the sixth incarnation of the Time Lord, had given a brief biography of him, and had even pointed out that his appointment quashed rumours that the next Doctor would be a woman, claiming that BBC chiefs had even described the kind of woman that they had been looking for!

The next major press call was on Tuesday 10 January 1984, when Colin's new costume was unveiled to the waiting lenses of Fleet Street. The following day, 'The Tasteless Time Lord' and 'Who's the height of bad taste?' were the headlines as John Nathan-Turner was quoted describing the Doctor's outfit as 'totally tasteless'. Almost every newspaper covered the story, many of them in colour. Then, not long afterwards, yet another photo-call was arranged to publicise the first episode of *The Twin Dilemma*. All in all, Colin Baker probably had more press coverage to launch his Doctor than did any of his predecessors.

A part of this interest was a story run in the *Sun* and the *Daily Star* concerning the fact that Colin and his wife Marion had lost their first child, Jack, to the Sudden Infant Death Syndrome four months previously. Although the *Sun* had run the news of Jack's birth in October 1983, and had also covered the tragic death in November, they considered the story worth repeating, apparently with additional comments from Colin. Colin was determined to use the exposure that *Doctor Who* was to give him to campaign and raise money for the Foundation for the Study of Infant Deaths.

Further media interest was created when John Nathan-Turner 'accidentally' let slip that the Doctor would be getting rid of the TARDIS's familiar shape as most viewers no longer knew what a police box was. This resulted in a deluge of viewers' letters to the BBC and newspapers jumping on the 'Save the TARDIS' bandwagon. One paper even ran a competition to design an exterior for the Doctor's timeship. In the event, of course, even though the Doctor got the TARDIS to change shape a couple of times in *Attack of the Cybermen*, it otherwise remained in the trusty form viewers knew and loved. The *Sun* claimed that this was totally down to its campaign, proclaiming on 17 November 1983 that it had saved the TARDIS from the scrap heap.

For the 22nd season, there was press interest aplenty when Prince Andrew's ex-girlfriend, photographer Koo Stark, was announced as featuring in the new series. This guest appearance was not to be, however, the *Sun* explaining on 18 June 1984 that Stark had been dropped from the role after a row over publicity.

Despite this setback, *Doctor Who*'s aptitude for attracting top names to its cast meant that the BBC soon had further media personalities to parade before the press. On 3 July, comedienne and impressionist Faith Brown was announced as a forthcoming guest star, and on 15 July, Sarah Berger was reported to be replacing Koo Stark as one of the Cryons in *Attack of the Cybermen*. Another Cryon was to be played by ex-*Blue Peter* presenter Sarah Greene. 'Koo missed out on a lot of fun,' said Greene.

Further names announced in the *Daily Star* on 5 January 1985 were Alexei Sayle, Eleanor Bron, Terence Alexander, Martin Jarvis, Frazer Hines, Jason Connery and Jacqueline Pearce. Colin Baker was reported as having the 'best job on television'. 'It's like being a grown-up who is getting paid to play cowboys and Indians, it's great fun,' he said.

As the season progressed, *The Mark of the Rani* received coverage because of the presence of the Master, while *The Two Doctors* made the news, because Frazer Hines apparently needed hardly any make-up to re-create his role as Jamie.

Of course, while *The Two Doctors* was being shown, news of a far more dramatic nature broke: *Doctor Who* was being rested for eighteen months. The full story of this turbulent period in *Doctor Who*'s history is covered in chapter 7 of this book.

After all the media hype about the postponement had died down, the press turned its attention to publicising the 23rd season. The series was heralded as coming back 'for a laugh', those anonymous 'BBC chiefs' that the newspapers loved quoting having felt that it was too violent and needed an injection of humour. This approach was apparently confirmed by the casting of *Carry On . . .* actress Joan Sims in the first segment of the story. Some interest was also shown because of the Trial theme of the season, which echoed the feelings of those BBC chiefs. The guest stars found themselves the centre of attention, as once again the programme was promoted on its ability to attract star names. This time it was the turn of Michael Jayston, Lynda Bellingham, Joan Sims, Tony Selby, Brian Blessed, Patrick Ryecart, Geoffrey Hughes, Christopher Ryan, Honor Blackman and Michael Craig who all featured in the reports.

Ultimately, following all the press coverage of the postponement, which included in the *Sun* some damning indictments by Colin Baker of BBC1's Controller Michael Grade, the news broke on 13 December 1986 that Baker had been 'sacked' from the role of the Doctor, reportedly because of these comments. His contract had not been renewed, but Bonnie Langford's had. It later transpired that Colin had been offered four episodes at the start of the 24th season to make a final story, but had declined them, not wishing to have to forego other work in the interim.

The hunt was now on for Doctor number seven.

Companions

As always, the press were very keen to feature the Doctor's companions, mainly because they tended to be pretty young women. In the case of Nicola Bryant, the tabloids had a field day.

'Naughty Nicola' screamed the headline in the *Daily Star*, which reported that fans were apparently up in arms because her outfits were too sexy. This outcry came as *Vengeance on Varos* was being screened, and Nicola's tight blue leotard-top and shorts left little to the imagination. 'Red-faced mums and dads want her to wear more modest outfits and hide her ample charms,' said Geoff Baker, writing in the *Daily Star* on 26 January 1985. Sexy the outfits may have been, but the show had again managed to achieve almost a full two-page spread, advertising the series, on the day it was transmitted.

When reporting Nicola's departure from the series, some newspapers even found some photographs of her posing with nothing but a smile and a towel. It is perhaps inevitable that the tabloid press will latch on to anything if it is sold to them with a little sex appeal – a fact that the *Doctor Who* production office knew and used to maximise publicity.

When Bonnie Langford was announced on 23 January 1986 as being the replacement for Nicola, the press were, for once, a little confounded. Here they were presented with a 'name', someone of whom they had all heard, and who was arguably more famous than the actor playing the Doctor. There was also no way they could present Bonnie Langford as a sex object, which, given their established attitude towards 'the *Doctor Who* girl', also caused them difficulties. To introduce Langford to the public, the BBC staged a press call at the London theatre where Langford was appearing in *Peter Pan*. Colin Baker, looking somewhat chubby after five or so months with little work, was squeezed into a flying harness, and the two of them were photographed clowning about against a starry background.

Picking up on Colin's apparent increase in weight, the *Daily Record* provided the news that the first thing Langford would do in the series was to put the Doctor on a diet.

The introduction of Bonnie's character Mel in *The Trial of a Time Lord* was followed up with another press call, this time with Colin sporting a moustache and a beard, grown following his departure from the series. The pair fooled about on this occasion with a pair of garden shears.

Personal appearances

While *Doctor Who* may not have been as popular with the viewing public at this point as perhaps it had been in the past, the producer and his stars were out and about almost constantly promoting the series.

John Nathan-Turner appeared on the BBC1 children's show *Saturday Superstore* talking to presenter Mike Reid about the TARDIS's police box shape being replaced. He said that the office was being bombarded with petitions, but stressed that no decision had yet been taken – he and his team were just thinking about it.

The Kenilworth Agricultural Show over the August bank holiday weekend in 1984 played host to a number of *Doctor Who* stars during its three-day run. These included Colin Baker and Nicola Bryant, who turned out to promote both the programme and John Nathan-Turner's forthcoming pantomime production, *Cinderella*, in which they would both appear.

The week before part one of *The Twin Dilemma* was transmitted, Colin Baker appeared on *Blue Peter* to publicise the story. A lengthy clip was shown of Mestor in his throne room speaking to Azmael and of the Doctor and Peri investigating the wreckage of Hugo Lang's ship. This was followed by a further clip of the Doctor attacking Peri in the TARDIS. Presenter Janet Ellis explained that both Colin and Nicola would be on *Saturday Superstore* that coming weekend. There, the pair answered questions and took phone calls, including one from 'the Master' (actor Anthony Ainley), who warned that he would be coming from the depths of hell to haunt the Doctor. He challenged the Doctor in his new guise to settle their feud once and forever. Colin (as the Doctor) accepted the challenge, and the Master then rang off.

Later in the programme, Colin's handwriting was analysed by an expert in that field. Not knowing whose it was, she came to the conclusion that he was well travelled, well educated and had a very inquiring mind. She recommended a job in which he could do his own thing, as he was too independent to go along with group decisions. She also felt that he saw his rightful place as being at the top, that he had a great sense of timing and presentation and that he appeared to have an affinity for detailed analytical work. She suggested that he would make a good barrister. She added that he liked to work things out for himself, that he liked to cut a dash, and that his clothing would have a certain panache as a result. Colin felt that this summation was partly accurate.

The same week, Colin, together with Peter Davison, also appeared on *Harty*, the weekly chat show presented by Russell Harty; and, on the actual morning of the day of the first episode's transmission, he and Nicola guested on the BBC's *Breakfast Time* show with Selina Scott and Frank Bough.

Take Two, a children's version of the *Did You See* viewers' correspondence programme, spoke to John Nathan-Turner about the series. Children they had interviewed felt that Colin Baker was too young to play the Doctor, and that Peri whined too much and had a disagreeable accent. They didn't appear to be frightened by the monsters, and cited the Daleks and the Cybermen as their favourites. However, the feeling was expressed that *Doctor Who* was shown too early for younger children. Nathan-Turner explained that the show was going out later than it ever had been, and that the intention was not to terrify, just occasionally to scare.

As the 22nd season got under way, Colin, Nicola, Mary Tamm and Jacqueline Pearce all appeared on the *Saturday Superstore* of 5 January 1985 to promote John Nathan-Turner's *Cinderella* pantomime, which was playing in Southampton at the time. They did, however, find time to answer questions from viewers about *Doctor Who*.

Towards the end of 1985, Lenny Henry turned his satirical eye on *Doctor Who* and presented in the edition of *The Lenny Henry Show* broadcast on 2 October a sketch featuring himself as the Doctor. The TARDIS – in fact the Master's TARDIS control room set from *Planet of Fire* – brings the Doctor and Peri to Earth in the future. The planet is now controlled by the most ruthless woman in the Universe, Thatchos, who threatens to have them privatised. They escape in the TARDIS, where Peri wants to use the fact that they are no longer on television to get to know the Doctor better.

Shortly after this, on 22 November, the BBC's annual *Children In*

Need fund-raising telethon saw no fewer than twenty *Doctor Who* stars presenting a cheque for £1000 to Terry Wogan. The money had been collected earlier in the year at the *Doctor Who* exhibition on Blackpool's Golden Mile, during a special appearance by Colin Baker and Nicola Bryant to sign autographs and meet the fans.

In the studio to present the cheque were Patrick Troughton, Carole Ann Ford, Maureen O'Brien, Peter Purves, Michael Craze, Adrienne Hill, Jon Pertwee, Caroline John, Nicholas Courtney, Richard Franklin, John Levene, Elisabeth Sladen, Louise Jameson, Ian Marter, Peter Davison, Janet Fielding, Matthew Waterhouse, Mark Strickson, Nicola Bryant and Colin Baker. This was the biggest assembly of *Doctor Who* cast members ever achieved in this country. A cheque for £100 was also presented by Patrick Troughton on behalf of the *Doctor Who* Appreciation Society.

The *Doctor Who* exhibition at Blackpool had been running for ten years, but at the end of October 1985 it closed its doors for the last time. The lease on the building in which it was housed had expired, and many of the costumes and props contained there were needed to fit out a massive *Doctor Who* exhibition bus which was to tour America. The new exhibition was contained in a trailer, 48 feet long, which was too large to travel on Britain's roads. It was designed by BBC designer Tony Burrough. Artist Andrew Skilleter created huge *Doctor Who* murals for the sides and interiors and the whole thing was sent over to America, where, on 9 May 1986, it was launched on its tour by Peter Davison and Michael Grade in New York. The tour was joined at various points by stars from the programme, including Tom Baker and Colin Baker, and was very well received.

Doctor Who appeared on ice in 1986 when, from 14 June until 1 November, an eight-minute *Doctor Who* segment was included in the annual Ice Spectacular show at Blackpool.

Also in 1986, the French TV network TF1 bought *Doctor Who* to the screen in their *Temps X* programme. To publicise the series, they put together a documentary called *Who is Who*, and even arranged for some of the *Doctor Who* novels to be reprinted in French, featuring the two presenters of *Temps X* on the covers.

On 25 August 1986, Colin Baker and Lynda Bellingham appeared on *Wogan* talking about Colin's acting career and the new season of *Doctor Who* starting on 6 September. The show also featured a Mandrel (from *Nightmare of Eden*) and a Sea Devil Warrior (from *Warriors of the Deep*) wandering about the studio.

Bonnie Langford made an appearance on *The Saturday Picture Show* on 6 September 1986, primarily to talk about the tour of *Peter Pan*, although *Doctor Who* did get a brief mention. A clip from the end of *Revelation of the Daleks* was shown – strangely, as Langford did not appear in it – leading into a brief clip from the start of the new series.

Colin Baker appeared as the Doctor on 13 September to introduce Roland Rat at the start of that week's episode of *Roland Rat – The Series*.

The next major *Doctor Who* feature on TV was again on *Saturday Superstore*, Sarah Greene and Mike Reid playing host on 29 November 1986 to a TARDIS full of *Doctor Who* monsters and Time Lords to celebrate 23 years of *Doctor Who*. To fill the *Doctor Who* costumes, the producers of *Saturday Superstore* contacted the DWAS, and arranged for a group of fans to come along and wander about dressed as Cybermen, Mandrels, Sea Devils and Time Lords. Colin Baker was also in the studio to talk about the series, and the regular 'pop panel' was enlivened by 'Tony the Cyberman' (played by DWAS Co-ordinator Tony Jordan and voiced by David J. Howe) commenting on the videos and attempting to destroy Mike Reid in the process. The programme ended with the cutting of a special TARDIS-shaped cake.

America

In the mid-eighties, *Doctor Who* was amongst the top ten bestselling British TV programmes overseas, reaching 54 different countries and attaining world-wide viewing figures estimated at 110 million. One of the series' most important markets was the United States of America.

Since the start of the eighties, *Doctor Who* had become more and more popular with American fans, and this popularity peaked during the period when the sixth Doctor was appearing on British television screens.

As with Peter Davison and Nicola Bryant before him, Colin Baker's first convention appearance was in the USA, at Panopticon West in Ohio in July 1984, and he also guested at the massive annual convention in Chicago in November of that year, organised by the commercial Spirit of Light company. This frustrated and infuriated the organisers of Britain's *Doctor Who* Appreciation Society (DWAS), who felt that their members were losing out to their American counterparts, as had been the case the previous year when no Doctors had been available for the biggest British fan convention to celebrate the series' twentieth anniversary as they were all being paid to attend the convention in Chicago. *Doctor Who* was, as usual, generally not being repeated in Britain – the latest repeats had been *The King's Demons, The Awakening* and *The Five Doctors* in 1984 during the break between the 21st and 22nd seasons – but in America it was being shown almost non-stop every day on Public Broadcasting Service channels. The fact that the American fans were now meeting new Doctors before their British counterparts added to the sense of injustice which many of the latter felt.

What British fans often overlooked, however, was the fact that their fellow devotees in the States outnumbered them by at least ten to one at this point. The *Doctor Who* Fan Club of America boasted some 30,000 members and could reasonably be considered to have been the hub of *Doctor Who* fandom in the mid-eighties.

The early US convention appearances by Colin Baker – who would later be extremely generous with his time in attending numerous British events – were partly down to the influence of John Nathan-Turner, who had apparently foregone British fandom in his desire to woo the Americans with the programme and its stars. The BBC themselves were certainly not going to object to this as they were gaining valuable overseas sales of the show, not to mention a sizeable income from the masses of licensed merchandise being produced in the States. By June 1985, *Doctor Who* was being seen in 146 American markets, covering 70 per cent of the country.

New Zealand

New Zealand was another country in which *Doctor Who* was extremely popular during the mid-eighties – and for this section we are grateful to Paul Scoones and Jon Preddle of the New Zealand *Doctor Who* fan club for information and research assistance.

1984, the year that Colin Baker took over as the Doctor, was also the first time since 1964 that Television New Zealand (TVNZ) had shown no *Doctor Who* at all. However, in July of that year, TVNZ promised that *Doctor Who* would be back towards the end of the year with a special season of repeats. These repeats actually started on 12 April 1985 with *The Mind Robber* and *The Krotons*, and continued with the first fifteen Pertwee stories up to *The Three Doctors*. The episodes were screened two at a time, back to back, and TVNZ had edited them slightly, adjusting the title sequences. The stories shown were a mixture of black and white and colour. Stories from which episodes were available in both black and white and colour (*The Ambassadors of Death* and *The Daemons*) were transmitted in black and white throughout.

1986 saw the start of the longest uninterrupted run of *Doctor Who* episodes on TVNZ, lasting over three years and consisting of 273 episodes. The episodes were variously screened at once a week, then twice a week. They started with *Carnival of Monsters* and went right through to *Snakedance*, with some screenings in November 1988 to celebrate the 25th anniversary of *Doctor Who: The Dalek Invasion of Earth*, *The Seeds of Death*, *Revelation of the Daleks* and *Silver Nemesis*.

This epic schedule included stories which had never been screened in New Zealand before (*Genesis of the Daleks, Horror of Fang Rock, The Sun Makers* and *The Invasion of Time*, as well as all the 25th anniversary stories listed above) and also netted a first for New Zealand. Their transmission of *Silver Nemesis* was partly prior to the UK transmission. In the UK, part 1 was shown on 23 November, with parts two and three on 30 November and 7 December respectively. In New Zealand, all three episodes were shown on 25 November. This is only the second time that *Doctor Who* episodes have not premiered in the UK. The first occasion was when *The Five Doctors* was first screened in America two days before the UK transmission to celebrate the 20th anniversary of the show.

The first that New Zealand viewers saw of Colin Baker's Doctor was the screening of *Revelation of the Daleks* in 1988 – the story being chosen as it featured the Daleks. The remainder of the Season 22 stories were held over until the following year, 1989, when *The Twin Dilemma* through to *Timelash* were shown in 25-minute episodes. *The Trial of a Time Lord* and also a repeat of *Revelation of the Daleks* were screened in 1990.

While the 22nd season was being criticised in the UK by the National Viewers' and Listeners' Association, headed by Mary Whitehouse, viewers in New Zealand had to contend with both the Australian ABC and TVNZ taking their scissors to several episodes. *Vengeance on Varos* lost a total of 8 minutes 31 seconds, with just over 5 minutes cut from part three. *The Two Doctors* had 4 minutes 36 seconds cut from episodes two to six, *The Mark of the Rani* lost 15 seconds from episodes two to four and *Timelash* lost 4 minutes 11 seconds in total. *Revelation of the Daleks* had been cut by ABC prior to it being transmitted on TVNZ, and while TVNZ removed some additional footage before its first transmission, the second time around just the ABC cuts were in evidence, totalling 3 minutes 43 seconds (NB figures unavailable for part two). Both *Vengeance on Varos* and *The Two Doctors* were also cut by both ABC and TVNZ.

For *The Trial of a Time Lord*, only parts nine (2 minutes 30 seconds) and fourteen (8 minutes 11 seconds) were edited, the latter presumably in part because of its extended running time.

The ratings system in New Zealand is somewhat different from that in the UK. Stories are given a percentage based on an assumed potential viewing audience of 3,038,000 people. The top-rated programmes usually receive around one million viewers (33%). No ratings are available for episodes since November 1989, and they are derived from each quarter of an hour of viewing time. For the *Doctor Who* ratings listed here they have been averaged out, and then the single episode results averaged to give an overall story average. The figures were compiled by David Bishop from the official AGB:McNair television ratings collected each week from sample surveys in New Zealand.

For the Colin Baker stories screened in New Zealand, the ratings were as follows:

The Twin Dilemma – 8%
Attack of the Cybermen – 6.2%
Vengeance on Varos – 6.5%
The Two Doctors – 6.7%
The Mark of the Rani – 4.5%
Timelash – 3.2%

By way of comparison, the top-rated *Doctor Who* stories in the repeats from 1985 to 1989 were *The Hand of Fear* (14.1%), *The Robots of Death* (13.4%) and *The Deadly Assassin* (12.4%). Analysis of all the ratings suggests that the fluctuation is due mainly to the time of year the stories were transmitted – better ratings during the winter months – rather than from any value judgement taking place. The timeslot is also considered to be of importance, with a Friday/

Tuesday/Wednesday slot doing well, but a Thursday/Friday slot faring badly. Incidentally, for this period, the lowest rating was received by *The Seeds of Death* (2.4%) during the 25th anniversary week, with *Timelash* close behind it.

Overall, viewers in New Zealand have fared far better than their UK counterparts, with *Doctor Who* screened almost non-stop over a three-year period, featuring every available story from the third to the sixth Doctor, together with a few gems from the first and second Doctors thrown in for good measure.

Fandom

As already noted, the main *Doctor Who* fan activity during the Colin Baker era took place in the USA. In addition to the numerous conventions, the *Doctor Who* Fan Club of America – a commercial organisation run by Ron Katz and Chad Roark – offered their members, reported to number some 30,000, a regular newspaper, *The Whovian Times*. This contained interviews with the series' stars and columns by John Nathan-Turner and, providing all the latest British news, writer Jeremy Bentham. The pages of the newspaper also featured numerous adverts for the masses of BBC-licensed (and, in some cases, possibly unlicensed) merchandise items produced in the States at this time, including T-shirts, jackets, mugs, key-fobs, pens, model kits and towels. Readers were even given regular invitations to join an organisation called the Gallifrey Beach and Body Club!

In Britain, the *Doctor Who* Appreciation Society (DWAS), the only official fan group in this country, was still growing steadily following publicity gained at the twentieth anniversary BBC convention at Longleat in 1983 and subsequent advertising in Marvel Comics' *Doctor Who Magazine*. The Society's newsletter, *Celestial Toyroom*, continued to appear on a regular monthly basis, and the news, as one would expect, covered all the major events of the time.

Apart from Marvel's official *Doctor Who Magazine*, in which news was scant and consisted mainly of brief details about forthcoming stories, the other main source of *Doctor Who* information was a monthly fanzine, *Doctor Who Bulletin*, edited and published by Gary Levy (who later changed his name to Gary Leigh). Levy had started *DWB* because he was interested in magazines and their production, and also in *Doctor Who*. He was a member of the DWAS and felt that he could improve on the news aspect of their newsletter. In contrast to *Celestial Toyroom* and *Doctor Who Magazine*, which tended to report news and current events without comment, *DWB*'s editorial style was highly outspoken and controversial. Also unlike the other two publications, *DWB* showed no hesitation in printing information before it had been either confirmed or denied officially. *DWB* started out with a fairly positive attitude towards *Doctor Who* and its producer but, following the postponement of Season 23, the fanzine took on a far more critical and negative stance.

The influence of American fandom made itself known to British fans in July of 1984 when the planned annual DWAS convention, Panopticon VI, scheduled for 23, 24 and 25 November 1984, had to be postponed as on those dates all the potential guests were going to be at the huge commercial Spirit of Light convention in America, which had just had its dates rescheduled from October. The British event was eventually moved to 26, 27 and 28 July 1985 and took place at the Brighton Metropole hotel. The event was notable for featuring the first and only British fan convention appearance of Patrick Troughton. While the convention went ahead and was reasonably successful, when it was all over the DWAS was left with a hefty bill to pay and insufficient funds to do so. The society's newsletter reported that the convention's finances had been mismanaged by its organisers.

As the DWAS' Co-ordinator, David Saunders, had resigned just prior to the convention, his successor, Tony Jordan, together with the rest of the DWAS Executive, now had to recover the Society from the brink of bankruptcy, while continuing to provide members with a reasonable service. To this end, the newsletter and the Society magazine, *TARDIS*, were merged, and the membership fee increased from six to eight pounds a year. With these measures in place, planning tentatively started towards the end of 1985 on the next big convention, this time with an edict to put the Society back on a sound financial footing, and with a new team doing the organising.

The resultant convention, Panopticon VII, was praised by fans as being the best the DWAS had ever organised. There was the added bonus for attendees of being able to watch the first episode of *The Trial of a Time Lord* on a big convention screen along with 500 of their fellow devotees. This screening was for some the highlight of the event and was described as 'electrifying' by those present.

At the end of 1986, after a great deal of hard work, the Society was again financially stable, and Tony Jordan, feeling that he had done what he was brought onto the Executive to do, moved on. He was succeeded by Andrew Beech, who was to steer the DWAS into yet another new era of *Doctor Who*.

One other UK fan activity of note from this period is Fan Aid. This was the brainchild of Paul Cornell, who decided to raise money for famine relief in Ethiopia spurred on by the Live Aid concert and Band Aid record for the same cause. Paul, along with many other helpers and assistants, organised a very successful convention in Bath, released some interesting and informative fanzines, and managed to raise £2,165.

Merchandise

While popularity in the programme may have been slipping somewhat as far as the ratings and the BBC were concerned, from the point of view of the merchandisers, things had never looked better.

There were just over 200 individual items of merchandise issued during the Colin Baker era, which is 100 per cent more than was released in the whole of the sixties. Whereas in the sixties the items were very diverse, in the mid-eighties the releases tended to be concentrated in three areas: books, metal miniatures and videos.

W. H. Allen continued releasing novelisations of *Doctor Who* stories, and when Nigel Robinson took over as editor of the range, he started to look into the past for the books rather than to the present series. Under Robinson's enthusiastic editorship, novels of first and second Doctor stories started appearing, as well as filling in the gaps for all the other Doctors.

When W. H. Allen contacted Colin Baker's agent about using his likeness on the covers of the books, they offered a single fee in lieu of a royalty. Baker's agent asked if a royalty could be negotiated instead but the publishers refused and did not contact the agent again. As a result, Baker's face did not appear on any of the first-edition covers of the novelisations of his stories. An illustration of the sixth Doctor, intended for the novelisation of *The Twin Dilemma*, was not used on the book and artist Andrew Skilleter was asked by the publishers to paint a new cover illustration at short notice.

W. H. Allen were, along with all the other merchandisers, reaping the rewards of the increased popularity of *Doctor Who* in America, and all manner of 'factual' books appeared, some with only a very tenuous connection with the series. This, however, did not appear to matter, as if the product had 'Doctor Who' on the cover it sold. Hence we saw the *Doctor Who Cookbook* compiled by Gary Downie, who had choreographed the dance sequences in *Black Orchid* and who had also worked as production assistant on several *Doctor Who* stories (recipes provided by numerous *Doctor Who* cast and production members); *Travel Without the TARDIS*, written by two American fans (an American's guide to visiting *Doctor Who* locations in Britain); *Doctor Who* quiz books; and, most obscure of all, the *Doctor Who Pattern Book* by Joy Gammon (knitting and sewing patterns – make your own woolly cybermat!). Even John Nathan-Turner turned his hand to writing and brought us *Doctor Who – The TARDIS Inside Out*, in which he presented his memories of the actors who have played the Doctor, and *Doctor Who – The Companions* where he did the same for the companions. While not being as bad as some of the other publications, these volumes were a little slim, and in the case of the companions volume, some additional research on those actors and actresses with whom Nathan-Turner had not worked would not have gone amiss.

There were some highly acclaimed books, too, and top of the pile was J. Jeremy Bentham's *Doctor Who – The Early Years*. Published by W. H. Allen, this told of the factual creation of the Daleks, and presented numerous design drawings and photographs from the extensive collection of ex-BBC designer Raymond P. Cusick. Bentham had organised the *Doctor Who* Appreciation Society's reference department for many years in the seventies, and was considered by many to be one of the stalwart historians of *Doctor Who*.

Another good publication was Mat Irvine's *Doctor Who Special Effects*, published by Beaver Books. Irvine was an effects designer at the BBC and had worked extensively on *Doctor Who* as well as on many other programmes. This book collected anecdotes and photographs from his own collection and provided an illuminating glimpse into the world of *Doctor Who* special effects.

Lastly on this subject, there were a number of 'game books' released featuring the sixth Doctor. In the US, the FASA Corporation in 1986 published *Doctor Who and the Rebel's Gamble* by William H. Keith Jr. Described as a 'solo-play adventure game', it involved the Doctor and Peri arriving in the middle of the American Civil War to find that history has been changed. In the UK, meanwhile, Severn House published six 'Make Your Own Adventure' books in the same year. These featured the Doctor alongside a number of TV and original characters in stories written by William Emms, Philip Martin, David Martin and Pip and Jane Baker, all of whom had contributed scripts to *Doctor Who*, and also one by Michael Holt. William Emms's *Mission to Venus* was a particularly notable example, as it was based on a script, *The Imps*, which had been planned for inclusion in Season 4 of the TV series.

The second major product type of the mid-eighties were cast metal miniatures of characters from *Doctor Who*. These were produced by Fine Art Castings out of their small workshop near Andover. The company had previously concentrated on military models, and were keen to branch into another market. There were three basic ranges of *Doctor Who* figures: 80mm figures, 40mm figures and a few 20mm figures, the latter two designed for role-playing games. With the help of David J. Howe and Mark Stammers (then involved in running the DWAS reference and graphics departments respectively), the figures were as accurate as could be represented given their dimensions and, before long, all six Doctors were available, as well as most of the companions, and a great number of the monsters and villains, from the Daleks and Cybermen right through to the Borad and Drathro.

The company also produced two limited edition bust sets, the first of all six Doctors and the second of a monster or villain from each of the Doctor's eras. In the three or so years that Fine Art Castings issued the figures, over 70 different characters from *Doctor Who* were released.

BBC Video decided to release more *Doctor Who* adventures on to the general public following their successful debut launch of *The Revenge of the Cybermen* in 1983. Unfortunately, all of the titles from this period were edited in one way or another, but stories included the black and white Troughton story *The Seeds of Death* as well as *Day of the Daleks* from the Pertwee era, and *Pyramids of Mars* and *The Robots of Death* from Tom Baker's era.

As well as the BBC, another major contributor to the video market was a new company called Reeltime Pictures. Reeltime Pictures had been set up by Keith Barnfather who had been working at both the BBC and Channel 4 for over eight years before leaving to move into business television production. Reeltime Pictures was set up to provide film and video production facilities for corporate customers and, as Keith

Barnfather was also a big fan of *Doctor Who*, he decided to put together some video interviews with the stars of that programme.

He started in 1984 with Michael Wisher (Davros) and John Leeson (voice of K-9), and when those were well received, moved on to such popular actors as Nicholas Courtney (the Brigadier), Janet Fielding (Tegan) and Nicola Bryant (Peri). Each tape improved on the one before, becoming more ambitious, with location recording and limited scope for visual effects. None of the tapes was ever made solely for profit – they were done primarily for fun and, as the fans seemed to like them, there seemed no reason to stop as long as their production costs were being covered.

Other items of interest released during the sixth Doctor's era included the incredible Dalek hat (a rather sorry felt construction which fell apart rather quickly); the *Doctor Who The Music 2* record which followed on from the success of the first release and which contained music up to *The Caves of Androzani*; more art prints from Who Dares Publishing, and from the same company a rather nice book celebrating the *Doctor Who* work of artist Frank Bellamy.

There were two sixth-Doctor artwork jigsaws released by Arrow, a set of *Doctor Who* plates from Royal Doulton, a rubber playmat was produced by Sport and Playbase Ltd which featured a large panoramic illustration of the sixth Doctor and Peri surrounded by Daleks and Cybermen. (As an interesting side note, the same product was also issued for the American market with the fourth Doctor and Leela replacing the then-current UK equivalents.) There were even two computer games – *The Mines of Terror* (Micro Power Ltd) and *Warlord* (BBC Software) released.

Doctor Who merchandise was still selling well and, despite the apparent slump in the television programme's ratings, there was no sign of it decreasing.

Ratings

During the eighties, ratings as a true means of gauging the public's reaction to a television series became less and less reliable. For one thing, they didn't take into account the boom in home video which was occurring across the world; in the past, if you didn't watch a programme you would then either miss it or wait for a repeat, but with a video recorder, you could happily tape your favourite show to keep, while watching the more transient but still entertaining fare on the other channel.

Towards the end of Tom Baker's tenure as the Doctor, the ratings dropped alarmingly, going from a maximum of 16.1 million viewers in his penultimate season, to 8.3 maximum, 3.7 minimum in his last. Through the Peter Davison era, which included the first Colin Baker story, *The Twin Dilemma*, at the end of the 21st season, the ratings tended to hover around the 6-7 million mark.

The 22nd season, the first full season for the sixth Doctor, continued this pattern, receiving between 6 and 7 million viewers; however, the return of the programme to Saturday evenings with season 23 proved disastrous for the ratings.

The reasons for this were simple. Having foregone its regular Saturday slot, ITV were quick to establish an effective and popular line-up of shows. So by the time *Doctor Who* returned, there was little impact that it could make against the opposition, especially when that opposition consisted of *The A-Team* and *Blind Date*.

The Saturday evening line-up on BBC for the duration of the 23rd season was, first of all, *Roland Rat – The Series*, then *Doctor Who* and then finally *The Late, Late Breakfast Show* for the first ten weeks, a film (*One of Our Dinosaurs is Missing*) and then *All Creatures Great and Small*. ITV's viewing for the same time period was *Blockbusters* followed by *The A-Team* and rounded off with *Blind Date*.

The average ratings (chart positions) for these programmes for the duration of the 23rd season of *Doctor Who* were as follows:

Blockbusters	7.8 (Pos 48.8)
The A-Team	11.8 (Pos 13.8)
Blind Date	14.8 (Pos 3.9)
Roland Rat – The Series	unrated (Pos >100)
Doctor Who	4.8 (Pos 87.3)
Late Breakfast	8.0 (Pos 45.4)*

*figure includes the film and *All Creatures Great And Small*.

As can be seen, *Blind Date* was not only ITV's top-rated show, it was frequently in the top three shows on television, and a few times it was second only to the BBC's *EastEnders* which was pulling in around 21 million viewers. There is no way that *Doctor Who* – or any programme for that matter – could compete with this, and as *Blind Date* followed directly on from *The A-Team*, another high-rated show, which started ten minutes before *Doctor Who*, viewers tended to be hooked to ITV for the whole of the early-evening period. If they videoed *Doctor Who* to watch later, then these figures were not reflected in the ratings.

Doctor Who was also not helped by being placed after *Roland Rat – The Series*, a short-lived puppet show which only entered the TV chart once during season 23's run, polling 4.8 million viewers and coming 91st in the chart for the week of the final episode of *The Trial of a Time Lord*. As this episode was also the highest rated *Doctor Who* episode of the season, it is interesting to speculate whether the Rat's ratings were boosted by viewers waiting to watch the final episode of the 23rd season. It may also be significant that *Blind Date* was not shown on that final Saturday and whatever was shown in its place did not appear in the TV chart at all.

Another contributing factor to the poor showing of the 23rd season is that *The Trial of a Time Lord* was one, long fourteen-part story. Viewers who had missed earlier episodes, would not be too concerned about watching later ones as they would not necessarily realise that there were self-contained stories within the season. Also, despite the voice-over explanations preceeding all but the first two episodes of the season, anyone coming into the series midway through would have had a hard job understanding exactly what was going on.

Overall, despite an eighteen-month break, supposedly to put the show back on the rails, little was apparently achieved except for dramatically lowering the ratings. The press coverage cannot be faulted – there was lots of it – and many commentators had wished for a return to the familiar Saturday evening slot since the programme moved from it back in 1982. It certainly looked, at least from the ratings point of view, as though *Doctor Who* might have had its day.

Table of Sixth Doctor Episodes in Order of Viewing Figures (Millions)

8.9	Attack of the Cybermen 1
7.7	Revelation of the Daleks 2
7.6	The Twin Dilemma 1
7.4	Timelash 2
7.4	The Twin Dilemma 2
7.4	Revelation of the Daleks 1
7.3	Mark of the Rani 2
7.2	Vengeance on Varos 1
7.2	Attack of the Cybermen 2
7.0	Vengeance on Varos 2
7.0	The Twin Dilemma 3
6.9	The Two Doctors 3
6.7	Timelash 1
6.6	The Two Doctors 1
6.3	Mark of the Rani 1
6.3	The Twin Dilemma 4
6.0	The Two Doctors 2
5.6	The Trial of a Time Lord 14
5.3	The Trial of a Time Lord 11
5.2	The Trial of a Time Lord 9
5.2	The Trial of a Time Lord 12
5.1	The Trial of a Time Lord 7
5.0	The Trial of a Time Lord 8
4.9	The Trial of a Time Lord 2
4.9	The Trial of a Time Lord 1
4.8	The Trial of a Time Lord 5
4.6	The Trial of a Time Lord 10
4.6	The Trial of a Time Lord 6
4.4	The Trial of a Time Lord 13
3.9	The Trial of a Time Lord 3
3.7	The Trial of a Time Lord 4

Table of Sixth Doctor Episodes in Order of Chart Position

58	Revelation of the Daleks 2
59	The Twin Dilemma 3
65	Revelation of the Daleks 1
66	The Two Doctors 3
66	The Twin Dilemma 1
67	The Twin Dilemma 4
69	The Trial of a Time Lord 1
69	Timelash 1
71	Attack of the Cybermen 1
71	The Twin Dilemma 2
75	The Trial of a Time Lord 2
76	The Trial of a Time Lord 5
79	Timelash 2
80	The Trial of a Time Lord 14
84	The Trial of a Time Lord 8
84	Mark of the Rani 2
85	The Trial of a Time Lord 9
86	The Trial of a Time Lord 11
87	The Trial of a Time Lord 7
87	The Trial of a Time Lord 6
89	The Trial of a Time Lord 12
90	The Two Doctors 2
92	The Two Doctors 1
93	The Trial of a Time Lord 10
97	The Trial of a Time Lord 4
98	The Trial of a Time Lord 13
98	The Trial of a Time Lord 3
104	Attack of the Cybermen 2
108	Vengeance on Varos 2
110	Vengeance on Varos 1
111	Mark of the Rani 1

Afterword

The news that Colin Baker would not be returning for the 24th season of *Doctor Who* was broken to the general public in early December 1986. The press once again took an interest in the series with the *Sun*'s Charles Catchpole interviewing Baker for a rather sensationalist three-part centre-page special. Fan reaction to Colin Baker's departure was, on the whole, muted. Although there was a widespread feeling that he had been very badly treated, many apparently saw the casting of a new Doctor as a sign of hope for the future and an escape from the troubled times of recent years.

This feeling of a bad time best forgotten has perhaps dissuaded fans from looking back and re-evaluating the eight stories produced during Colin Baker's incumbency. It is often forgotten that Season 22 received an average audience of 7.12 million viewers with a high appreciation rating. It could be argued that, had Season 23 continued as originally planned, Baker would have settled comfortably into the role of the Doctor and viewers would have become used to this flamboyant portrayal of the Time Lord. It is also interesting to speculate what might have happened with the arrival of a new script editor for Season 24. Under Andrew Cartmel's aegis, the sixth Doctor may have taken on a slightly darker nature, a change in characterisation that Colin Baker has indicated he would have been happy with had it taken place. In fact, this concept has been taken up by the BBC Film Club in a series of video dramas, produced and directed by Bill Baggs, in which Colin Baker plays the Stranger alongside Nicola Bryant's Miss Brown. While having no visible connection – other than the casting – with *Doctor Who*, these tapes present an interesting counterpoint to Baker's tenure as the Doctor.

It is inevitable to conclude that the eighteen-month hiatus and the public vilification of the programme by the Controller of BBC1, Michael Grade, did immense damage to *Doctor Who*. The changes of scheduling and scripting which were supposed to tackle the perceived need to revitalise the programme's style and direction had precisely the opposite effect, leading to a sharp drop to an average viewing figure of 4.8 million.

It is unfortunate that Colin Baker's departure from the role of the Doctor was the only remaining, and highly visible, action that could be taken to give the viewing public the impression that changes were being made to improve the series for the future. In this way, fan and press attention could be diverted from any other reasons for the falling viewing figures and instead blame, by implication, the series' lead actor for the programme's woes. Whether this strategy came about by design or by accident is not known, but it worked.

The beginning of Season 24 saw the arrival of a new Doctor in the earthly form of Sylvester McCoy. As Colin Baker had turned down the option of making a regeneration story, the change-over of Doctors was achieved by McCoy donning a blonde curly wig and lying on the floor of the TARDIS dressed in the sixth Doctor's costume. Colin's understandable decision to bow out when he did meant that the last line delivered by the sixth Doctor was the immortal phrase: 'Carrot juice, carrot juice, carrot juice!'

A rather less than fitting epitaph for the sixth Doctor.

Production Credits

TITLE	AUTHOR	DIRECTOR	COSTUME	MAKE-UP	VISUAL EFFECTS	MUSIC	DESIGNER
			SEASON TWENTY-ONE				
			Producer – John Nathan-Turner, Script Editor – Eric Saward				
6S The Twin Dilemma	Anthony Steven	Peter Moffatt	Pat Godfrey	Denise Baron	Stuart Brisdon	Malcolm Clarke	Val Warrender
			SEASON TWENTY-TWO				
6T Attack of the Cybermen	Paula Moore (Ian Levine)*	Matthew Robinson	Anushia Nieradzik	Linda McInnes	Chris Lawson	Malcolm Clarke	Marjorie Pratt
6V Vengeance on Varos	Philip Martin	Ron Jones	Anne Harding	Cecile Hay-Arthur / Dorka Nieradzik	Charles Jeanes	Jonathan Gibbs	Tony Snoaden
6X The Mark of the Rani	Pip and Jane Baker	Sarah Hellings	Dinah Collin	Catherine Davies	David Barton	Jonathan Gibbs	Paul Trerise
6W The Two Doctors	Robert Holmes	Peter Moffatt	Jan Wright	Catherine Davies	Steven Drewett	Peter Howell	Tony Burrough
6Y Timelash	Glen McCoy	Pennant Roberts	Alun Hughes	Vanessa Poulton	Kevin Molloy	Elizabeth Parker	Bob Cove
6Z Revelation of the Daleks	Eric Saward	Graeme Harper	Pat Godfrey	Dorka Nieradzik	John Brace	Roger Limb	Alan Spalding
			SEASON TWENTY-THREE – The Trial of a Time Lord				
7A (Parts One to Four)	Robert Holmes	Nicholas Mallett	Ken Trew	Denise Baron	Mike Kelt	Dominic Glynn	John Anderson
7B (Parts Five to Eight)	Philip Martin	Ron Jones	John Hearne	Dorka Nieradzik	Peter Wragg	Richard Hartley	Andrew Howe-Davies
			No Script Editor				
7C (Parts Nine to Twelve)	Pip and Jane Baker	Chris Clough	Andrew Rose	Shaunna Harrison	Kevin Molloy	Malcolm Clarke	Dinah Walker
			Script Editor – Eric Saward				
(Part Thirteen)	Robert Holmes	Chris Clough	Andrew Rose	Shaunna Harrison	Kevin Molloy	Dominic Glynn	Michael Trevor
			No Script Editor				
(Part Fourteen)	Pip and Jane Baker	Chris Clough	Andrew Rose	Shaunna Harrison	Kevin Molloy	Dominic Glynn	Michael Trevor

NOTES:

*Ian Levine provided some story suggestions.

It must be presumed throughout that the script editor had input into all the scripts to a greater or lesser degree.

DOCTOR WHO THE HANDBOOK
THE FOURTH DOCTOR

Howe-Stammers-Walker

Doctor Who is the world's longest running science fiction series, and Tom Baker was the longest-serving of the actors who portrayed the title role.

This volume covers the reign of the fourth Doctor, from 1974 to 1981, when the programme achieved its highest ratings in Britain, and became a sensation in the United States.

As well as interviews with Tom Baker, the book includes an in-depth study of the production processes and location work used, and an episode by episode guide to the era.

The Handbook is a must for every *Doctor Who* fan – and for everyone whose favourite Doctor is the curly-haired chap with the teeth and the long scarf.

ISBN 0 426 20369 0

DOCTOR WHO – THE SIXTIES

Howe-Stammers-Walker

The Sixties is the definitive record of *Doctor Who*'s early years, from the broadcast of its first episode on 23 November 1963, to its change into colour with the beginning of the Jon Pertwee era.

Illustrated throughout with colour and black and white photographs, most of which have never been published before, this is a meticulous record of the beginning of a cultural phenomenon. It is also a lovingly assembled history of the art of television in a decade perhaps less jaded than our own.

'. . . for the Science Fiction fan who's always wanted one book about the series, but who has been put off by the plethora of titles available, this is the one to get.'

Starburst

'This will probably rank as the ultimate book on the subject . . .'

Doctor Who Magazine

ISBN 0 86369 707 0   Paperback

DOCTOR WHO – TIMEFRAME

David J. Howe

Thirty years ago, a programme called *Doctor Who* first appeared on British television. It has since become a British institution.

Twenty years ago, three *Doctor Who* novels – originally written in the sixties – were reissued, beginning an unbroken programme of book publishing that has produced over 150 novelisations, with eight million copies sold, and a growing series of New Adventures following the Doctor's travels beyond the television series.

This volume celebrates that double anniversary with a remarkable collection of photographs, cuttings, and full-page original artwork in the most highly illustrated and comprehensive *Doctor Who* book ever published.

ISBN 1 85227 427 1

WHO ARE YOU?

Help us to find out what you want.
No stamp needed – free postage!

Name   _____

Address   _____

Town/County _____

Postcode   _____

Home Tel No. _____

About Doctor Who Books

How did you acquire this book?
Buy	☐	Borrow ☐
Swap	☐	

How often do you buy Doctor Who books?
1 or more every month ☐	3 months	☐
6 months ☐	12 months	☐

Roughly how many Doctor Who books have you read in total?

_____

Would you like to receive a list of all past and forthcoming Doctor Who titles?
Yes ☐   No ☐

Would you like to be able to order the Doctor Who books you want by post?
Yes ☐   No ☐

Doctor Who Exclusives

We are intending to publish exclusive Doctor Who editions which may not be available from booksellers and available only by post.

Would you like to be mailed information about exclusive books?
Yes ☐   No ☐

About You

What other books do you read?

Other character-led books (which characters?) _____

Science Fiction ☐ Thriller/Adventure ☐
Horror ☐
Non-fiction subject areas (please specify) _____

Male ☐ Female ☐

Age:
Under 18 ☐ 18–24 ☐
25–34 ☐ 35+ ☐

Married ☐ Single ☐
Divorced/Separated ☐

Occupation _____

Household income:
Under £12,000 ☐ £13,000–£20,000 ☐
£20,000+ ☐

Credit Cards held:
Yes ☐ No ☐

Bank Cheque guarantee card:
Yes ☐ No ☐

Is your home:
Owned ☐ Rented ☐

What are your leisure interests? _____

Thank you for completing this questionnaire. Please tear it out carefully and return to: **Doctor Who Books, FREEPOST, London, W10 5BR** (no stamp required)